D0473706

The

BIG BOOK of BOOK
SOCKS

The **ULTIMATE** Beyond-the-Basics
GUIDE TO KNITTING SOCKS

Kathleen Taylor

The Taunton Press

CALGARY PUBLIC LIBRARY

SEP - 2009

Text © 2009 by Kathleen Taylor
Photographs © 2009 by Burcu Avsar and Zach DeSart
Illustrations © 2009 by The Taunton Press, Inc.

All rights reserved.

The Taunton Press
Inspiration for hands-on living®

The Taunton Press, Inc., 63 South Main Street,
PO Box 5506, Newtown, CT 06470-5506
e-mail: tp@taunton.com

Editors: Erica Sanders-Foege, Alex Bandon
Copy Editor: Betty Christiansen
Indexer: Lynne Lipkind
Cover design: L49 Design
Interior design and layout: L49 Design
Illustrator: Christine Erikson
Photographers: Burcu Avsar and Zach DeSart

Library of Congress Cataloging-in-Publication Data

Taylor, Kathleen, 1953-
  The big book of socks : the ultimate beyond-the-basics guide to knitting socks /
Kathleen Taylor.
      p. cm.
  Includes index.
  ISBN 978-1-60085-085-1
  1. Knitting--Patterns. 2. Socks. I. Title.
  TT825.T35 2009
  746.43'2--dc22
                              2009016381

Printed in the United States of America
10 9 8 7 6 5 4 3 2 1

CraftStylish™ is a trademark of The Taunton Press, Inc., registered in the U.S. Patent
and Trademark Office.

The following names/manufacturers appearing in *The Big Book of Socks* are trade-
marks: Berroco®, Berroco Comfort™, Blue Moon Fiber Arts®, Blue Moon Fiber Arts
Socks That Rock®, Knit Picks®, Knit Picks Andean Silk™, Knit Picks Crayon™, Knit
Picks Essential™, Knit Picks Essential Kettle-Dyed™, Knit Picks Essential Tweed™,
Knit Picks Felici™, Knit Picks Gloss™, Knit Picks Palette™, Knit Picks Risata™, Knit
Picks Swish™, Knit Picks Telemark™, Knit Picks Wool of the Andes™, Knit Picks
Wool of the Andes Hand-Dyed™, Knit Picks Wool of the Andes Kettle-Dyed™, Lion
Brand® Yarn, Patons®, SeaCell®, Soysilk®, Tencel®

To Betty Clay, Dana Locken, and all
the wonderful friends of Knitters Etc.

ACKNOWLEDGMENTS

Even the most solitary writers need assistance and support, and I had both
in abundance. My agent, Stacey Glick, was always there to hold my hand.
My editors Erica Sanders-Foege, Alex Bandon, and Catherine Levy guided
and improved this book immeasurably. Test knitters Anne Leedham, Toby
Sanders, and Edith Murphy saved me from a world of embarrassment. And
as always, Terry, Shirley, Ann, and Melanie kept me centered and working
when what I really wanted to do was goof off.

TABLE

~ of ~

CONTENTS

1

The
WONDERFUL
Madness
~ THAT IS ~
SOCK
KNITTING

People are never surprised to see me knitting socks, which is why I was so excited when my wonderful editor, Erica, approached me about writing a big, honkin' book of sock patterns. The process of putting them together was exhilarating and exhausting. For months, I knitted nothing except socks. What was the first thing I cast on when I was finished working on the book? Socks.

I doubt there's a single sock knitter out there who hasn't heard, "You know, you can buy those for two dollars a pair." I knit socks because knitting socks makes me happy. That's the only reason I need, but of course, there are many more. Socks are small and portable. You can tuck the yarn, needles, and pattern into your purse and take them anywhere, whipping them out whenever you have a few spare minutes. Hand-knitted socks are long-lasting and unique. They can be made by beginners and by people who can knit in their sleep. They can be knitted slowly with needles that resemble wire and yarn that resembles thread, or quickly with large needles and fat yarn. But no matter. Hand-knitted socks are hugs for the feet. Who needs more reason than that?

SOCK *style*: A PRIMER

All non-tube socks have the same components: The cuff, the heel, the foot, and the toe. The cuff, which often has ribbing or an upper hem, extends from the top of the sock to the heel. The heel is the bend in the sock that accommodates the wearer's heel. The foot is the area between the heel and the place where the toe decreases begin. On most socks, the foot is divided into the sole, which is the bottom of the foot, and the instep, which is the top. The toe begins at the decreases and ends with the closing of the sock.

Tube socks are a good choice when you want to knit socks for someone whose shoe size is uncertain, since the heel is not specifically located. Tube socks are a good choice for babies and small children, whose feet grow quickly.

A sock with a heel that is knit after the body of the sock is completed has an Afterthought Heel. Socks with Afterthought Heels are also good projects for beginning knitters or first-time sock knitters.

A Flap and Gusset Heel has three components: the flap, the heel turn, and the gusset. Socks with Flap and Gusset Heels are excellent for beginning sock knitters, and they provide a good and durable fit. This style is especially well suited for yarns and patterns that don't provide a lot of elasticity, because it allows extra room in the instep. See Appendix 1 on page 170 for more information.

There are many styles of Short-Row Heels, but we're only featuring one in this book: a No-Wrap Short-Row Heel. You work the short rows without decreases, and the only component to a Short-Row Heel is the heel itself. A Short-Row Heel is generally considered an advanced technique, and Short-Row Heel patterns are especially well suited for use with self-patterning yarns because the stitch number does not change; therefore, the patterning is not disrupted by the gusset.

Hand-knitted socks can also be classified by construction style: flat or round.

Flat (or two-needle) socks are knitted flat, back and forth on

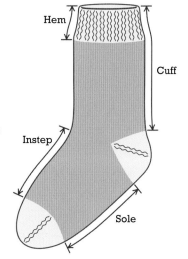

two straight needles, and then seamed after the knitting is complete. Flat socks are a good choice for knitters who are not comfortable working in the round, nor with double-pointed needles. You knit **round** socks seamlessly, in the round, using double-pointed needles or one or two circular needles. Socks are traditionally knit in the round.

Yarn SELECTION

There are hundreds of yarns out there produced specifically for sock knitting. Fingering weight superwash wool (meaning the yarn can be machine-washed and -dried), with a percentage of nylon spun into the yarn for durability, is the most common. Then there are sock yarns made from wool blended with man-made or other natural fibers, such as Tencel®, bamboo, SeaCell®, Soysilk®, silk, and cotton. All make lovely yarns for sock knitting. One hundred percent wool is available, too.

Non-superwash wool yarns (the kind that will felt if you put them in a washing machine) are also suitable for socks and are readily available. An advantage of feltable wool socks is that the sole of the sock will felt a little bit just from wear. For heavier socks, almost any worsted weight wool yarns work well.

For knitters who don't like to work with wool, or for recipients who prefer not to wear it, there are other fibers that can be knitted into socks: cotton and cotton blends, synthetic fibers, and blends of assorted fibers. These yarns come in many weights and sizes and knit up into lovely socks. The best sock yarns, regardless of weight or fiber content, are those that are tightly spun and plied, and have a little bounce (or stretch). Those yarns hold up well to wear and repeated washings, whether by hand or machine. A good, firm fabric is the most important ingredient for long-lasting socks.

A NOTE ABOUT
YARN AVAILABILITY

It is likely that some of the yarns and colors shown in this book will no longer be available by the time you read this. Yarn manufacturers tend to rotate their catalog to entice sock knitters with new lines and colorways. If the sock yarns shown in this book are not available, many others—equally beautiful—will be.

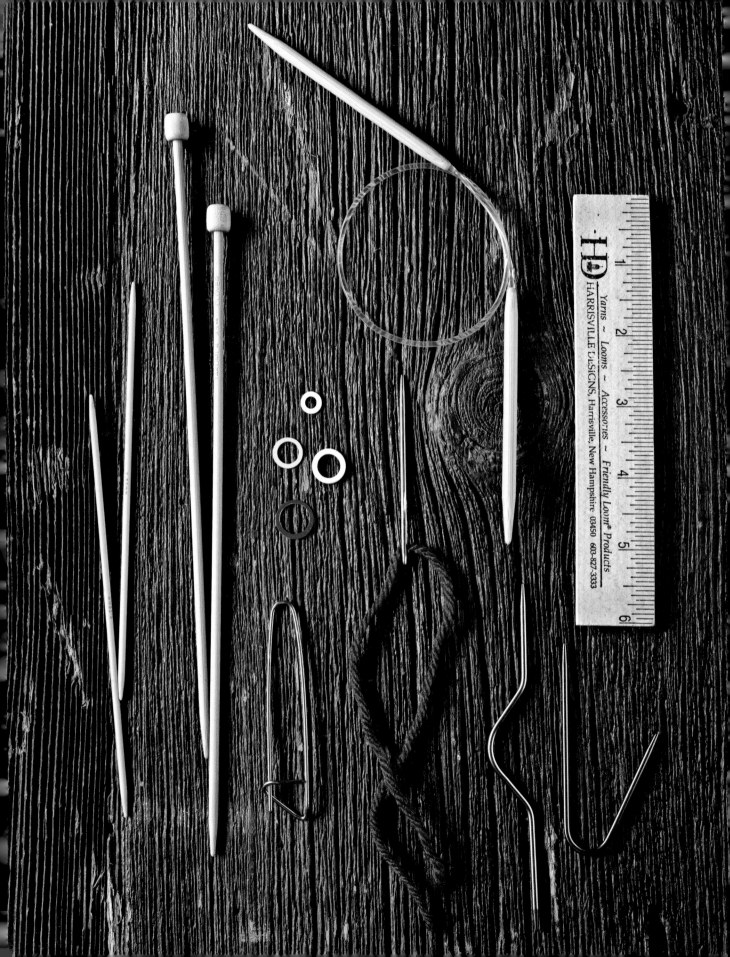

NEEDLES

I'm a confirmed double-pointed needle (dpn) fan. I use them nearly exclusively in my sock knitting. I usually knit with four dpns, rather than five, and I know that many sock knitters favor circular needles. All of the patterns in this book have been written to accommodate both techniques.

In general, you cast the full number of stitches onto a separate needle (often one size larger than the size you'll be using to knit the sock), and then place the stitches on your chosen needle type. With dpns, you divide the stitches equally on three or four needles, and join the needles in a triangle or a square after making certain that the stitches are not twisted around any of the needles. When using two circular needles, you divide the stitches evenly—half on one needle, half on the other. When using one long circular needle, you place all of the stitches on a single needle, but you pull the needle cable itself out into a loop and use it to divide the stitches in half. You then join the stitches.

Sock-knitting needles come in metal, wood, or bamboo. There are also needles made from acrylic, plastic, glass, and other materials. I prefer my needles to be very slick, so I like to use nickel-plated needles with very sharp points. But needle preference is a personal matter, so whichever needle you enjoy using is the right one for you. When using circular needles, make sure that the cable is thin and flexible and that the place where the cable joins to the needles is smooth, without jogs or snags.

OTHER *tools*

Needles and yarn are the most important tools for knitting socks, but there are a few other things you will want to have handy: a short ruler, scissors, a crochet hook for picking up dropped stitches, a large-eye blunt needle, stitch markers, a cable needle, and a few safety pins to mark rows.

It's nice to have a sock-knitting bag, a portable box, or even just a resealable plastic bag to hold all of your tools, needles, and yarn. For charted designs, it is helpful to photo copy the chart and anchor it to a flat metal sheet with magnetic strips, which you move after each row or round.

GAUGE

In general, ignore the gauge listed on the labels of most sock yarns. The manufacturer-recommended gauge for most sock yarns is too loose for me. A gauge ranging between 8 and 10 stitches per inch with fingering weight yarns, on needles sized from 0 to 3, makes

NEEDLE SIZE ISN'T IMPORTANT; WHAT MATTERS IS THE NUMBER OF STITCHES PER INCH

If you need a size 4 needle to get 6.5 stitches per inch with worsted weight yarn, use it. If you need a size 7 needle to get 6.5 stitches per inch with worsted weight yarn, use it. If you need a size 0 needle to get 8 stitches per inch with fingering weight yarn, then stock up on size 0 needles.

a good, sturdy fabric for long-wearing socks. Most worsted weight yarns weren't intended for sock knitting, so the listed gauge is geared toward sweaters and other outerwear. For worsted weight yarns, 6 to 7 stitches per inch with size 4 to 6 needles works for most of the patterns.

Row gauge isn't quite as important as the stitch gauge because, in most cases, you just knit until the piece is long enough. But the norm for fingering weight socks runs from 9 to 12 rows/rounds per inch on the same needle sizes as listed on page 7. For worsted weight yarns, the gauge averages 7 to 8 rows/rounds per inch. Most of the sock patterns in this book list gauge measurements for Stockinette stitch, and that's how you should measure your gauge. But some patterns list the gauge measurement over the patterning. Knit your swatch in the stitch that is listed in order to test your gauge.

SWATCHING

Yeah, you need to swatch. In addition to discovering where your knitting stands in comparison to the pattern gauge, you'll know whether you actually like the look and feel of the finished fabric after washing. Since gauge differs when you knit flat or in the round, knit your swatch the same way that you will knit your socks: flat if they're two-needle socks, in the round if they're knitted in the round.

It's important to measure your swatch, and record your gauge before washing as well, so that you can adjust your knitting if the yarn shrinks or stretches after washing. Wash your swatch the same way you will wash your finished socks. Unless noted otherwise, all of the pattern gauges in this book were calculated after washing.

MEASUREMENTS

Unless otherwise noted, do not stretch the fabric when measuring the width of your piece. Unless otherwise noted in the individual pattern, length measurements do not include the needle. Measure length from the point specified in the pattern up to the needle for the proper length.

Pattern notations: Unless otherwise noted, all needle and shoe sizes are U. S. equivalents throughout.

Laundry DAY

Wear hand-knitted socks no more than twice before laundering. The knitted fabric stretches on the foot. Washing the sock restores the natural fiber and stitch elasticity. Superwash wool yarn is yarn that has been treated to prevent felting.

If your socks are knit from any fiber blend that can be machine-washed, turn the socks inside out (to reduce pilling) and toss them in the washer, then into the dryer.

If your socks can't be machine-dried, turn the clean socks right side out, and either block them or smooth them on a flat surface to dry. Socks will usually air-dry overnight.

If your socks are knit from a fiber that can be *neither* machine-washed *nor* machine-dried, wash them by hand, inside out, in a sink full of warm water with soap (laundry soap, dish soap, or liquid soap). Don't agitate or scrub the socks. Drain the water, then immerse the socks in fresh water to rinse. Drain the rinse water, squeeze the moisture from the socks, then block them or smooth them out on a flat surface to dry. Always wash your socks before the first wearing.

TO *Block* OR NOT TO BLOCK

All of the patterns in this book end with the words *Wash and block the socks*. Blocking shapes air-dried socks. When I block socks, I use handmade blockers made from plastic-coated wire hangers to prevent the wire from rusting.

A fully blocked sock will look wider and longer than one that has been machine-dried because a blocked sock has been stretched. A sock that has been hung to dry will look smaller because the natural elasticity of the yarn has not been counteracted. A sock that has been smoothed flat on the top of the dryer generally looks larger than a machine-dried sock and smaller than one that was formally blocked. Those differences are cosmetic; the size of the sock is the size of the sock, however you block it.

SOCK *repair*

Sooner or later, you're going to end up with holes in your socks. Heels are often the first to go. Toes are usually next on the disaster list, with thinning soles coming in third. Don't toss the socks. You can fix almost every sock disaster and wring a few more months, or even years, of wear out of your beloved socks.

It's best to repair thin spots before they become actual holes. You can Duplicate stitch over the existing fabric easily and quickly (see Glossary on page 178 for instructions).

Don't worry about not having the same yarn—use whatever closely matching yarn of the same weight and washability that you have on hand.

If you have worn out an Afterthought Heel, just take the heel out and knit another (with the same yarn, or contrasting). If you don't want to repair thin toe sections, you can cut the toe off, pick up stitches, and knit a new toe.

If the foot of your sock is truly irreparable, cut the foot from the cuff, pick up the stitches, and knit an entire new heel and foot.

SOCK-KNITTING *tips* YOUR KNITTING TEACHER *might* TELL YOU

- A 6-inch knitting needle makes a handy substitute for a 6-inch ruler.
- K1, P1 ribbing isn't as elastic as other knit-and-purl ribbings. You may need to work K1, P1 ribbing with a larger-size needle.
- If you have gaps where the heel stitches meet the instep after working a Short-Row Heel, reach inside the sock with your left needle, pick up a nearby purl loop, and knit that with the first stitch after the heel.
- *Knitting back backward* is a handy technique for knitting flat (back and forth) without turning your needles. At the end of a row, keep the needles in the same hands, insert the left needle into the first stitch of the right needle, catch and pull the yarn back through that stitch, and place the new loop on the left needle. Then drop the first stitch from the right needle. Continue across.

A SOCK-KNITTING *tip* YOUR KNITTING TEACHER *won't* TELL YOU

- Sometimes it's hard to remember which side of the gusset or toe or wedge heel uses a K2tog decrease and which side uses an SSK decrease. One slants to the left, one slants to the right. It's more important to be consistent with whichever one you use.

Finally, don't worry if your finished socks don't look exactly like the ones pictured in this book. You knit your way, and I knit my way, and we'll all have lovely socks and warm feet when we get done. So, knitters, start your needles!

2

BASIC SOCKS

Here are the Plain Vanilla socks, the workhorses of your sock pattern stable boiled down to their basic structure: cuff, heel (if there is one), foot, and toe. And these are the building blocks from which other sock patterns and styles are made. You'll cruise through these designs in order to get on to the flashier, fiddly ones in the later chapters, but you'll be back. These are the ones I keep close at hand, the kind I can carry on a conversation (or watch a movie) as I knit.

Basic sock patterns let the yarn be the star, and with all the gorgeous yarns available, there are plenty of contenders for that role.

We'll play with both fingering and worsted weight yarns, and start with super-simple tube socks, then work our way through two-needle flat socks, Flap and Gusset socks, and, finally, No-Wrap Short-Row Heel basic sock.

Are you excited? I know I am. Let's get to work.

Tweed Worsted
Weight

Reverse Stockinette
Worsted Weight

Contrast Cuff and Toe
Worsted Weight

TUBE SOCKS

Tube socks have no heel, no bend, no complicated-looking short rows or gussets. You can knit tube socks one at a time or two at a time (with either one or two circular needles or two sets of double-pointed needles). In fact, a tube sock can even be knitted flat. (See Appendix 1: Heels & Toes, page 170, for further instructions.)

Tweed Worsted Weight
TUBE SOCK

PATTERN DIFFICULTY: Easy/Beginner

YARN: Cascade 220 Tweed, 90% Peruvian highland wool/ 10% Donegal tweed, 100 g, 220 yd., #7619 Charcoal Tweed, 1 (1, 1, 2, 2, 2) skeins

YARN WEIGHT: Worsted

NEEDLES: Size 5 (U.S.)/ 3.75 mm, or size needed to obtain gauge 1 or 2 circulars or 4 or 5 dpns, as desired

TOOLS: Large-eye blunt needle

PATTERN SIZES: Infant (newborn–18 months), Child (8–13), Youth (1–4), Women's (5–10), Men's Average, Men's Wide (8–12)

MEASUREMENTS: Approx Width (lying flat) over Stockinette st: Infant: 2¼ in., Child: 2½ in., Youth: 3 in., Women's: 3½ in., Men's Average: 3¾ in., Men's Wide: 4¼ in.; Approx Length: Infant: 5½ in., Child: 10¼ in., Youth: 13 in., Women's: 15 in., Men's Average: 17 in., Men's Long: 19 in.

HEEL STYLE: None

GAUGE: 7 sts = 1 in., 9 rnds = 1 in. in Stockinette st

With size 5 needles, CO 30 (36, 42, 48, 54, 60) sts. Divide on 1 or 2 circulars or 3 or 4 dpns as desired. Without twisting the sts, join.

CUFF Work 10 (10, 12, 16, 20, 20) rnds in K3, P3 ribbing.

Work even in Stockinette st until sock measures 5 in. (9 in., 11½ in., 14 in., 15 in., 17 in.), or your desired length.

TOE Work 30 (36, 42, 48, 54, 60)-st Star Toe as instructed on page 177.

FINISHING Cut a tail 12 in. long. Thread the tail in a large-eye blunt needle, pull the needle through the remaining loops, and tighten. Tie off on the inside of the sock. Weave all loose ends in on the inside of the sock. Wash and block the socks.

Work out your own tube sock pattern for any weight of yarn or needle size by knitting a gauge swatch and then calculating the number of stitches you need for the foot/leg circumference (minus about an inch to keep the sock fitted). Cast on that number of stitches, work an inch or two of ribbing, and then knit the tube and decrease for the toe. When you reach the desired length, just decrease for the toe and finish it off.

Tube

Reverse Stockinette Worsted Weight
TUBE SOCK

PATTERN DIFFICULTY:
Easy/Beginner

YARN: Knit Picks® Swish™,
100% superwash Merino wool,
50 g, 110 yd., #23873 Aloe,
1 (2, 2, 3, 3, 4) balls

YARN WEIGHT: Worsted

NEEDLES: Size 5 (U.S.)/
3.75 mm, or size needed to obtain
gauge 1 or 2 circulars or 4 or
5 dpns, as desired

TOOLS: Large-eye blunt needle

PATTERN SIZES: Infant
(newborn–18 months), Child
(8–13), Youth (1–4), Women's
(5–10), Men's Average, Men's
Wide (8–13)

MEASUREMENTS: Approx
Width (lying flat) over Stockinette
st: Infant: 2¼ in., Child: 2¾ in.,
Youth: 3¼ in., Women's: 3½ in.,
Men's Average: 4 in., Men's

Wide: 4½ in.; Approx Length:
Infant: 5½ in., Child: 10¼ in.,
Youth: 13 in., Women's: 15 in.,
Men's Average: 17 in., Men's
Long: 19 in.

HEEL STYLE: None

GAUGE: 6.5 sts = 1 in., 8 rnds =
1 in. in Stockinette st

With size 5 needles, CO 30 (36, 42, 48, 54, 60) sts. Distribute on 1 or 2 circulars or 3 or 4 dpns, as desired. Without twisting the sts, join.

CUFF Work 10 (10, 12, 16, 20, 20) rnds in K3, P3 ribbing.

Work even in Stockinette st until sock measures 5 in. (9 in., 11½ in., 14 in., 15 in., 17 in.), or your desired length.

TOE Work 30 (36, 42, 48, 54, 60)-st Star Toe as instructed on page 177.

FINISHING Cut a tail 12 in. long. Thread the tail in a large-eye blunt needle, pull the needle through the remaining loops, and tighten. Tie off on the **outside** (knit side) of the sock. Weave all loose ends in on the **outside** of the sock. Turn sock to the purl side for the right side of the sock. Wash and block the socks.

Contrast Cuff and Toe Worsted Weight
TUBE SOCK

PATTERN DIFFICULTY: Easy/Beginner

YARN: Knit Picks Wool of the Andes™, 100% Peruvian wool, 110 yd., 50 g, #23425 Cranberry, 1 ball for all sizes; Knit Picks Wool of the Andes Hand-Dyed™, 100% Peruvian wool, 50 g, 110 yd., #24087 Buchanan, 1 (1, 2, 2, 3, 4) balls

YARN WEIGHT: Worsted

NEEDLES: Size 5 (U.S.)/ 3.75 mm, or size needed to obtain gauge 1 or 2 circulars or 4 or 5 dpns, as desired

TOOLS: Large-eye blunt needle

PATTERN SIZES: Infant (newborn–18 months), Child (8–13), Youth (1–4), Women's (5–10), Men's Average, and Men's Wide (8–13).

MEASUREMENTS: Approx Width (lying flat) over Stockinette St: Infant: 2¼ in., Child: 2¾ in., Youth: 3¼ in., Women's: 3½ in., Men's Average: 4 in., Men's Wide: 4½ in.; Approx Length: Infant: 5½ in., Child: 10¼ in., Youth: 13 in., Women's: 15 in., Men's Average: 17 in., Men's Long: 19 in.

HEEL STYLE: None

GAUGE: 6.5 sts = 1 in., 8 rnds = 1 in. in Stockinette st

With Cranberry and size 5 needles, CO 30 (36, 42, 48, 54, 60) sts. Distribute on 1 or 2 circulars or 3 or 4 dpns, as desired. Without twisting the sts, join.

CUFF Work 12 (12, 16, 20, 20, 20) rnds in K3, P3 ribbing.

Cut Cranberry. Change to Buchanan. Work in Stockinette st until sock measures 4¼ in. (8 in., 10½ in., 13 in., 14 in., 16 in.). Cut Buchanan. Change to Cranberry. Work 1 in. in Stockinette st for all sizes.

TOE Work 30 (36, 42, 48, 54, 60)-st Star Toe as instructed on page 177.

FINISHING Cut a tail 12 in. long. Thread the tail in a large-eye blunt needle, pull the needle through the remaining loops, and tighten. Tie off on the inside of the sock. Weave all loose ends in on the inside of the sock. Wash and block the socks.

Ribbon Eyelet Worsted Weight
TUBE SOCK

PATTERN DIFFICULTY:
Easy/Beginner
YARN: Knit Picks Crayon™,
100% Pima cotton, 50 g, 128 yd.,
#23817 Azure, 1 (1, 2, 3) balls
YARN WEIGHT: Worsted
NEEDLES: Size 5 (U.S.)/
3.75 mm, or size needed to obtain
gauge 1 or 2 circulars or 4 or
5 dpns, as desired

NOTIONS: 1 (1, 1, 2) yd.
grosgrain ribbon, ⅛ in. wide
TOOLS: Large-eye blunt needle
PATTERN SIZES: Infant
(newborn–18 months), Child
(8–13), Youth (1–4), Women's
(5–10)
MEASUREMENTS: Approx
Width (lying flat) over Stockinette
St: Infant: 2½ in., Child: 3 in.,

Youth: 3½ in., Women's: 4 in.;
Approx Length: Infant: 5½ in.,
Child: 10¼ in., Youth: 13 in.,
Women's: 15 in.
HEEL STYLE: None
GAUGE: 6 sts = 1 in., 8 rnds =
1 in. in Stockinette st

Note: Securely attach the ribbon to Infant size socks—by sewing or knotting—or omit it altogether to prevent a choking hazard.

With size 5 needles, CO 30 (36, 42, 48) sts. Distribute on 1 or 2 circulars or 3 or 4 dpns, as desired. Without twisting the sts, join.
CUFF Work 6 (6, 10, 12) rnds in Stockinette st.
EYELET RND 1: *K2 tog, YO*, rep around.
EYELET RND 2: K, working each YO as a st.
Work even in Stockinette st until sock measures 5 in. (9 in., 11½ in., 14 in.), or your desired length.
TOE Work 30 (36, 42, 48)-st Star Toe as instructed on page 177.
FINISHING Cut a tail 12 in. long. Thread the tail in a large-eye blunt needle, pull the needle through the remaining loops, and tighten. Tie off on the inside of the sock. Weave all loose ends in on the inside of the sock. Wash and block the socks. If you desire, with a large-eye blunt needle, thread 18 in. (18 in., 18 in., 24 in.) of ⅛-in.-wide grosgrain ribbon through the eyelets. Tighten slightly and tie in a bow. Trim ends.

4 x 2 Ribbed Worsted Weight
TUBE SOCK

PATTERN DIFFICULTY:
Easy/Beginner

YARN: Patons® SWS,
70% wool/30% soy, 80 g, 110 yd.,
#70605 Natural Green, 1 (2, 2,
3, 4, 4) balls

YARN WEIGHT: Worsted

NEEDLES: Size 5 (U.S.)/
3.75 mm, or size needed to obtain
gauge 1 or 2 circulars or 4 or
5 dpns, as desired

TOOLS: Large-eye blunt needle

PATTERN SIZES: Infant
(newborn–18 months), Child
(8–13), Youth (1–4), Women's
(5–10), Men's Average, Men's Wide
(8–13)

MEASUREMENTS: Approx
Width (lying flat, unstretched) over
4 x 2 Ribbing: Infant: 1½ in.,
Child: 1¾ in., Youth: 2 in.,
Women's: 2¼ in., Men's Average:

2½ in., Men's Wide: 2¾ in.;
Approx Length: Infant: 5½ in.,
Child: 10¼ in., Youth: 13 in.,
Women's: 15 in., Men's Average:
17 in., Men's Long: 19 in.

HEEL STYLE: None

GAUGE: 11 sts = 1 in., 8 rnds =
1 in. in K4, P2 ribbing

Note: If you want matching socks, it might be a good idea to buy an extra ball of this yarn, because the stripe repeats are very long.

With size 5 needles, CO 30 (36, 42, 48, 54, 60) sts. Distribute on 1 or 2 circulars or 3 or 4 dpns, as desired. Without twisting the sts, join.

CUFF Work entire sock, until the toe decreases, in 4 x 2 (K4, P2) ribbing until desired length, as for Tweed Worsted Weight Tube Sock on page 15.

TOE K 1 rnd. Work 30 (36, 42, 48, 54, 60)-st Star Toe as instructed on page 177.

FINISHING Cut a tail 12 in. long. Thread the tail in a large-eye blunt needle, pull the needle through the remaining loops, and tighten. Tie off on the inside of the sock. Weave all loose ends in on the inside of the sock. Wash and block the socks.

Picot Hem
Fingering Weight

Basic Fingering Weight

FINGERING WEIGHT TUBE SOCKS

Like worsted weight tube socks, tube socks knit with fingering weight yarn are also perfect for mindless knitting. Fingering weight socks generally fit in any shoe or sandal, and cotton and synthetic-blend yarns are great for spring and summer.

BASIC *Fingering Weight* TUBE SOCK

PATTERN DIFFICULTY: Easy/Beginner

YARN: Knit Picks Felici™, 75% superwash Merino wool/25% nylon, 50 g, 218 yd., #24114 Atmosphere, 1 (1, 2, 2, 2, 2) balls

YARN WEIGHT: Fingering

NEEDLES: Size 2 (U.S.)/2.75 mm, or size needed to obtain gauge 1 or 2 circulars or 4 or 5 dpns, as desired 1 size 3 (U.S.)/3.25 mm needle for casting on

PATTERN SIZES: Infant (newborn–18 months), Child (8–13), Youth (1–4), Women's (5–10), Men's Average (8–13), Men's Wide

MEASUREMENTS: Approx Width (lying flat) over Stockinette St: Infant: 2 in., Child: 2½ in., Youth: 2¾ in., Women's: 3½ in., Men's Average: 3¾ in., Men's Wide: 4¼ in.; Approx Length: Infant: 5½ in., Child: 10¼ in., Youth: 13 in., Women's: 15 in., Men's Average: 17 in., Men's Long: 19 in.

HEEL STYLE: None

GAUGE: 8.5 sts = 1 in., 10 rnds = 1 in. in Stockinette st

Note: To make matching socks from self-patterning yarns, begin your CO at the same spot in the color repeat for both socks.

With a size 3 needle, CO 36 (44, 52, 60, 64, 72) sts. Distribute on size 2 needles, 1 or 2 circulars or 3 or 4 dpns, as desired. Without twisting the sts, join. CUFF Work 12 (12, 12, 16, 20, 20) rnds in K2, P2 ribbing.

NEXT RND, MEN'S AVERAGE SIZE ONLY: Inc 2 sts evenly spaced in rnd. (66 sts)

Work even in Stockinette st until the sock measures 5 in. (9 in., 11 in., 14 in., 16 in., 17 in.).

2ND TO THE LAST FOOT RND, YOUTH SIZE ONLY: Dec 4 sts evenly spaced in the rnd. (48 sts rem)

2ND TO THE LAST FOOT RND, CHILD SIZE ONLY: Dec 2 sts evenly spaced in the rnd. (42 sts rem)

LAST FOOT RND, YOUTH AND CHILD: K.

TOE Work 36 (42, 48, 60, 66, 72)-st Star Toe as instructed on pages 176–177.

FINISHING Cut a tail 12 in. long. Thread the tail in a large-eye blunt needle, pull the needle through the remaining loops, and tighten. Tie off on the inside of the sock. Weave all loose ends in on the inside of the sock. Wash and block the socks.

Picot Hem Fingering Weight
TUBE SOCK

PATTERN DIFFICULTY: Easy/Beginner

YARN: Fleece Artist Sea Wool, 70% Merino/30% SeaCell, 112 g, 383 yd., Rose Garden, 1 (1, 1, 1, 2, 2) skeins

YARN WEIGHT: Fingering

NEEDLES: Size 2 (U.S.)/ 2.75 mm, or size needed to obtain gauge 1 or 2 circulars or 4 or 5 dpns, as desired,

TOOLS: Large-eye blunt needle

PATTERN SIZES: Infant (newborn–18 months), Child (8–13), Youth (1–4), Women's (5–10), Men's Average, Men's Wide (8–13)

MEASUREMENTS: Approx Width (lying flat) over Stockinette st: Infant: 2¼ in., Child: 2¾ in., Youth: 3¼ in., Women's: 3¾ in., Men's Average: 4¼ in.,

Men's Wide: 4½ in.; Approx Length: Infant: 5½ in., Child: 10¼ in., Youth: 13 in., Women's: 15 in., Men's Average: 17 in., Men's Long: 19 in.

HEEL STYLE: None

GAUGE: 8 sts = 1 in., 10 rnds = 1 in. in Stockinette st

Note: This pattern may be adapted for boys and men by omitting the picot rnd and substituting a purl rnd, also called a hem fold rnd.

With a size 2 needle, CO 36 (44, 52, 60, 66, 72) sts. Distribute on 1 or 2 circulars or 3 or 4 dpns, as desired. Without twisting the sts, join.

HEM K 12 rnds.

GIRLS' AND WOMEN'S PICOT RND: *K2 tog, YO*, rep around.

GIRLS' AND WOMEN'S NEXT RND: K, working each YO as a stitch.

BOYS' AND MEN'S PURL RND: P.

BOYS' AND MEN'S NEXT RND: K.

Work even in Stockinette st until the sock measures 5 in. (9 in., 11 in., 14 in., 16 in., 17 in.) from the Picot or Purl Rnd.

2ND TO THE LAST FOOT RND, YOUTH SIZE ONLY: Dec 4 sts evenly spaced in the rnd. (48 sts rem)

2ND TO THE LAST FOOT RND, CHILD SIZE ONLY: Dec 2 sts evenly spaced in the rnd. (42 sts rem)

LAST FOOT RND, YOUTH AND CHILD: K.

TOE Work 36 (42, 48, 60, 66, 72)-st Star Toe Decrease as instructed on pages 176–177.

FINISH HEM Fold the hem down and in along the Picot or Purl Rnd. With yarn threaded in a large eye needle, loosely tack the hem in place. Weave the loose end in on the inside of the hem. Wash and block the socks.

Contrast Cuff and Toe Fingering-Weight
TUBE SOCK

PATTERN DIFFICULTY:
Easy/Beginner

YARN: DG Confetti, 75% super-wash wool/25% polyamide, 50 g, 230 yd., #181, 1 (1, 2, 2, 2, 2) balls; Phildar Preface, 70% wool/30% polyamide, 50 g, 211 yd., #500236-0043 Gris Moyen, 1 ball for all sizes

NEEDLES: Size 2 (U.S.)/ 2.75 mm, or size needed to obtain gauge 1 or 2 circulars or 4 or 5 dpns, as desired

1 size 3 (U.S.)/3.25 mm needle for casting on

TOOLS: Large-eye blunt needle

PATTERN SIZES: Infant (newborn–18 months), Child (8–13), Youth (1–4), Women's (5–10), Men's Average, Men's Wide (8–13)

MEASUREMENTS: Approx Width (lying flat) over Stockinette st: Infant: 2 in., Child: 2½ in., Youth: 2¾ in., Women's: 3½ in.,

Men's Average: 3¾ in., Men's Wide: 4¼ in.; Approx Length: Infant: 5½ in., Child: 10¼ in., Youth: 13 in., Women's: 15 in., Men's Average: 17 in., Men's Long: 19 in.

HEEL STYLE: None

GAUGE: 8.5 sts = 1 in., 10 rnds = 1 in. in Stockinette st

With size 3 needle and Preface, CO 36 (44, 52, 60,66, 72) sts. Distribute on size 2 needles, 1 or 2 circulars or 3 or 4 dpns, as desired. Without twisting the sts, join.
C U F F Work 12 (12, 12, 16, 20, 20) rnds in K1, P1 ribbing.

Cut Preface and change to Confetti. Work even in Stockinette st until the sock measures 4 in. (8 in., 10 in., 13 in., 15 in., 16 in.).

Cut Confetti and change to Preface.

ALL SIZES: Work 1 in. in Stockinette st (sock measures 4 in., 8 in., 10 in., 13 in., 15 in., 16 in.).

Cut Confetti and change to Preface.

ALL SIZES: Work 1 in. in Stockinette st (sock measures 5 in., 9 in., 11 in., 14 in., 16 in., 17 in.).

2ND TO THE LAST FOOT RND, YOUTH SIZE ONLY: Dec 4 sts evenly spaced in the rnd. (48 sts rem)

2ND TO THE LAST FOOT RND, CHILD SIZE ONLY: Dec 2 sts evenly spaced in the rnd. (42 sts rem)

LAST FOOT RND, YOUTH AND CHILD: K.

T O E Work 36 (42, 48, 60, 66, 72)-st Star Toe as shown on pages 176–177.

FINISHING Cut a tail 12 in. long. Thread the tail in a large-eye blunt needle, pull the needle through the remaining loops, and tighten. Tie off on the inside of the sock. Weave all loose ends in on the inside of the sock. Wash and block the socks.

2 x 2 Ribbed Fingering-Weight
TUBE SOCK

PATTERN DIFFICULTY:
Easy/Beginner

YARN: Zitron Trekking XXL,
75% superwash wool/25% nylon,
100 g, 459 yd., #90 (brown/black),
1 ball for all sizes

NEEDLES: Size 1 (U.S.)/
2.50 mm, or size needed to obtain
gauge 1 or 2 circulars or 4 or
5 dpns, as desired

TOOLS: Large-eye blunt needle

PATTERN SIZES: Infant
(newborn–18 months), Child
(8–13), Youth (1–4), Women's
(5–10), Men's Average, Men's Wide
(8–13)

MEASUREMENTS: Approx
Width (lying flat) over Ribbing,
Unstretched: Infant: ¾ in., Child:
1 in., Youth: 1¼ in., Women's: 1½ in.,

Men's Average: 1¾ in., Men's Wide:
2 in.; Approx Length: Infant: 5½ in.,
Child: 10¼ in., Youth: 13 in.,
Women's: 15 in., Men's Average:
17 in., Men's Long: 19 in.

HEEL STYLE: None

GAUGE: 20 sts = 1 in., 12 rnds
= 1 in. in K2, P2 ribbing

With size 1 needles, CO 36 (44, 52, 60, 68, 72) sts.

CUFF Work even in 2 x 2 ribbing (K2, P2) until the
sock measures 5 in. (9 in., 11 in., 14 in., 16 in., 17 in.).

LAST FOOT RND, MEN'S AVERAGE SIZE ONLY: K, dec
2 sts evenly spaced in the rnd. (66 sts rem)

LAST FOOT RND, YOUTH SIZE ONLY: K, dec 4 sts
evenly spaced in the rnd. (48 sts rem)

LAST FOOT RND, CHILD SIZE ONLY: K, dec 2 sts
evenly spaced in the rnd. (42 sts rem)

LAST FOOT RND, ALL OTHER SIZES: K.

TOE Work 36 (42, 48, 60, 66, 72)-st Star Toe as shown
on pages 176–177.

FINISHING Cut a tail 12 in. long. Thread the tail in
a large-eye blunt needle, pull the needle through the
remaining loops, and tighten. Tie off on the inside of
the sock. Weave all loose ends in on the inside of the
sock. Wash and block the socks.

AFTERTHOUGHT HEEL SOCKS

Afterthought Heels are just what the name implies: heels that you knit after the rest of the sock is completed. You can work Two-Needle Afterthought Heel socks flat with a slit indicating the placement for the heel stitches that you will pick up and knit. The entire sock, heel and all, is seamed afterward. Remember that the toe decreases are worked on the right-side knit rows only, with purl rows on the wrong side in between the decrease rows. (For instructions, see Appendix 1: Heels & Toes, page 170.)

Two-Needle Worsted-Weight
AFTERTHOUGHT HEEL SOCK

PATTERN DIFFICULTY:
Easy/Beginner
YARN: Crystal Palace Merino 5, 100% superwash wool, 50 g, 110 yd., #9809 Fall Herbs, 1 (2, 2, 3, 3) balls, and #5236 Khaki, 1 (1, 1, 1, 2) balls
YARN WEIGHT: Worsted
NEEDLES: 1 pair 10-in. size 5 (U.S.)/3.75 mm straight needles, or size needed to obtain gauge
TOOLS: Large-eye blunt needle, stitch marker, small safety pin

PATTERN SIZES: Child (10–11, 12–13), Youth (1–2, 3–4), Women's (5–6, 7–8, 9–10), Men's Average, Men's Wide (8–9, 10–11, 12–13)
MEASUREMENTS: Cuff Width, Unsewn: Child: 5½ in., Youth: 6½ in., Women's: 7¼ in., Men's Average: 8¼ in., Men's Wide: 9¼ in.; Cuff Length: Child: 4 in., Youth: 5 in., Women's: 6 in., Men's: 7 in.; Length from Heel-to-Toe, Sewn: Child Shoe Size 10–11: 5½ in., Child Shoe Size 12–13:

6¼ in., Youth Shoe Size 1–2: 7 in., Youth Shoe Size 3–4: 7½ in., Women's Shoe Size 5–6: 9 in., Women's Shoe Size 7–8: 9½ in., Women's Shoe Size 9–10: 10 in., Men's Shoe Size 8–9: 10½ in., Men's Shoe Size 10–11: 11 in., Men's Shoe Size 12–13: 12 in.
HEEL STYLE: Two-Needle Afterthought
GAUGE: 6.5 sts = 1 in., 8 rows = 1 in. in Stockinette st

Note: **Women's Wide** can be worked as for **Men's Average**; adjust cuff and foot length for shoe size. **Women's Narrow** can be worked as for **Youth**; adjust cuff and foot length for shoe size.

Note: The side seam is visible when you use variegated yarns (it won't show as much with a solid color yarn), and it does create a small ridge. That ridge doesn't bother my feet, but sensitive tootsies might object to the seam.

RIGHT SOCK With size 5 needle and Khaki, CO 36 (42, 48, 54, 60) sts. Work 10 (12, 16, 20, 20) rows in K3, P3 ribbing. Change to Fall Herbs and work in Stockinette st until cuff measures 4 in. (5 in., 6 in., 7 in.), ending with a P row.
RIGHT SOCK HEEL OPENING ROW 1 (RS): BO 18 (21, 24, 27, 30) sts, K remainder of row. Mark end of row with a small safety pin.

RIGHT SOCK HEEL OPENING ROW 2: P 18 (21, 24, 27, 30) sts, CO 18 (21, 24, 27, 30) sts.

F O O T Work foot in Stockinette st until it measures from the Heel Opening: Child Shoe Size 10–11: 2½ in., Child Shoe Size 12–13: 3 in., Youth Shoe Size 1–2: 3½ in., Youth Shoe Size 3–4: 3¾ in., Women's Shoe Size 5–6: 4½ in., Women's Shoe Size 7–8: 5 in., Women's Shoe Size 9–10: 5½ in., Men's Shoe Size 8–9: 5½ in., Men's Shoe Size 10–12: 6 in., Men's Shoe Size 13: 6½ in.

Change to Khaki and work 1 in. in Stockinette st (all sizes), end with a P row.

T O E Work a 36 (42, 48, 54, 60)-st Star Toe as instructed on page 177.

LEFT SOCK Work ribbing and cuff as for Right Sock, end with a K row.

LEFT SOCK HEEL OPENING ROW 1 (WS): BO 18 (21, 24, 27, 30) sts, P remainder of row. Mark end of row with a small safety pin.

LEFT SOCK HEEL OPENING ROW 2: K 18 (21, 24, 27, 30) sts, CO 18 (21, 24, 27, 30) sts. Complete foot as for Right Sock.

H E E L On both socks, work Two-Needle Afterthought Heel as follows:

AFTERTHOUGHT HEEL ROW 1: With Khaki, on the wrong side of the sock, pick up and P 18 (21, 24, 27, 30) sts along one edge of the heel opening, place marker; along the other edge of the heel opening, pick up and P 18 (21, 24, 27, 30) sts. (36, 42, 48, 54, 60 sts)

AFTERTHOUGHT HEEL ROW 2: SSK, K to within 2 sts of the marker, K2 tog, move marker, SSK, K to within 2 sts of the end of the row, K2 tog. (4 sts dec)

AFTERTHOUGHT HEEL ROW 3: P.

Rep Afterthought Heel Rows 2–3 until there are 20 (22, 24, 26, 28) sts left. Divide the rem sts on 2 needles so that the decreases are at the beginning and the end of each needle. You may need to work half of the sts so that the yarn is at the working end of the needle. Close the heel with the Kitchener st (see Glossary for instructions). Tighten and tie off.

F I N I S H I N G Match the heel side seam and sew it with yarn threaded in a large-eye blunt needle, using the Mattress st (see Glossary for instructions). Match the row marked with the safety pin to the seam of the sewn heel. Using the Mattress st, and yarn threaded in a large-eye needle, sew the sock side seam. Tie off ends, and weave all loose ends in on the inside of the sock. Wash and block the socks.

Two-Needle Fingering Weight
AFTERTHOUGHT HEEL SOCK

PATTERN DIFFICULTY: Easy/Beginner

YARN: Blue Moon Fiber Arts® Socks That Rock® Lightweight, 100% superwash Merino wool, 127 g, 360 yd., Fire on the Mountain, 1 (1, 1, 2, 2) skeins

YARN WEIGHT: Fingering

NEEDLES: 1 pair 10-in. size 2 (U.S.)/2.75 mm straight needles, or size needed to obtain gauge 1 size 3 (U.S.)/3.25 mm needle for casting on

TOOLS: Large-eye blunt needle, stitch marker, small safety pin

PATTERN SIZES: Child (10–11, 12–13), Youth (1–2, 3–4), Women's (5–6, 7–8, 9–10), Men's Average, Men's Wide (8–9, 10–11, 12–13)

MEASUREMENTS: Cuff Length: Child: 4 in., Youth: 5 in., Women's: 6 in., Men's: 7 in.; Cuff Width, Unsewn: Child: 5½ in., Youth: 6½ in., Women's: 7 in., Men's Average: 7½ in., Men's Wide: 8½ in.; Length from Heel-to-Toe: Child Shoe Size 10–11: 5½ in., Child Shoe Size 12–13: 6¼ in., Youth Shoe Size 1–2: 7 in., Youth Shoe Size 3–4: 7½, Women's Shoe Size 5–6: 9 in., Women's Shoe Size 7–8: 9½ in., Women's Shoe Size 9–10: 10 in., Men's Shoe Size 8–9: 10½ in., Men's Shoe Size 10–11: 11 in., Men's Shoe Size 12–13: 12 in.

HEEL STYLE: Two-Needle Afterthought

GAUGE: 8.5 sts = 1 in., 12 rows = 1 in. in Stockinette st

Note: **Women's Wide** can be worked as for **Men's Average**; adjust cuff and foot length for shoe size. **Women's Narrow** can be worked as for **Youth**; adjust cuff and foot length for shoe size.

Note: The side seam is visible when you use variegated yarns (it won't show as much if you use a solid color yarn), and it does create a small ridge. That ridge doesn't bother my feet, but sensitive tootsies might object to the seam.

RIGHT SOCK With size 3 needle, CO 48 (56, 60, 64, 72) sts. Change to size 2 needle, work 10 (12, 16, 20, 20) rows in K2, P2 ribbing.

YOUTH SIZE ONLY: Dec 2 sts evenly spaced on the last ribbing row. (54 sts)

MEN'S AVERAGE SIZE ONLY: Inc 2 sts evenly spaced on the last ribbing row. (66 sts)

Work Stockinette st (K 1 row, P 1 row) until cuff measures 4 in. (5 in., 6 in., 7 in.), ending with a P row.

RIGHT SOCK HEEL OPENING ROW 1 (RS): BO 24 (27, 30, 33, 36) sts, K remainder of row. Mark end of row with a small safety pin.

RIGHT SOCK HEEL OPENING ROW 2: P 24 (27, 30, 33, 36) sts, CO 24 (27, 30, 33, 36) sts.

FOOT Work foot in Stockinette st until it measures: Child Shoe Size 10–11: 3½ in., Child Shoe Size 12–13: 4 in., Youth Shoe Size 1–2: 4½ in., Youth Shoe Size 3–4: 4¾ in., Women's Shoe Size 5–6: 5 ½ in., Women's Shoe Size 7–8: 6 in., Women's Shoe Size 9–10: 6½ in., Men's Shoe Size 8–9: 6½ in., Men's Shoe Size 10–12: 7 in., Men's Shoe Size 13: 7½ in.

TOE Work a 48 (54, 60, 66, 72)-st Star Toe as instructed on pages 176–177.

LEFT SOCK Work ribbing and cuff as for Right Sock, end with a **Knit** row.

LEFT SOCK HEEL OPENING ROW 1 (WS): BO 24 (27, 30, 33, 36) sts, **Purl** remainder of row. Mark end of row with a small safety pin.

LEFT SOCK HEEL OPENING ROW 2: Knit 24 (27, 30, 33, 36) sts, CO 24 (27, 30, 33, 36) sts.

Complete foot as for Right Sock.

HEEL Work Two-Needle Afterthought Heel as follows:

ROW 1: On the wrong side of the sock, pick up and P 24 (27, 30, 33, 36) sts along one edge of the heel opening, place marker; along the other edge of the heel opening, pick up and P 24 (27, 30, 33, 36) sts. (48, 54, 60, 66, 72 sts)

ROW 2: SSK, K to within 2 sts of the marker, K2 tog, move marker, SSK, K to within 2 sts of the end of the row, K2 tog. (4 sts dec)

ROW 3: P.

Rep Rows 2–3 until there are 20 (26, 28, 34, 36) sts left. Divide the remaining sts on 2 needles so that the decreases are at the beginning and the end of each needle. You may need to work half of the sts so that the yarn is at the working end of the needle. Close the heel with the Kitchener st (see Glossary for instructions). Tighten and tie off.

FINISHING

Match the heel side seam and sew it with yarn threaded in a large-eye blunt needle, using the Mattress st (see Glossary for instructions). Match the row marked with the safety pin to the seam of the sewn heel. Using the Mattress st, and yarn threaded in a large-eye needle, sew the sock side seam. Tie off ends, and weave all loose ends in on the inside of the sock. Wash and block the socks.

Round Worsted-Weight
AFTERTHOUGHT HEEL SOCK

PATTERN DIFFICULTY:
Beginner

YARN: Knit Picks Wool of the Andes, 100% Peruvian highland wool, 50 g, 110 yd., #24074 Pampas Heather, Toddler: 1 (Child: 1; Youth: 2; Women's, Men's Average, and Men's Wide up to shoe size 10–11: 2; Men's Wide shoe size 12–13: 3) balls; #23896 Firecracker Heather Toddler: 1 (Child: 1; Youth, Women's, Men's Average, and Men's Wide: 2) balls; 18 in. of contrasting waste yarn in a similar weight

YARN WEIGHT: Worsted
NEEDLES: Size 5 (U.S.)/ 3.75 mm or size needed to obtain gauge 1 or 2 circulars or 4 or 5 dpns, as desired

TOOLS: Large-eye blunt needle, 2 stitch markers

NOTIONS: 36 in. worsted weight contrasting waste yarn

PATTERN SIZES: Toddler (6–8), Child (10–11, 12–13), Youth (1–2, 3–4), Women's (5–6, 7–8, 9–10), Men's Average, Men's Wide (9, 10–11, 12–13)

MEASUREMENTS: Cuff Width: Toddler: 2 in., Child: 3 in., Youth: 3½ in., Women's: 4 in., Men's Average: 4½ in., Men's Wide: 5 in.; Cuff Length: Toddler: 4 in., Child: 4½ in., Youth: 5 in., Women: 6 in., Men: 7 in.; Heel-to-Toe Length: Toddler: 5½ in., Child Shoe Size 10–11: 5¾ in., Child Shoe Size 12–13: 6¼ in., Youth Shoe Size 1–2: 6½ in., Youth Shoe Size 3–4: 6¾ in., Women's Shoe Size 5–6: 7¼ in., Women's Shoe Size 7–8: 8¼ in., Women's Shoe Size 9–10: 9¼ in., Men's Shoe Size 9–10: 9½ in., Men's Shoe Size 11–12: 10 in., Men's Shoe Size 13: 11 in.

HEEL STYLE: Afterthought
GAUGE: 6 sts = 1 in., 8 rnds = 1 in. in Stockinette st

Note: **Women's Wide** can be worked as for **Men's Average**; adjust cuff and foot length for shoe size. **Women's Narrow** can be worked as for **Youth**; adjust cuff and foot length for shoe size.

Note: You knit these socks exactly like tube socks, except you mark the heel location by knitting those stitches with a waste yarn that you carefully remove after the sock is completed. You then pick up the stitch loops, and knit this style of Afterthought Heel exactly like a Wedge Toe knitted in the round.

With size 5 needle and Firecracker Heather, CO 24 (36, 42, 48, 54, 60) sts. Distribute on 1 or 2 circulars or 3 or 4 dpns, as desired. Without twisting the sts, join. **CUFF** Work 8 (10, 12, 16, 20, 20) rnds K3, P3 ribbing. Cut Firecracker Heather and change to Pampas Heather. Work in Stockinette st until cuff measures: Toddler: 4 in., Child: 4½ in., Youth: 5 in., Women's: 6 in., Men's: 7 in.

WASTE YARN HEEL MARK RND: With 18 in. contrasting waste yarn, K 12 (18, 22, 24, 26, 30) sts. Pull the loose ends of the waste yarn to the outside of the sock. Do not tie the waste yarn at either edge. Slide the 12 (18, 22, 24, 26, 30) sts back on the left needle, and K with the sock yarn.

Work even in Stockinette st until the foot measures from waste yarn: Toddler: 2 in., Child Shoe Size 10–11: 2½ in., Child Shoe Size 12–13: 3 in., Youth Shoe Size 3–4: 3½ in., Women's Shoe Size 5–6: 4 in., Women's Shoe Size 7–8: 4½ in., Women's Shoe Size 9–10: 5 in., Men's Shoe Size 9–10: 5 in., Men's Shoe Size 11–12: 5½ in., Men's Shoe Size 12–13: 6 in.

Cut Pampas Heather. Change to Firecracker Heather. Work even 1 in. Foot will measure from waste yarn: Toddler: 3 in., Child Shoe Size 10–11: 3½ in., Child Shoe Size 12–13: 4 in., Youth Shoe Size 3–4: 4½ in., Women's Shoe Size 5–6: 5 in., Women's Shoe Size 7–8: 5½ in., Women's Shoe Size 9–10: 6 in., Men's Shoe Size 9–10: 6 in., Men's Shoe Size 11–12: 6½ in., Men's Shoe Size 12–13: 7 in.

NEXT RND: K 6 (9, 10, 12, 13, 15) sts, place marker, K 12 (18, 21, 24, 27, 30) sts, place marker, K rem 6 (9, 11, 12, 14, 15) sts.

T O E Work Wedge Toe Decrease as instructed on page 177.

H E E L Work Round Afterthought Heel as follows: Using a size 5 needle, pick up 1 loop of each st above the waste yarn.

With a 2nd needle and beginning at one edge, pick up 1 loop from the first 5 sts below the waste yarn. Carefully remove the waste yarn for those sts. Continuing along the waste yarn, pick up 1 loop from the next 5 sts, and repeat. Continue across the entire set of waste sts. You will have 1 less st on the bottom needle than on the top needle.

Distribute the picked-up heel sts on 1 or 2 circulars or 3 or 4 dpns, as desired, marking the division between the top and the bottom rows of sts with stitch markers or by dividing the sts on separate needles. (23, 35, 41, 47, 53, 59 sts)

RND 1: With Firecracker Heather, K around, pick up and K 1 st in the gap either directly before or after the lower line of heel sts to increase 1 st. (24, 36, 42, 48, 54, 60 sts)

RND 2: K to within 2 sts of the first marker, K2 tog, move marker, SSK, K to within 2 sts of the 2nd marker, K2 tog, move marker, SSK, K to end. (4 sts dec)

RND 3: K.

Rep Rnds 2–3 until there are 16 (20, 22, 24, 26, 28) sts left. If the sts are not already divided in half, divide them on 2 needles, so that the decs are at either side of each needle. You may need to knit to the end of one needle.

F I N I S H I N G Use Kitchener st (see Glossary for instructions) to close the heel. Weave in all loose ends on the inside of the sock. Wash and block the socks.

Round Fingering Weight
AFTERTHOUGHT HEEL SOCK

PATTERN DIFFICULTY:
Beginner

YARN: Blue Moon Fiber Arts Socks That Rock Lightweight, 100% superwash Merino wool, 127 g, 360 yd., Calico, Toddler through Women's sizes: 1 skein (Men's sizes: 2 skeins); 36 in. of contrasting waste yarn in a similar weight

YARN WEIGHT: Fingering

NEEDLES: Size 2 (U.S.)/ 2.75 mm, or size needed to obtain gauge1 or 2 circulars or 4 or 5 dpns, as desired

1 size 3 (U.S.)/3.25 mm needle for casting on

TOOLS: Large-eye blunt needle, 2 stitch markers

PATTERN SIZES: Toddler (6–8), Child (10–11, 12–13), Youth (1–2, 3–4), Women's Average (5–6, 7–8, 9–10), Men's Average, Men's Wide (9, 10–11, 12–13)

MEASUREMENTS: Cuff Width: Toddler: 2¼ in., Child: 2¾ in., Youth/Women's Narrow: 3¼ in., Women's Average: 3¾ in., Women's Wide/Men's Average: 4 in., Men's Wide: 4½ in.; Cuff Length: Toddler: 4 in., Child: 4½ in., Youth: 5 in.,

Women's: 6 in., Men's: 7 in.; Heel-to-Toe Length: Toddler: 5½ in., Child Shoe Size 10–11: 5¾ in., Child Shoe Size 12–13: 6¼ in., Youth Shoe Size 1–2: 6½ in., Youth Shoe Size 3–4: 6¾ in., Women's Shoe Size 5–6: 7¼ in., Women's Shoe Size 7–8: 8¼ in., Women's Shoe Size 9–10: 9¼ in., Men's Shoe Size 9–10: 9½ in., Men's Shoe Size 11–12: 10 in., Men's Shoe Size 13: 11 in.

HEEL STYLE: Afterthought

GAUGE: 8 sts = 1 in., 11 rnds = 1 in. in Stockinette st

Note: **Women's Wide** can be worked as for **Men's Average**; adjust cuff and foot length for shoe size. **Women's Narrow** can be worked as for **Youth**, adjust cuff and foot length for shoe size.

Note: You knit these socks exactly like tube socks, except you mark the heel location by knitting those stitches with a waste yarn that you carefully remove after the sock is completed. You then pick up the stitch loops, and knit this style of Afterthought Heel exactly like a Wedge Toe knitted in the round.

With a size 3 needle, CO 36 (44, 52, 60, 64, 72) sts. Transfer the stitches to size 2 needles, 1 or 2 circulars or 3 or 4 dpns, as desired. Without twisting the sts, join.

CUFF Work 10 (12, 12, 16, 20, 20) rnds in K2, P2 ribbing.

Work in Stockinette st until cuff measures 4 in. (4½ in., 5 in., 6 in., 7 in.).

WASTE YARN HEEL MARK RND: With contrasting waste yarn, K 18 (22, 26, 30, 32, 36) sts. Pull the loose ends of the waste yarn to the outside of the work. Do not tie the waste yarn at either edge. Slide the 18 (22, 26, 30, 32, 36) sts back on the left needle, and K with the sock yarn.

Work even in Stockinette st until the foot measures from waste yarn: Toddler: 3 in., Child Shoe Size 10–11: 3½ in., Child Shoe Size 12–13: 4 in., Youth Shoe Size 1–2: 4½ in., Youth Shoe Size 3–4: 4½ in., Women's Shoe Size 5–6: 5 in., Women's Shoe Size 7–8: 5½ in., Women's Shoe Size 9–10: 6 in., Men's Shoe Size 9–10: 6 in., Men's Shoe Size 11–12: 6½ in., Men's Shoe Size 12–13: 7 in.

NEXT RND: K 9 (11, 13, 15, 16, 18) sts, place marker, K 18 (22, 26, 30, 32, 36) sts, place marker, K rem 9 (11, 13, 15, 16, 18) sts.

TOE Work Wedge Toe Decrease as instructed on page 177.

HEEL Work Round Afterthought Heel as follows: Using a size 2 needle, pick up one loop of each st above the waste yarn.

With a 2nd needle, and beginning at one edge below the waste yarn, pick up one loop from the first 5 sts. Carefully remove the waste yarn for those sts. Continuing along the waste yarn, pick up one loop from the next 5 sts, and repeat. Continue across the entire set of waste sts. You will have 1 less st on the bottom needle than on the top needle.

Distribute the picked-up heel sts on 1 or 2 circulars or 3 or 4 dpns, as desired, marking the division between the top and the bottom rows of sts with stitch markers or by dividing the sts on separate needles. (35, 43, 51, 59, 63, 71 sts)

RND 1: K around, pick up and K 1 st in the gap either directly before or after the lower line of heel sts to increase 1 st. (36, 44, 52, 60, 64, 72 sts)

RND 2: K to within 2 sts of the first marker, K2 tog, move marker, SSK, K to within 2 sts of the 2nd marker, K2 tog, move marker, SSK, K to end. (4 sts dec)

RND 3: K.

Rep Rnds 2–3 until there are 16 (20, 24, 28, 32, 36) sts left. If the sts are not already divided in half, divide them on 2 needles, so that the decs are at either side of each needle. You may need to knit to the end of one needle.

FINISHING Close the heel with Kitchener st (see Glossary for instructions). Weave all loose ends in on the inside of the sock. Wash and block the socks.

FLAP & GUSSET SOCKS

A Flap and Gusset Heel consists of a heel flap that you work back and forth with roughly half of the cuff stitches (with exceptions), a turned heel, and a gusset. The gusset consists of stitches that you pick up along the outside edges of the heel flap, which you then decrease so that you knit the rest of the foot with (usually) the same number of stitches that you had on the cuff. You set aside the instep stitches (those that aren't used for the heel) on a stitch holder or separate needle while you work the heel. (For instructions, see Appendix 1: Heels & Toes, page 170.)

Purl when Ready
Adult-Size
Worsted Weight

Basic Adult-Size
Worsted Weight
Ragg Wool

Self-Patterning
Adult-Size
Worsted Weight

Contrast Rib-Heel-
Toe Child-Size
Worsted Weight

Basic Adult-Size Worsted Weight Ragg Wool
FLAP AND GUSSET SOCK

PATTERN DIFFICULTY:
Advanced Beginner
YARN: Jarbo Garn Raggi, 100 g,
166 yd., 70% wool/30% nylon,
#34226, 2 (2, 3) balls
YARN WEIGHT: Worsted
NEEDLES: Size 5 (U.S.)/
3.75 mm, or size needed to
obtain gauge 1 or 2 circulars or
4 or 5 dpns, as desired.

TOOLS: Large-eye blunt needle
PATTERN SIZES: Women's
Average (5–6, 7–8, 9–10), Men's
Average, Men's Wide (8–9, 10–11,
12–13)
MEASUREMENTS: Cuff Width:
Women's: 3½ in., Men's Average:
4 in., Men's Wide: 4½ in.; Cuff
Length: Women's: 6½ in., Men's:
7 in.; Heel-to-Toe Length: Women's

Shoe Size 5–6: 9 in., Women's
Shoe Size 7–8: 9½ in., Women's
Shoe Size 9–10: 10 in., Men's
Shoe Size 8–9: 10½ in., Men's
Shoe Size 10–11: 11 in., Men's
Shoe Size 12–13: 12 in.
HEEL STYLE: Flap and Gusset
GAUGE: 6.25 sts = 1 in., 8 rnds
= 1 in. in Stockinette st

s **Narrow** sizes can be knit using
ock patterns (see pages 37–39).
for shoe size. You may need to
's **Wide** may be worked as for
d foot length for shoe size.

(54, 60) sts. Distribute
r 3 or 4 dpns, as desired,
es aren't twisted, join.
s K3, P3 ribbing. Work
es 6½ in. (all Women's
siz

HE for the heel. Place
the or separate needle
for tl

HEEL FLAP ROW 1: Turn. Sl 1, P across, turn.
HEEL FLAP ROW 2: *Sl 1, K1*, rep across, turn.
Work Heel Flap Rows 1–2, 8 (9, 10) times more. End
with a P row, turn.

HEEL Work 24 (28, 30)-st Flap and Gusset Heel as
instructed on page 172.

GUSSET RND 1, ALL SIZES: Pick up, twist, and K 11 (12,
13) sts along edge of heel flap, place marker, work
across instep sts, place marker, pick up, twist, and K
11 (12, 13) sts along other edge of heel flap, K 7 (8, 9).

GUSSET RND 2, ALL SIZES: K to within 2 sts of marker,
SSK, move marker, work across instep sts, move
marker, K2 tog, K to end. (2 sts dec)
GUSSET RND 3, ALL SIZES: K.

Rep Gusset Rnds 2–3 until 48 (54, 60) sts rem. Redistribute sts on needles if desired.

Work in Stockinette st until foot measures for Women's sizes from the beginning of the gusset: Shoe
Sizes 5–6: 4½ in., Shoe Sizes 7–8: 5½ in., Shoe Sizes
9–10: 6 in.; for Men's sizes from the beginning of the
gusset: Shoe Sizes 8–9: 6½ in., Shoe Sizes 10–11: 7 in.,
Shoe Sizes 12–13: 7½ in.

LAST FOOT RND: K 12 (13, 15) sts, place marker, K 24
(27, 30) sts, place marker, K 12 (14, 15) sts.

TOE **WEDGE TOE DECREASE RND 1:** K to within 2 sts
of marker, SSK, move marker, K2 tog, K to within 2 sts of
marker, SSK, move marker, K2 tog, K to end. (4 sts dec)
WEDGE TOE DECREASE RND 2: K.

Rep Wedge Toe Decrease Rnds 1–2 until 24 (26, 28)
sts rem. K to the next marker, close the rem sts with
Kitchener st.

FINISHING Weave all ends in on the inside of the
sock. Wash and block the socks.

Self-Patterning Adult-Size Worsted Weight
FLAP AND GUSSET SOCK

~~~~~~

YARN: Adriafil Knitcol, 100% superwash Merino wool, 50 g, 137 yd., #43 Degas Phantasy, 2 (3, 3) balls

NEEDLES: As for Basic Adult-Size Worsted Weight Ragg Wool Flap and Gusset Sock

SIZES: As for Basic Adult-Size Worsted Weight Ragg Wool Flap and Gusset Sock

MEASUREMENTS: Cuff and Heel-to-Toe Length: As for Basic Worsted Weight Ragg Wool Flap and Gusset Sock; Approx Cuff Width

(lying flat): Women's: 3½ in., Men's Average: 3¾ in., Men's Wide: 4¼ in.

GAUGE: 7 sts = 1 in., 8 rnds = 1 in. in Stockinette st

~~~~~~

Knit as for Basic Adult-Size Worsted Weight Ragg Wool Flap and Gusset Sock.

Purl When Ready Adult-Size Worsted Weight
FLAP AND GUSSET SOCK

~~~~~~

YARN: Lion Brand® Yarn Lion® Wool Prints, 100% wool, 78 g, 143 yd., #820-201 Autumn Sunset, 2 (3, 3) balls

NEEDLES: As for Basic Adult-Size Worsted Weight Ragg Wool Flap and Gusset Sock

SIZES: As for Basic Adult-Size Worsted Weight Ragg Wool Flap and Gusset Sock

MEASUREMENTS: Cuff and Heel-to-Toe Length: As for Basic Worsted Weight Ragg Wool Flap and Gusset Sock; Approx Width:

Women's: 3½ in., Men's Average: 3¾ in., Men's Wide: 4¼ in.

GAUGE: 7 sts = 1 in., 8 rnds = 1 in. in Stockinette st

~~~~~~

Note: This variation requires a variegated yarn with short color repeats.

Knit as for Basic Adult-Size Worsted Weight Ragg Wool Flap and Gusset Sock, working the Purl When Ready Patterning on the cuff and instep. Work the sole and toe in plain Stockinette st.

PURL WHEN READY PATTERNING

Select any color from the variegation on the yarn. Any time on the cuff or instep when you encounter loops of your selected color on the needle, ready to be knit (not when you knit the yarn of that color, just when you come up to the already-knitted loops on the needle), purl those stitches. This makes a very interesting random bit of texture and color interest all along the sock.

Contrast Rib-Heel-Toe Child-Size Worsted Weight
FLAP AND GUSSET SOCK

PATTERN DIFFICULTY: Easy/Intermediate

YARN: Crystal Palace Bunny Hop, 50% microacrylic/42% micronylon/8% angora, 50 g, 113 yd., #2210 Baby Lilac, 1 ball for all sizes; #2308 Baby Sherbet, 1 ball for Toddler, Child, and Youth up to Shoe Size 1–2; 2 balls for Youth Shoe Size 3–4

YARN WEIGHT: Worsted

NEEDLES: Size 5 (U.S.)/ 3.75 mm, or size needed to obtain gauge 1 or 2 circulars or 4 or 5 dpns, as desired

TOOLS: Large-eye blunt needle, stitch markers

PATTERN SIZES: Toddler (6–8), Child (10–11, 12–13), Youth (1–2, 3–4)

MEASUREMENTS: Cuff Length: Toddler: 4 in., Child: 4½ in., Youth: 5¼ in.; Cuff/Foot Width: Toddler: 2½ in., Child: 3 in., Youth: 3½ in.; Heel-to-Toe Length: Toddler: 5½ in., Child Shoe Size 10–11: 5¾ in., Child Shoe Size 12–13: 6¼ in., Youth Shoe Size 1–2: 6½ in., Youth Shoe Size 3–4: 6¾ in.

HEEL STYLE: Flap and Gusset

GAUGE: 6 sts = 1 in., 9 rnds = 1 in. in Stockinette st

With Baby Lilac and size 5 needles, CO 30 (36, 42) sts. Distribute on 1 or 2 circulars or 3 or 4 dpns, as desired. Without twisting sts, join.

CUFF Work 10 (12, 12) rnds in K3, P3 ribbing. Cut Baby Lilac and change to Baby Sherbet.

Work even in Stockinette st for 3½ in. (4 in., 5 in.). Cut Baby Sherbet, change to Baby Lilac.

HEEL SETUP K 16 (18, 20) sts. Place rem 14 (18, 22) sts on a separate needle or holder for the instep.

HEEL FLAP ROW 1: Turn. Sl 1, P across.

HEEL FLAP ROW 2: *Sl 1, K1*, rep across.

Rep Heel Flap Rows 1–2, 5 (6, 7) times more, end with a P row, turn.

HEEL Work 16 (18, 20)-st Flap and Gusset Heel as instructed on page 173.

GUSSET RND 1: K 5 (5, 6) sts, pick up, twist, and K 7 (9, 10) sts along heel flap edge, place marker, K across instep sts, place marker, pick up, twist, and K 7 (9, 10) sts along other heel flap edge, K 5 (5, 6) sts.

GUSSET RND 2: K to within 2 sts of marker, SSK, move marker, K across instep sts, move marker, K2 tog, K to end. (2 sts dec)

GUSSET RND 3: K.

Rep Gusset Rnds 2–3 until 30 (36, 42) sts rem.

Work even until foot measures: Toddler: 2 in., Child Shoe Size 10–11: 3 in., Child Shoe Size 12–13: 3½ in., Youth Shoe Size 1–2: 4 in., Youth Shoe Size 3–4: 4½ in. Cut Baby Sherbet, change to Baby Lilac. Work ½ in. (all sizes). On the last rnd, K 8 (9, 11) sts, place markers K 15 (18, 21) sts, place marker, K 7 (9, 10) sts.

TOE **WEDGE TOE DECREASE RND 1:** K to within 2 sts of first marker, K2 tog, move marker, SSK, K to within 2 sts of 2nd marker, K2 tog, move marker, SSK, K to end. (4 sts dec)

WEDGE TOE DECREASE RND 2: K.

Rep Wedge Toe Decrease Rnds 1–2 until 18 (20, 22) sts rem. You may need to K to a marker or side.

FINISHING Cut yarn, leaving a 12-in. tail. Close the remaining sts with Kitchener st (see Glossary for instructions). Weave all loose ends in on the inside of the sock. Wash and block the socks.

Purl Bump Child-Size Worsted Weight
FLAP AND GUSSET SOCK

PATTERN DIFFICULTY:
Easy/Intermediate
YARN: Knit Picks Wool of
the Andes Kettle-Dyed™,
100% Peruvian highland wool,
50 g, 110 yd., #24292 Grasshopper Kettle, 1 (2, 2) balls
YARN WEIGHT: Worsted
NEEDLES: Size 5 (U.S.)/
3.75 mm, or size needed to obtain

gauge 1 or 2 circulars or 4 or
5 dpns, as desired
TOOLS: Large-eye blunt needle,
stitch markers
PATTERN SIZES: Toddler (6–8),
Child (10–11, 12–13), Youth (1–2,
3–4)
MEASUREMENTS: Cuff Length:
Toddler: 3½ in., Child: 4 in., Youth:
5 in.; Width: Toddler: 2⅛ in., Child:
2⅝, Youth: 3 in.; Heel-to-Toe

Length: Toddler: 5½ in., Child
Shoe Size 10–11: 5¾ in., Child
Shoe Size 12–13: 6¼ in., Youth
Shoe Size 1–2: 6½ in., Youth Shoe
Size 3–4: 6¾ in.
HEEL STYLE: Flap and Gusset
GAUGE: 7 sts = 1 in., 8 rnds =
1 in. in Stockinette st
7 sts = 1 in., 9 rnds = 1 in. in Purl
Bump Pattern

*N*ote: **Youth** pattern may also fit **Women's Narrow**; adjust
foot and cuff length for shoe size, and purchase extra yarn.

PURL BUMP PATTERN (3-st, 4-rnd repeat)
RNDS 1–3: K.
RND 4: *K2, P1*, rep around.
Work Purl Bump Pattern over cuff and instep.

With Grasshopper Kettle and size 5 needles, CO 30
(36, 42) sts. Distribute on 1 or 2 circulars or 3 or
4 dpns, as desired. Without twisting sts, join.
Work 10 (12, 12) rnds in K3, P3 ribbing.
Work Purl Bump Pattern until cuff measures 3½ in.
(4 in., 5 in.).
HEEL SETUP: K 16 (18, 20) sts. Place rem 14 (18, 22) sts
on a separate needle or holder for the instep.
HEEL **HEEL FLAP ROW 1:** Turn. Sl 1, P across.
HEEL FLAP ROW 2: *Sl 1, K1*, rep across.
Rep Heel Flap Rows 1–2, 5 (6, 7) times more, end with
a P row, turn.
Work a 16 (18, 20)-st Flap and Gusset Heel as
instructed on page 173.

Work foot, continuing in established patt with Purl
Bump patterning on the instep and plain Stockinette
st on the sole, until foot measures from gusset edge:
Toddler: 2½ in.; Child Shoe Size 10–11: 3 in., Child
Shoe Size 12–13: 3½ in., Youth Shoe Size 1–2: 4 in.,
Youth Shoe Size 3–4: 4½ in.
On the last foot rnd, K8 (9, 11), place marker, K15 (18,
21), place marker, K7 (9, 10).
TOE **WEDGE TOE DECREASE RND 1:** K to within 2 sts
of first marker, K2 tog, move marker, SSK, K to within
2 sts of 2nd marker, K2 tog, move marker, SSK, K to
end. (4 sts dec)
WEDGE TOE DECREASE RND 2: K.
Rep Wedge Toe Decrease Rnds 1–2 until 18 (20, 22)
sts rem. You may need to K to a marker or side.
FINISHING Cut yarn, leaving a 12-in. tail. Close
the rem sts with Kitchener st. Weave all loose ends in
on the inside of the sock. Wash and block the socks.

Mini Broken Rib Child-Size Worsted Weight
FLAP AND GUSSET SOCK

PATTERN DIFFICULTY: Easy/Intermediate

YARN: Knit Picks Swish, 100% superwash wool, 50 g, 110 yd., #23879 Bubblegum, 1 (2, 2) balls

YARN WEIGHT: Worsted

NEEDLES: Size 5 (U.S.)/ 3.75 mm, or size needed to obtain gauge

1 or 2 circulars or 4 or 5 dpns, as desired

TOOLS: Large-eye blunt needle, stitch markers

PATTERN SIZES: Toddler (6–8), Child (10–11, 12–13), Youth (1–2, 3–4)

MEASUREMENTS: Cuff Length: Toddler: 4 in., Child: 4½ in., Youth: 5¼ in.; Other Measurements: As for

Contrast Rib-Heel-Toe Child Size Worsted Weight Flap and Gusset Sock

HEEL STYLE: Flap and Gusset

GAUGE: 6 sts = 1 in., 9 rnds = 1 in. in Stockinette st

7 sts = 1 in., 10 rnds = 1 in. in Mini Broken Rib Pattern

Note: Youth pattern may also fit **Women's Narrow**; adjust foot and cuff length for shoe size, and purchase extra yarn.

MINI BROKEN RIB PATTERN
(2-st, 2-row repeat)

ROW 1: *K1, P1*, rep around.

ROW 2: K.

Cast on, knit, and finish as for Contrast Rib-Heel-Toe Child-Size Worsted Weight Flap and Gusset Sock working Mini Broken Rib Pattern over cuff and instep.

Adult-Size Fingering
Weight Flap and
Gusset Anklet

Basic Adult-Size
Fingering Weight

Lightly Textured
Adult-Size
Fingering Weight

Basic Adult-Size Fingering Weight
FLAP AND GUSSET SOCK

PATTERN DIFFICULTY:
Advanced Beginner
YARN: Berroco Comfort™ Sock,
50% superfine nylon/50% superfine acrylic, 100g, 447 yd.,
#1814 Dunedin, 1 ball for all sizes
YARN WEIGHT: Fingering
NEEDLES: Size 2 (U.S.)/
2.75 mm, or size needed to obtain
gauge 1 or 2 circulars or 4 or
5 dpns, as desired

1 size 3 (US)/3.25 mm needle for
casting on
TOOLS: Large-eye blunt needle
PATTERN SIZES: Women's
Average (5–6, 7–8, 9–10), Men's
Average, Men's Wide (9–10,
11–12, 13)
MEASUREMENTS: Cuff Length:
Women's: 6 in., Men's Average:
6½ in., Men's Wide: 7 in.; Approx
Width: Women's: 3¼ in., Men's

Average: 3¾ in., Men's Wide: 4 in.;
Heel-to-Toe Length: Women's Shoe
Size 5–6: 7¼ in., Women's Shoe
Size 7–8: 8¼ in., Women's Shoe
Size 9–10: 9¼ in., Men's Shoe
Size 9–10: 9½ in., Men's Shoe
Size 11–12: 10 in., Men's Shoe
Size 13: 11 in.
HEEL STYLE: Flap and Gusset
GAUGE: 9 sts = 1 in., 11 rnds =
1 in. in Stockinette st

Note: To make matching socks with self-patterning yarns,
note the spot in the repeat where you cast on the first sock.
Cast on the mate in the same spot in the repeat.

With a size 3 needle, CO 60 (64, 72) sts. Being careful
not to twist the sts, join. Distribute on size 2 needles,
1 or 2 circulars or 3 or 4 dpns, as desired.
CUFF Work 20 rnds in K2, P2 ribbing.
NEXT RND, MEN'S AVERAGE WIDTH ONLY: Inc 2 sts
evenly spaced in rnd. (66 sts)
Work even in Stockinette st until cuff measures 6 in.
(6½ in., 7 in.).
HEEL SETUP K 30 (34, 36) sts. These are the
heel sts. Place the other 30 (30, 36) sts on a separate
needle or stitch holder for the instep.
HEEL FLAP ROW 1, ALL SIZES: Turn, Sl 1, P
across, turn.
HEEL FLAP ROW 2, ALL SIZES: *Sl 1, K1*, rep
across, turn.
Rep Heel Flap Rows 1–2, 13 (14, 15) more times, end
with a P row.

HEEL Work 30 (34, 36)-st Flap and Gusset Heel as
instructed on page 171–172.
GUSSET RND 1: K 9 (11, 11) sts, pick up, twist, and
K 15 (16, 17) sts along the edge of the heel flap, place
marker, work across the instep sts, place marker, pick
up, twist, and K 15 (16, 17) sts along the other edge of
the heel flap, K 9 (11, 11) sts.
GUSSET RND 2: K to within 2 sts of marked spot, SSK,
work across instep sts, K2 tog, K to end.
GUSSET RND 3: K.
Rep Gusset Rnds 2–3 until 60 (66, 72) sts rem.
Work foot in Stockinette st until it measures from the
edge of the heel flap: Women's Shoe Size 5–6: 5 in.,
Women's Shoe Size 7–8: 6 in., Women's Shoe Size
9–10: 6½ in., Men's Shoe Size 9–10: 6½ in., Men's
Shoe Size 11–12: 7 in., Men's Shoe Size 13: 7½ in.
TOE Work a 60 (66, 72)-st Star Toe as instructed
in the Fingering Weight Tube Sock patterns in this
chapter, or see page 176–177 for instructions.
FINISHING Weave all loose ends in on the inside
of the sock. Wash and block the socks.

Adult-Size Fingering Weight
FLAP AND GUSSET ANKLET

PATTERN DIFFICULTY:
Advanced Beginner

YARN: Knit Picks Risata™,
42% Cotton/39% superwash
wool/13% polyamide/6% Elite
elastic, 50 g, 196 yd.,
#24109 Buttermilk, 2 (3, 3) balls

YARN WEIGHT: Fingering

NEEDLES: Size 2 (U.S.)/
2.75 mm, or size needed to obtain
gauge 1 or 2 circulars or 4 or
5 dpns, as desired

1 size 3 (U.S.)/3.25 mm needle for
casting on

TOOLS: Large-eye blunt needle

PATTERN SIZES: Women's
Average (5–6, 7–8, 9–10), Men's
Average, Men's Wide (9–10,
11–12, 13)

MEASUREMENTS: Cuff Length:
Women's: 1 in., Men's: 1½ in.;
Approx Width: Women's: 3¼ in.,
Men's Average: 3¾ in., Men's
Wide: 4 in.; Heel-to-Toe Length:

Women's Shoe Size 5–6: 7¼ in.,
Women's Shoe Size 7–8: 8¼ in.,
Women's Shoe Size 9–10: 9¼ in.
Men's Shoe Size 9–10: 9½ in.,
Men's Shoe Size 11–12: 10 in.,
Men's Shoe Size 13: 11 in.

HEEL STYLE: Flap and Gusset

GAUGE: 9 sts = 1 in., 11 rnds =
1 in. in Stockinette st.

CO as for Basic Adult-Size Fingering Weight Flap and
Gusset Sock. Work 8 (10, 10) rnds K2, P2 ribbing.

NEXT RND, MEN'S AVERAGE ONLY: Inc 2 sts evenly
spaced in rnd. (66 sts)

ALL SIZES: K 3 rnds.

Work heel and finish as for Basic Adult-Size
Fingering Weight Flap and Gusset Sock. Wash
and block the socks.

Lightly Textured Adult-Size Fingering Weight
FLAP AND GUSSET SOCK

PATTERN DIFFICULTY:
Advanced Beginner

YARN: Knit Picks Essential
Kettle-Dyed™, 75% superwash
Merino wool/25% nylon, 50 g,
231 yd., #24388 Eggplant Kettle,
2 (2, 3) balls

YARN WEIGHT: Fingering

NEEDLES: Size 2 (U.S.)/2.75mm,
or size needed to obtain gauge
1 or 2 circulars or 4 or 5 dpns,
as desired

1 size 3 (U.S.)/3.25 mm needle for
casting on

TOOLS: Large-eye blunt needle

PATTERN SIZES: Women's
Average (5–6, 7–8, 9–10), Men's
Average, Men's Wide (9–10,
11–12, 13)

MEASUREMENTS: Cuff Length:
Women's: 6 in., Men's Average:
6½ in., Men's Wide: 7 in.; Approx
Cuff Width: Women's: 2½ in.,
Men's Average: 3¼ in., Men's
Wide: 3¾ in.; Heel-to-Toe Length:

Women's Shoe Size 5–6: 7¼ in.,
Women's Shoe Size 7–8: 8¼ in.,
Women's Shoe Size 9–10: 9¼ in.,
Men's Shoe Size 9–10: 9½ in.,
Men's Shoe Size 11–12: 10 in.,
Men's Shoe Size 13: 11 in.

HEEL STYLE: Flap and Gusset

GAUGE: 8.5 sts = 1 in., 11 rnds
= 1 in. in Stockinette st
10 sts = 1 in., 12 rnds = 1 in. in
Texture Pattern

TEXTURE PATTERN (6-st, 6-row repeat)

PATTERN ROWS 1–2: *K3, P3*, rep around.

PATTERN ROWS 3–6: K.

CO and work ribbing as for Basic Adult-Size
Fingering Weight Flap and Gusset Sock.

NEXT RND, MEN'S AVERAGE ONLY: Inc 2 sts evenly
spaced in rnd. (66 sts)

ALL SIZES: K 4 rnds. Work in Texture Pattern until cuff
measures 6 in. (7 in. 7½ in.).

Divide sts for heel as for Basic Adult-Size Fingering
Weight Flap and Gusset Sock. Adjust the 30 (32, 36)

instep sts so that they will begin with P1 (2, 2) *K3,
P3* on the next Texture Pattern Rnds 1–2.

HEEL Work the remaining 30 (34, 36) sts as for the
Basic Adult-Size Fingering Weight Flap and Gusset
Sock. Work the gusset and foot as for the Basic Adult-
Size Fingering Weight Adult Flap and Gusset Sock,
continuing the established patt along the instep, until
the toe decs. Work the toe decs and finish as for the
Basic Adult-Size Fingering Weight Flap and Gusset
Sock. Wash and block the socks.

Picot Edge Child-Size Fingering Weight
SLOUCH SOCK

PATTERN DIFFICULTY: Easy/Intermediate

YARN: Knit Picks Essential™, 75% superwash Merino wool/ 25% nylon, 50 g, 231 yd., 1 ball each of #24352 Jester Multi and #24343 Granny Smith

YARN WEIGHT: Fingering

NEEDLES: Size 2 (U.S.)/ 2.75 mm, or size needed to obtain gauge 1 or 2 circulars or 4 or 5 dpns, as desired 1 size 3/ 3.25 mm needle for casting on

TOOLS: Large-eye blunt needle, stitch markers

PATTERN SIZES: Toddler (6–8), Child (10–11, 12–13), Youth (1–2, 3–4)

MEASUREMENTS: Cuff Length: Toddler: 4 in., Child: 4½ in., Youth: 5¼ in.; Cuff Width: Toddler: 2¾ in., Child: 3 in., Youth: 3¼ in.; Heel-to-Toe Length: Toddler: 5½ in., Child Shoe Size 10–11: 5¾ in., Child Shoe Size 12–13: 6¼ in., Youth Shoe Size 1–2: 6½ in., Youth Shoe Size 3–4: 6¾ in.

HEEL STYLE: Flap and Gusset

GAUGE: 8.5 sts = 1 in., 12 rnds = 1 in. in Stockinette st

Note: **Youth** pattern may also fit **Women's Narrow**; adjust foot and cuff length for shoe size, and purchase additional yarn.

With Jester Multi and size 3 needle, CO 48 (52, 56) sts. Arrange sts on size 2 needles, 1 or 2 circulars or 3 or 4 dpns, as desired, making sure sts are not twisted, and join.

K 14 rnds.

CONTRAST CUFF Change to Granny Smith, K 1 rnd.

PICOT RND 1: *K2 tog, YO*, rep around.

PICOT RND 2: K around, working each YO as a st. K next 15 rnds.

Change to Jester Multi. Work even in Stockinette st (K all rnds) until cuff measures 4 in. (4½ in., 5¼ in.) from Picot Rnd 1.

HEEL SETUP K 24 (26, 28) sts for the heel. Place remaining 24 (26, 28) sts on a separate needle or holder for the instep.

HEEL FLAP ROW 1: Change to Granny Smith, turn work. Sl 1, P across, turn.

HEEL FLAP ROW 2: *Sl 1, K1*, rep across, turn.

Rep Heel Flap Rows 1–2, 7 (8, 10) more times, end with a P row.

HEEL Work 24 (26, 28)-st Flap and Gusset Heel as instructed on page 172.

GUSSET RND 1: Change to Jester Multi. K 7 (7, 8) sts, pick up, twist, and K 10 (11, 13) sts along flap edge, place marker, K across instep sts, place marker, pick up, twist, and K 10 (11, 13) sts along other flap edge, K 7 (7, 8) sts.

GUSSET RND 2: K to within 2 sts of first marker, SSK, move marker, K across instep sts, move marker, K2 tog, K to end of rnd. (2 sts dec)

GUSSET RND 3: K.

Repeat Gusset Rnds 2–3 until there are 12 (13, 14) sts before the first marker, and after the last marker. You will have the same number of sts as on the cuff. (48, 52, 56 sts)

Work even until foot measures: Toddler: 3 in., Child Shoe Size 10–11: 3¼ in., Child Shoe Size 12–13: 3½ in., Youth Shoe Size 10–12: 3¾ in., Youth Shoe Size 3–4: 4 in. from heel flap edge.

NEXT RND: Change to Green Apple. K, placing markers after the first and before the last 12 (13, 14) sts.

TOE **TOE DECREASE RND 1:** K to within 2 sts of the first marker, K2 tog, move marker, SSK, K to within 2 sts of the 2nd marker, K2 tog, move marker, SSK, K to end. (4 sts dec)

TOE DECREASE RND 2: K.

Rep Toe Decrease Rnds 1–2 until there are 16 (20, 24) sts left. If the sts are not already divided in half, divide them on 2 needles, so that the decs are at either side of each needle. You may need to knit to the end of one needle.

FINISHING Close the toe with Kitchener st (see Glossary for instructions). Fold hem in at the picot edge, and stitch down on the inside of the sock. Weave all the loose ends in on the inside of the sock. Wash and block the socks.

Folded Cuff
Child-Size
Fingering Weight

Picot Edge
Child-Size
Fingering Weight
Slouch Sock

Folded Cuff Child-Size
FINGERING WEIGHT SOCK

PATTERN DIFFICULTY: Easy/Intermediate

YARN: Lime & Violet Sasquatch, 75% superwash wool/25% nylon, 100 g, 425 yd., Shim Sham, 1 skein for all sizes

YARN WEIGHT: Fingering

NEEDLES: Size 2 (U.S.)/2.75 mm, or size needed to obtain gauge 1 or 2 circulars or 4 or 5 dpns, as desired

1 size 3 needle for casting on

TOOLS: Large-eye blunt needle, stitch markers

PATTERN SIZES: Toddler (6–8), Child (10–11, 12–13), Youth (1–2, 3–4)

MEASUREMENTS: Cuff Length: All Sizes: 5¼ in.; Heel-to-Toe Length: Toddler: 5½ in., Child Shoe Size 10–11: 5¾ in., Child

Shoe Size 12–13: 6¼ in., Youth Shoe Size 1–2: 6½ in., Youth Shoe Size 3–4: 6¾ in.

HEEL STYLE: Flap and Gusset

GAUGE: 8.5 sts = 1 in., 11 rnds = 1 in. in Stockinette St

Note: **Youth** pattern may also fit **Women's Narrow**; adjust foot and cuff length for shoe size, and purchase additional yarn.

With size 3 needles, CO and redistribute sts on size 2 needles as for Picot Edge Child-Size Fingering Weight Slouch Sock. Work 3 in. in K 2, P 2 ribbing.

NEXT RND: Turn entire cuff inside out, pick up a loop from the previous needle, and K that loop together with the first st of the new rnd. Continue to work K2, P2 ribbing until cuff measures 5¼ in. You may fold the cuff to reduce bulk.

HEEL SETUP Divide sts for heel as for Picot Edge Child-Size Fingering Weight Slouch Sock, making sure that the instep sts begin and end with purl sts (that may involve rearranging the stitches to center the instep properly).

HEEL Work Heel as for Picot Edge Child-Size Fingering Weight Slouch Sock.

GUSSET Work gusset as for Picot Edge Child-Size Fingering Weight Slouch Sock, continuing the K2, P2 ribbing on the instep sts, and Stockinette st on the sole.

Work the foot and toe decs as for Picot Edge Child-Size Fingering Weight Slouch Sock.

FINISHING Weave all loose ends in on the inside of the sock. Wash and block the socks.

Basic Child-Size
FLAP AND GUSSET SOCK

PATTERN DIFFICULTY: Easy/Intermediate

YARN: Schoeller Stahl Fortissima Colori Socka, 75% superwash wool/25% polyamide, 50 g, 229 yd., #9048 Safari, 1 (1, 2) balls

YARN WEIGHT: Fingering

NEEDLES: Size 2 (U.S.)/ 2.75 mm, or size needed to obtain gauge 1 or 2 circulars or 4 or 5 dpns, as desired 1 size 3 needle for casting on

TOOLS: Large-eye blunt needle, stitch markers

PATTERN SIZES: Toddler (6–8), Child (10–11, 12–13), Youth (1–2, 3–4)

MEASUREMENTS: Cuff Length: Toddler: 4 in., Child: 4½ in., Youth 5¼ in.; Cuff Width: Toddler: 2¾ in., Child: 3 in., Youth: 3¼ in.;

Heel-to-Toe Length: Toddler: 5½ in., Child Shoe Size 10–11: 5¾ in., Child Shoe Size 12–13: 6¼ in., Youth Shoe Size 1–2: 6½ in., Youth Shoe Size 3–4: 6¾ in.

HEEL STYLE: Flap and Gusset

GAUGE: 8.5 sts = 1 in., 11 rnds = 1 in. in Stockinette st

Note: **Youth** pattern may also fit **Women's Narrow**; adjust foot and cuff length for shoe size, and purchase additional yarn.

Note: To make matching socks from self-patterning yarns, note the spot in the pattern repeat where you began your first sock CO, and begin the second sock in the same place.

With size 3 needles, CO and redistribute on size 2 needles as for Picot Edge Child-Size Fingering Weight Slouch Sock. Work 10 (12, 12) rnds in K2, P2 ribbing. Work rem cuff in Stockinette st. Work the heel flap, gusset, foot, and toe as for Picot Edge Child-Size Fingering Weight Slouch Sock. Weave loose ends in on the inside of the sock. Wash and block the socks.

Basic 3 x 3 Rib
Worsted Weight

1 x 1 Rib Worsted Weight

NO-WRAP SHORT-ROW HEEL SOCKS

A Short-Row Heel is one that *turns* the direction of the sock without fussing with gussets and flaps. This heel is still worked back and forth on two needles, using roughly half of the total stitches, but there is no change in the total stitch number. A Short-Row Heel is not suitable for sock patterns that are designed to be nonstretchy (such as some cabled or stranded socks) or with yarn that has little or no elasticity. But it may be substituted for a Flap and Gusset Heel. Short-Row Heels are faster to knit, and they take less yarn than a Flap and Gusset Heel. (For more information, see Heels & Toes, page 173.)

Basic 1 x 1 Rib Worsted Weight
SHORT-ROW HEEL SOCK

PATTERN DIFFICULTY: Intermediate

YARN: Decadent Fibers Cookie Dough, 20% mohair/80% Merino wool, 227 g, 490 yd., Relish (variegated greens), 1 skein for all sizes

YARN WEIGHT: Worsted
NEEDLES: Size 5 (U.S.)/ 3.75 mm, or size needed to obtain gauge 1 or 2 circulars or 4 or 5 dpns, as desired
1 size 6 (U.S.)/4.0 mm needle for CO.

TOOLS: Large-eye blunt needle
PATTERN SIZES, MEASUREMENTS, AND GAUGE: As for Basic 3 x 3 Rib Worsted Weight Short-Row Heel Sock

Note: There is enough yarn in one skein to knit two pairs of socks in the women's and child sizes.

With a size 6 needle, CO as for Basic 3 x 3 Worsted Weight Short-Row Heel Sock. Distribute on size 5 needles, 1 or 2 circulars or 3 or 4 dpns, as desired, and without twisting sts, join.

Work 5 in. (6 in., 7 in.) in K1, P1 ribbing.
Work rem of sock as for Basic 3 x 3 Rib Worsted Weight Short-Row Heel Sock. Wash and block the socks.

Basic 3 x 3 Rib Worsted Weight
SHORT-ROW HEEL SOCK

PATTERN DIFFICULTY:
Intermediate

YARN: Decadent Fibers Cookie
Dough, 20% mohair/80% Merino
wool, 227 g, 490 yd., Nutmeg
(variegated browns), 1 skein for
all sizes

YARN WEIGHT: Worsted

NEEDLES: Size 5 (U.S.)/
3.75 mm, or size needed to obtain
gauge 1 or 2 circulars or 4 or
5 dpns as desired

TOOLS: Large-eye blunt needle

PATTERN SIZES: Child
(10–11, 12–13), Youth (1–2, 3–4),
Women's Average, Women's Wide
(5–6, 7–8, 9–10), Men's (8–9,
10–11, 12-13)

MEASUREMENTS: Cuff Length:
Child/Youth: 5 in., Women's: 6 in.,
Men's: 7 in.; Foot Width: Child:
2¾ in., Youth: 3¼ in., Women's
Average: 3½ in., Women's Wide:
4¼ in., Men's: 4½ in.; Heel-to-Toe
Length: Child Shoe Size 10–11:

6½ in., Child Shoe Size 12–13:
7 in., Youth Shoe Size 1–2: 7½ in.,
Youth Shoe Size 3–4: 8 in.,
Women's Shoe Size 5–6: 9 in.,
Women's Shoe Size 7–8: 9½ in.,
Women's Shoe Size 9–10: 10 in.,
Men's Shoe Size 8–9: 10½ in.,
Men's Shoe Size 10–11: 11 in.,
Men's Shoe Size 12–13: 12 in.

HEEL STYLE: Short Row

GAUGE: 6.5 sts = 1 in., 8 rnds =
1 in. in Stockinette st

Note: There is enough yarn in one skein to knit two pairs
of socks in the women's and child sizes.

With size 5 needles, CO 36 (42, 48, 54, 60) sts. Distribute on 1 or 2 circulars or 3 or 4 dpns, as desired, and without twisting sts, join.

Work in K3, P3 ribbing for 5 in. (6 in., 7 in.).

HEEL SETUP K 18 (20, 24, 26, 30) sts for the heel.
Place the remaining 18 (22, 24, 28, 30) sts on a stitch holder or separate needle for the instep.

HEEL Work 18 (20, 24, 26, 30)-st Short-Row Heel as instructed on pages 174–176.

FOOT Work even in Stockinette st until foot measures from heel: Child Shoe Size 10–11: 3½ in., Child Shoe Size 12–13: 4 in., Youth Shoe Size 1–2: 4½ in., Youth Shoe Size 3–4: 4¾ in., Women's Shoe Size 5–6: 5½ in., Women's Shoe Size 7–8: 6 in., Women's Shoe Size 9–10: 6½ in., Men's Shoe Size 8–9: 6½ in., Men's Shoe Size 10–11: 7 in., Men's Shoe Size 12–13: 7½ in.

TOE Work a 36 (42, 48, 54, 60)-st Star Toe as for the Worsted Weight Tweed Tube Socks in this chapter, or see instructions on page 177. Weave all loose ends in on the inside of the sock. Wash and block the socks.

Spiral Rib Worsted Weight
SHORT-ROW HEEL SOCK

PATTERN DIFFICULTY:
Intermediate

YARN: Knit Picks Wool of the Andes, 100% Peruvian highland wool, 50 g, 110 yd., #23896 Firecracker Heather, 2 balls for all sizes through Women's Shoe Size

5–6, 3 balls for Women's Shoe Size 7–8 through Men's Average Shoe Size 10–11, 4 balls for other Men's sizes

YARN WEIGHT: Worsted

NEEDLES: Size 5 (U.S.)/ 3.75 mm, or size needed to obtain gauge 1 or 2 circulars or 4 or 5 dpns, as desired

TOOLS: Large-eye blunt needle

PATTERN SIZES, MEASUREMENTS, AND GAUGE: As for Basic 3 x 3 Rib Worsted Weight Short-Row Heel Sock

SPIRAL RIB PATTERN
(6-st, 18-rnd repeat)

RNDS 1–3: *K3, P3*, rep around.

RNDS 4–6: P1, *K3, P3*, rep around, ending with P2.

RNDS 7–9: P2, *K3, P3*, rep around, ending with P1.

RNDS 10–12: *P3, K3*, rep around.

RNDS 13–15: K1, *P3, K3*, rep around, ending with K2.

RNDS 16–18: K2, *P3, K3*, rep around, ending with K1.

With a size 5 needle, CO as for Basic 3 x 3 Rib Worsted Weight Short-Row Heel Sock. Distribute on 1 or 2 circulars or 3 or 4 dpns, as desired; without twisting sts, join.

Work Spiral Rib Pattern for 5 in. (6 in., 7 in.).

Work rem of sock as for Basic 3 x 3 Rib Worsted Weight Short-Row Heel Sock. Wash and block the socks.

Basic Adult-Size Fingering Weight
SHORT-ROW HEEL SOCK

PATTERN DIFFICULTY:
Intermediate
YARN: Angora Valley Fibers
Natural Colored Cotton/Wool Yarn,
100 g (100 g, 150 g)
YARN WEIGHT: Fingering
NEEDLES: Size 2 (U.S.)/
2.75 mm, or size needed to
obtain gauge 1 or 2 circulars or
4 or 5 dpns, as desired

1 size 3 (U.S.)/3.25 mm needle for
casting on
TOOLS: Large-eye blunt needle
PATTERN SIZES: Women's
(5–6, 7–8, 9–10), Men's Average,
Men's Wide (9, 10–11, 12–13)
MEASUREMENTS: Cuff Length:
Women's: 6 in., Men's: 7 in.; Approx
Width: Women's: 3¾ in., Men's
Average: 4⅛ in., Men's Wide: 4½ in.;
Heel-to-Toe Length: Women's Length:

Women's Shoe Size 5–6: 7¼ in.,
Women's Shoe Size 7–8: 8¼ in.,
Women's Shoe Size 9–10: 9¼ in.
Men's Shoe Size 9–10: 9½ in.,
Men's Shoe Size 11–12: 10 in.,
Men's Shoe Size 13: 11 in.
HEEL STYLE: Short Row
GAUGE: 8 sts = 1 in., 10.5 rows
= 1 in. in Stockinette st (after
blocking)

With size 3 needle, CO 60 (64, 72 sts). Divide on size
2 needles, 1 or 2 circulars or 3 or 4 dpns, as desired.
Making sure that the sts are not twisted, join. Work
20 rnds in K2, P2 ribbing.
NEXT RND, MEN'S AVERAGE SIZE ONLY: K, inc 2 sts
evenly in rnd. (66 sts)

Work in Stockinette st until cuff measures 6 in.
(7 in., 7 in.).
HEEL SETUP K 30 (32, 36) sts. Place rem 30
(34, 36) sts on separate needle or holder for instep.
HEEL Work 30 (32, 36)-st Short-Row Heel as
instructed on pages 173–175.
FOOT Work even in Stockinette st until foot
measures: Women's Shoe Size 5–6: 5 in., Women's
Shoe Size 7–8: 5½ in., Women's Shoe Size 9–10: 6 in.,
Men's Shoe Size 9–10: 6 in., Men's Shoe Size 11–12:
6½ in., Men's Shoe Size 12–13: 7 in., from heel.
LAST FOOT RND: K 15 (17, 18) sts, place marker, K 30
(33, 36) sts, place marker, K 15 (16, 18) sts.
TOE **WEDGE TOE DECREASE RND 1:** K to within 2 sts
of marker, K2 tog, move marker, SSK, K to within
2 sts of marker, K 2 tog, move marker, SSK, K to end.
(4 sts dec)
WEDGE TOE DECREASE RND 2: K.
Rep Wedge Toe Decrease Rnds 1–2 until 28 (30, 32)
sts rem. You may need to knit to a marker.
FINISHING Cut a 12-in. tail, and close the
remaining sts with Kitchener st (see Glossary for
instructions). Weave all loose ends in on the inside of
the sock. Wash and block the socks.

Contrast Ribbing Heel and Toe
Adult-Size Fingering Weight
SHORT-ROW HEEL SOCK

PATTERN DIFFICULTY: Intermediate

YARN: Knit Picks Essential Tweed™, 65% superwash wool/25% nylon/10% Donegal tweed, 50 g, 231 yd., #23861 Flint (1 ball for all sizes), #23862 Inca Gold 1 (2, 2) balls

YARN WEIGHT: Fingering

NEEDLES: Size 2 (U.S.)/ 2.75 mm, or size needed to obtain gauge 1 or 2 circulars or 4 or 5 dpns, as desired 1 size 3 (U.S.)/3.25 mm needle for casting on

TOOLS: Large-eye blunt needle

PATTERN SIZES: As for Basic Adult-Size Fingering Weight Short-Row Heel Sock

MEASUREMENTS: Cuff Width (lying flat): Women's: 3½ in., Men's Average: 3¾ in., Men's Wide: 4 in.; all other measurements as for Basic Adult-Size Fingering Weight Short-Row Heel Sock

HEEL STYLE: Short Row

GAUGE: 9 sts = 1 in., 12 rnds = 1 in. in Stockinette st

With size 3 needles and Flint, CO as for Basic Adult-Size Fingering Weight Short-Row Heel Sock, redistribute sts on size 2 needles. Work 20 rnds K1, P1 ribbing. Change to Inca Gold.

NEXT ROW, MEN'S AVERAGE ONLY: K, inc 2 sts evenly spaced in rnd. (66 sts)

Work cuff and heel as for Basic Adult-Size Fingering Weight Short-Row Heel Sock, changing to Flint for the heel, and back to Inca Gold after the heel. Work the foot as for Basic Adult-Size Fingering Weight Short-Row Heel Sock until it measures: Women's Shoe Size 5–6: 4½ in., Women's Shoe Size 7–8: 5 in., Women's Shoe Size 9–10: 5½ in., Men's Shoe Size 9–10: 5½ in., Men's Shoe Size 11–12: 6 in., Men's Shoe Size 12–13: 6½ in., from the heel. Change to Flint, work even for ½ in.

Work Wedge Toe and finish as for Basic Adult-Size Fingering Weight Short-Row Heel Sock.

Purl Spiral Adult-Size Fingering Weight
SHORT-ROW HEEL SOCK

PATTERN DIFFICULTY:
Intermediate
YARN: Knit Picks Essential
Kettle-Dyed, 75% superwash
Merino wool/25% nylon, 50 g,
231 yd., #24387 Gold Kettle,
2 (2, 3) balls
YARN WEIGHT: Fingering

NEEDLES: Size 2 (U.S.)/
2.75 mm, or size needed to obtain
gauge 1 or 2 circulars or 4 or
5 dpns, as desired
1 size 3 (U.S.)/3.25 mm needle for
casting on
TOOLS: Large-eye blunt needle
PATTERN SIZES: As for Basic
Adult-Size Fingering Weight Short-
Row Heel Sock

MEASUREMENTS: Length:
As for Basic Adult-Size Fingering
Weight Short-Row Heel Sock; Cuff
Width (lying flat): Women's:
3½ in., Men's Average: 3¾ in.,
Men's Wide: 4¼ in.
HEEL STYLE: Short Row
GAUGE: 9 sts = 1 in., 11 rnds =
1 in. in Stockinette st
8.5 sts = 1 in., 10 rnds = 1 in. in
Purl Spiral Pattern

PURL SPIRAL PATTERN
(6-st, 6-rnd repeat)

RND 1: *K5, P1*, rep around.

RND 2: P1, *K5, P1*, around, end K5.

RND 3: K1, P1, *K5, P1*, rep around, end K4.

RND 4: K2, P1, *K5, P1*, rep around, end K3.

RND 5: K3, P1, *K5, P1*, rep around, end K2.

RND 6: K4, P1, *K5, P1*, rep around, end K1.

CO and work ribbing as for Basic Adult-Size Fingering Weight Short-Row Heel Sock.

NEXT RND, MEN'S AVERAGE ONLY: K, inc 2 sts
evenly spaced in rnd. (66 sts)

Work Cuff in Purl Spiral Pattern, as for Basic Short-
Row Heel Sock. Work Heel as for Basic Short-Row
Heel Sock. Work Foot as for Basic Short-Row Heel
Sock in Stockinette st, using Purl Spiral Pattern on
the instep. Work Wedge Toe as for Basic Short-
Row Heel Sock. Finish and block as for Basic
Short-Row Heel Sock.

Roll-Top Child-Size Fingering Weight
SHORT-ROW HEEL SOCK

PATTERN DIFFICULTY: Intermediate

YARN: Knit Picks Essential Tweed, 65% superwash Merino wool/25% nylon/10% Donegal tweed, 50g, 231 yd., #24339 Blue Ox, 1 ball for all sizes through Youth Shoe Size 1–2, 2 balls for Youth Shoe Size 3–4

YARN WEIGHT: Fingering

NEEDLES: Size 2 (U.S.)/ 2.75 mm, or size needed to obtain gauge 1 or 2 circulars and 4 or 5 dpns as desired 1 size 3 (U.S.)/3.25 mm needle for casting on

TOOLS: Large-eye blunt needle

PATTERN SIZES: Toddler (6–8), Child (10–11, 12–13), Youth (1–2, 3–4)

MEASUREMENTS: Cuff Length (including the naturally rolled top; do not unroll the upper edge for measuring): Toddler: 4 in., Child: 4½ in., Youth: 5 in.; Approx Width: Toddler: 2¾ in., Child: 3 in., Youth: 3¼ in.; Heel-to-Toe Length: Toddler: 5½ in., Child Shoe Size 10–11: 5¾ in., Child Shoe Size 12–13: 6¼ in., Youth Shoe Size 1–2: 6½ in., Youth Shoe Size 3–4: 6¾ in.

HEEL STYLE: Short Row

GAUGE: 8.5 sts = 1 in., 12 rnds = 1 in. in Stockinette st

Note: **Youth** pattern may also fit **Women's Narrow**; adjust foot and cuff length for shoe size, and purchase additional yarn.

With size 3 needle, CO 48 (52, 56) sts. Distribute on size 2 needles, 1 or 2 circular or 3 or 4 dpns, as desired. Being careful not to twist the sts, join. K 6 rnds.

Work 10 rnds K1, P1 ribbing.

Work even in Stockinette st until cuff measures 4 in. (4½ in., 5 in.) from the top of the rolled edge (do not unroll the edge for measuring).

HEEL SETUP K 24 (26, 28) sts for heel. Set rem 24 (26, 28) sts on a separate needle or holder for instep.

HEEL Work 24 (26, 28)-st Short-Row Heel as instructed on page 175.

FOOT Work even in Stockinette st until foot measures: Toddler: 3½ in., Child Shoe Size 10–11: 3¾ in., Child Shoe Size 12–13: 4 in.; Youth Shoe Size 1–2: 4½ in., Youth Shoe Size 3–4: 4¾ in.

2ND TO THE LAST FOOT ROW, YOUTH: Dec 2 sts evenly spaced in rnd. (54 sts rem)

2ND TO THE LAST FOOT ROW, CHILD: Dec 4 sts evenly spaced in rnd. (48 sts rem)

TOE Work 48 (48, 54)-st Star Toe as instructed in the Fingering Weight Tube Sock Knitting Instructions in this chapter, or see page 177 for instructions.

FINISHING Weave all loose ends in on the inside of the sock. Wash and block the socks.

Seed Stitch
Child-Size
Fingering Weight

Roll-Top Child-Size
Fingering Weight

Easy Basket Weave
Child-Size

Seed Stitch Child-Size Fingering Weight
SHORT-ROW HEEL SOCK

PATTERN DIFFICULTY:
Intermediate
YARN: Knit Picks Essential, 75% superwash wool/25% nylon, 50 g, 231 yd., #24037 Riverbed Multi, 1 (1, 2) balls

NEEDLES AND PATTERN SIZES: As for Roll-Top Child Size Fingering Weight Short-Row Heel Sock
MEASUREMENTS: As for Roll-Top Child-Size Fingering Weight Short-Row Heel Sock except Cuff

Width: Toddler: 2½ in., Child: 2¾ in., Youth: 3 in.
HEEL STYLE: Short Row
GAUGE: 8.5 sts = 1 in., 12 rnds = 1 in. in Stockinette st
9 sts = 1 in., 13 rnds = 1 in. in Seed st

CO as for Roll-Top Child-Size Fingering Weight Short-Row Heel Sock, join. Work 12 rnds in K1, P1 ribbing.

RND 1 SEED ST: *P1, K1*, rep around.
RND 2 SEED ST: *K1, P1*, rep around.
Rep Rnds 1–2 Seed st until cuff measures as for Roll-Top Child-Size Fingering Weight Short-Row Heel Sock, measuring from the end of the ribbing. Work Short-Row Heel as for Roll-Top Sock. Work foot as for Roll-Top Sock, working the instep in Seed st and the sole in Stockinette st. Work the toe, and finish as for Roll-Top Sock. Wash and block the socks.

Easy Basket Weave Child-Size
SHORT-ROW HEEL SOCK

PATTERN DIFFICULTY:
Intermediate
YARN: Knit Picks Essential, 75% superwash wool/25% nylon, 50 g, 231 yd., #63543 Rust, 1 (1, 2) balls

NEEDLES AND PATTERN SIZES: As for Roll-Top Child Size Fingering Weight Short-Row Heel Sock
MEASUREMENTS: As for Roll-Top Child-Size Fingering Weight Short-Row Heel Sock except Cuff

Width: Toddler: 2⅛ in., Child: 2¼ in., Youth: 2½ in.
HEEL STYLE: Short Row
GAUGE: 8 sts = 1 in., 10.5 rnds = 1 in. in Stockinette st
11 sts = 1 in., 10 rnds = 1 in. in Basket Weave Pattern

BASKET WEAVE PATTERN
(4-st, 8-rnd repeat)
BASKET WEAVE RNDS 1–4: *K2, P2*, rep around.
BASKET WEAVE RNDS 5–8: *P2, K2*, rep around.

CO as for Roll-Top Sock. Work 12 rnds K2, P2 ribbing. Work cuff in Basket Weave Pattern as for Roll-Top Sock. Work heel, foot, and toe as for Roll-Top Sock. Finish as for Roll-Top Sock. Wash and block the socks.

TOE-UP SOCKS

Almost any Short-Row Heel sock pattern, in any weight yarn, can be knitted from the toe up because a Short-Row Heel is identical worked from either direction. Most toe-up patterns use a Wedge Toe construction, but our worsted weight pattern on page 60 incorporates the Star Toe. You can close and tighten the toe opening as soon as you have an inch or so of the foot knitted, or you can wait until you're done with the whole sock.

Toe-Up Fingering Weight
SHORT-ROW TOE ANKLET

PATTERN DIFFICULTY:
Intermediate
YARN: Crystal Palace Panda Cotton, 59% bamboo/25% cotton/16% elastic nylon, 50 g, 182 yd., #0225 Pinto Pony, 1 (1, 2, 2, 3, 3) balls
YARN WEIGHT: Fingering
NEEDLES: Size 2 (U.S.)/2.75 mm, or size needed to obtain gauge 1 or 2 circulars or 4 or 5 dpns, as desired Size 3 (U.S.)/3.25 mm needle for binding off

TOOLS: Large-eye blunt needle
PATTERN SIZES: Toddler (6–8), Child (10–11, 12–13), Youth (1–2, 3–4), Women's Average (5–6, 7–8, 9–10), Men's Average, Men's Wide (9, 10–11, 12–13)
MEASUREMENTS: Approx Width: Toddler: 3 in., Child: 3¼ in., Youth: 3½ in., Women's: 3¾ in., Men's Average: 4⅛ in., Men's Wide: 4½ in.; Heel-to-Toe Length: Toddler: 5½ in., Child Shoe Size 10–11: 5¾ in., Child

Shoe Size 12–13: 6¼ in., Youth Shoe Size 1–2: 6½ in., Youth Shoe Size 3–4: 6¾ in., Women's Shoe Size 5–6: 7¼ in., Women's Shoe Size 7–8: 8¼ in., Women's Shoe Size 9–10: 9¼ in., Men's Shoe Size 9–10: 9½ in., Men's Shoe Size 11–12: 10 in., Men's Shoe Size 13: 11 in.
HEEL STYLE: Short Row
GAUGE: 8 sts = 1 in., 12 rnds = 1 in. in Stockinette st

This yarn is quite stretchy, so the heel-to-toe lengths are a bit shorter than for many sock patterns.

Note: **Youth** may fit **Women's Narrow**; adjust the cuff and foot length for shoe size and purchase additional yarn. **Women's Wide** and **Men's Average** sizes use the same number of sts; work the cuff length and the foot length as for the desired shoe size.

With size 2 needle, CO 24 (26, 28, 30, 32, 36) sts. Do not divide the sts on other needles, do not join.

ST SHORT-ROW TOE: Work as for 24 (26, 28, 30, 32, 36)-st Short-Row Heel as instructed on pages 173–175.
FOOT SETUP: Pick up and K 24 (26, 28, 30, 32, 36) sts across lower front toe CO edge. Distribute on 1 or 2 circulars or 3 or 4 dpns, as desired, for foot. (48, 52, 56, 60, 64, 72 sts)
FOOT Work even in Stockinette st until foot measures: Toddler: 3 in., Child Shoe Size 10–11: 3¼ in., Child Shoe Size 12–13: 3½ in. Youth Shoe Size 1–2: 4 in. Youth Shoe Size 3–4: 4¼ in. Women's Shoe Size 5–6: 5 in., Women's Shoe Size 7–8: 5½ in., Women's Shoe Size 9–10: 6 in., Men's Shoe Size 9–10:

6 in., Men's Shoe Size 11–12: 6½ in., Men's Shoe Size 12–13: 7 in. from end of picked-up edge.

HEEL Work heel as for toe, making sure that the Short-Row Heel and Short-Row Toe line up properly.

CUFF SETUP: Work as for Short-Row Heel Foot Setup

CUFF Work 1 in. in Stockinette st.

RIBBING: Work 10 (10, 12, 12, 16, 16) rnds in K2, P2 ribbing.

FINISHING With a size 3 needle, BO loosely. Weave in all loose ends on the inside of the sock. Wash and block the socks.

Toe-Up Star Toe
WORSTED WEIGHT SOCK

PATTERN DIFFICULTY: Intermediate

YARN: Knit Picks Wool of the Andes Kettle-Dyed, 100% Peruvian highland wool, 50 g, 110 yd., #24288 Wine Kettle, 2 (2, 3, 4) balls. **Note:** This yarn bled a bit in the wash. Hand-wash these socks separately.)

YARN WEIGHT: Worsted

NEEDLES: Size 5 (U.S.)/ 3.75 mm, or size needed to obtain gauge 1 or 2 circulars or 4 or 5 dpns, as desired

1 size 6 (U.S.)/4.0 mm needle for binding off

TOOLS: Large-eye blunt needle

PATTERN SIZES: Child (10–11, 12–13), Youth (1–2, 3–4), Women's Average, Women's Wide (5–6, 7–8, 9–10), Men's Average, Men's Wide (9, 10–11, 12–13)

MEASUREMENTS: Approx Cuff/ Foot Width: Child: 2¾ in., Youth: 3¼ in., Women's Narrow: 3¼ in., Women's Average: 3¾ in., Women's Wide and Men's Average: 4⅛ in., Men's Wide: 4½ in.; Cuff Length: Child: 4½ in., Youth: 5½ in.,

Women's: 6 in., Men's: 7 in.; Heel-to-Toe Length: Child Shoe Size 10–11: 5¾ in., Child Shoe Size 12–13: 6¼ in., Youth Shoe Size 1–2: 6½ in., Youth Shoe Size 3–4: 6¾ in., Women's Shoe Size 5–6: 7¼ in., Women's Shoe Size 7–8: 8¼ in., Women's Shoe Size 9–10: 9¼ in., Men's Shoe Size 9: 9½ in., Men's Shoe Size 10–11: 10 in., Men's Shoe Size 12–13: 11 in.

HEEL STYLE: Short Row

GAUGE: 6.5 sts = 1 in., 9 rnds = 1 in. in Stockinette st

Note: **Youth** may fit **Women's Narrow**; adjust the cuff and foot length for shoe size and purchase additional yarn. **Women's Wide** and **Men's Average** sizes use the same number of sts; work the cuff length and the foot length as for the desired shoe size.

With size 5 needles, CO 12 sts. Distribute on 1 or 2 circulars or 3 or 4 dpns, as desired. Without twisting sts, join.

RND 1: K.

RND 2: *K2, inc 1*, rep around. (18 sts)

RND 3: *K3, inc 1*, rep around. (24 sts)

RND 4 AND ALL EVEN RNDS: K.

RND 5: *K4, inc 1*, rep around. (30 sts)

RND 7: *K5, inc 1*, rep around. (36 sts—for Child, go to Foot)

RND 9: *K6, inc 1*, rep around. (42 sts—for Youth and Women's Narrow, go to Foot)

RND 11: *K7, inc 1*, rep around. (48 sts—for Women's Average, go to Foot)

RND 13: *K8, inc 1*, rep around. (54 sts—for Women's Wide and Men's Average, go to Foot)

RND 15: *K9, inc 1*, rep around. (60 sts—for Men's Wide, go to Foot)

FOOT SETUP: Divide sts on needles as desired and work Foot.

FOOT Work even in Stockinette st until foot measures from end of toe incs: Child Shoe Size 10–11: 3 in., Child Shoe Size 12–13: 3½ in., Youth Shoe Size 1–2: 4 in., Youth Shoe Size 3–4: 4½ in., Women's Shoe Size 5–6: 5 in., Women's Shoe Size 7–8: 6 in., Women's Shoe Size 9–10: 6½ in., Men's Shoe Size 9: 6¼ in., Men's Shoe Size 10–11: 6½ in., Men's Shoe Size 12–13: 7 in.

HEEL SETUP: K 18 (20, 24, 28, 30) sts for the heel. Set the rem 18 (22, 24, 26, 30) sts on a separate needle or holder for the instep.

HEEL Work 18 (20, 24, 28, 30)-st Short-Row Heel as instructed on pages 174–176.

CUFF SETUP: Divide sts on needles as desired and work Cuff.

CUFF Work even until cuff measures from heel:
Child: 3½ in., Youth: 4 in., Women's: 4½ in., Men's: 5 in.
RIBBING: Work 10 (12, 15, 20) rnds in K3, P3 ribbing.
With size 6 needle, BO in patt.

Thread original CO tail in a large-eye needle, sew through the first row of sts, tighten and tie off on the inside of the sock. Weave all loose ends in on the inside of the sock. Wash and block the socks.

3

Striped

SOCKS

Stripes can be so much more than a simple changing of the colors every few rows. That said, changing colors is simple: For stripes of four rounds or less, strand the unused yarn up the inside of the sock without cutting the original color between the stripes. For stripes of more than four rounds, I recommend cutting the old color yarn and tying the new color on, leaving at least a 3-in. tail.

There are lots of different ways to join new colors to existing knitting (type *new yarn* into any online search engine). My favorite is the easiest: Tie the new color to the old color with a plain old knot. After the sock is finished, I go back and tighten them and either retie the yarn ends, or, if I am worried about that little bump, and if the yarn is a nice and grabby wool, I just pull the ends tightly and weave them in without further tying or knotting.

Another method I use to join wool yarns is called a *spit splice*. You moisten the two yarns with spit (with your mouth), overlap them a couple of inches, and roll them briskly between your palms. The moisture, friction, and heat will felt the yarn ends, and you'll have a clean join. If you prefer, use tap water to moisten the yarn. A spit splice won't work if you're using superwash wool yarns—or yarns predominantly made of cotton, silk, or other man-made fibers—since they won't felt.

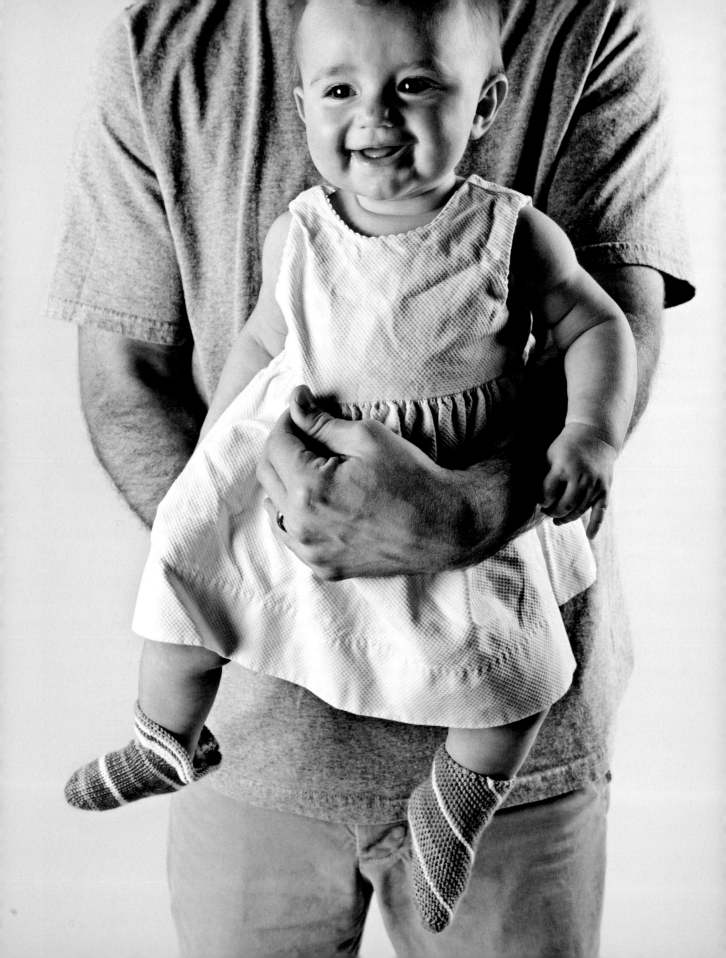

Sugar and Spice BOOTIE

Sugar and spice and everything stripes, that's what these adorable
two-needle, ruffle-top, toe-up tube booties are made from.

PATTERN DIFFICULTY:
Beginner
YARN: Dale of Norway Baby Ull,
100% Merino wool, 50 g, 180 yd.,
1 ball each of #4516 Fuchsia,
#0010 White, #9436 Kiwi
YARN WEIGHT: Fingering

NEEDLES: 1 pair 10-in. size
2 (U.S.)/2.75 mm straight needles,
or size needed to obtain gauge
1 size 3 (U.S.)/3.25 mm needle for
binding off
TOOLS: Large-eye blunt needle
PATTERN SIZES: Infant 0–3
Months, 3–6 Months, 6–12 Months

MEASUREMENTS: Width: 0–3
Months: 2¼ in., 3–6 Months:
2½ in., 6–12 Months: 2¾ in.;
Length: 0–3 Months: 5 in., 3–6
Months: 5½ in., 6–12 Months: 6 in.
HEEL STYLE: None
GAUGE: 8 sts = 1 in., 10 rows =
1 in. in Stockinette st

Note: Size 0–3 Months will reach required length before
final 6 Fuchsia rows are completed.

With Fuchsia and size 2 needles, CO 12 sts.

ROW 1: P, turn.

ROW 2: *K2, inc 1*, rep across, turn. (18 sts)

**ROW 3 AND ALL ODD ROWS UNTIL OTHERWISE
NOTED:** P, turn.

ROW 4: *K3, inc 1*, rep across, turn. (24 sts)

ROW 6: *K4, inc 1*, rep across, turn. (30 sts)

ROW 8: *K5, inc 1*, rep across, turn. (36 sts—for
0–3 Months size, go to Foot)

ROW 10: *K6, inc 1*, rep across, turn. (42 sts—for
3–6 Months size, go to Foot)

ROW 12: *K7, inc 1*, rep across, turn. (48 sts—for
6–12 Months size, go to Foot)

F O O T **ROW 1:** P across, turn.

FOOT STRIPE REPEAT: In Stockinette st (K 1 row, P 1
row), work the following sequence twice for all sizes:
*2 rows Kiwi, 6 rows Fuchsia, 2 rows White, 6 rows

Fuchsia*. Leave at least a 3-in. tail when tying on new
colors.

Work even in Stockinette st and Fuchsia until sock
measures 4 in. (4½ in., 5 in.) from toe, end with a
K row.

RIBBING Work 4 rows in K1, P1 ribbing. End on
RS row.

RUFFLE SETUP ROW (WS): *P1, inc 1*, rep across.
(72, 84, 96 sts)

RUFFLE On RS, tie on White. Work 4 rows White in
Garter st (K all rows), 2 rows Fuchsia, 2 rows White,
2 rows Kiwi.

FINISHING With Kiwi and size 3 needle, BO
loosely. Weave all ends in on the inside of the sock.
With yarn threaded in a large-eye needle, sew
through the CO loops at the toe and tighten. Using a
Mattress st (see Glossary for instructions), sew the
back seam. Weave end in on the inside of the sock.
Wash and block the socks.

$\mathcal{S}$nakes and $\mathcal{S}$nails BOOTIE

Snakes and snails and diagonal Garter stitch stripes—that's what these booties are made from. Knit the body of this little tube sock first, then pick up stitches for the toes. This construction is very stretchy; one size will fit most infants.

PATTERN DIFFICULTY: Beginner

YARN: Dale of Norway Baby Ull, 100% Merino wool, 50 g, 180 yd., 1 ball each of #6435 Lagoon, #0010 White, #9436 Kiwi

YARN WEIGHT: Fingering

NEEDLES: 1 pair 10-in. size 2 (U.S.)/2.75 mm straight needles, or size needed to obtain gauge

TOOLS: Large-eye blunt needle

PATTERN SIZE: Infant 3–12 Months

MEASUREMENTS: Unsewn Body: 5 in. square; Sewn Width: 2½ in.; Finished Length: 6 in.

HEEL STYLE: None

GAUGE: 10 sts = 1 in., 14 rows = 1 in. in Garter st

$\mathcal{N}$**ote:** The stripes will not line up on the back seam of the bootie.

With Lagoon and size 2 needles, CO 3.

INCREASE ROW 1: K across, turn.

INCREASE ROW 2: K2, inc 1, K1, turn.

INCREASE ROW 3: K to within 1 st of the end, inc 1, K1, turn.

Rep Increase Row 3 until there are 20 sts on the needle. Turn.

Cut Lagoon. Tie on Kiwi. Rep Increase Row 3 until there are 30 sts on the needle. Turn.

Do not cut Kiwi. Tie on White. Rep Increase Row 3 twice.

Cut White. With Kiwi, rep Increase Row 3 until there are 42 sts on the needle. Turn.

Cut Kiwi. Tie on Lagoon. Rep Increase Row 3 until there are 52 sts on the needle. Turn.

Do not cut Lagoon. Tie on White. K 2 rows even (no increases).

DECREASE ROW 1: Cut White. With Lagoon, K to within 2 sts of end, K2 tog. Turn.

DECREASE ROW 2: K to within 2 sts of end, K2 tog. Turn.

Rep Decrease Row 2 until there are 42 sts on the needle.

Cut Lagoon. Tie on Kiwi. Rep Decrease Row 2 until there are 32 sts on the needle.

Do not cut Kiwi. Tie on White. Rep Decrease Row 2 twice.

Cut White. With Kiwi, rep Decrease Row 2 until there are 20 sts on the needle.

Cut Kiwi. With Lagoon, rep Decrease Row 2 until there are 3 sts on the needle.

K 1 row even.

LAST ROW: Sl 1, K2 tog, PSSO.

Cut yarn, pull through remaining loop, and tighten. Weave all loose ends in on the wrong side of the work.

TOE Select the edge of the diagonally knit body that is the neatest looking. That will be the cuff edge of the bootie. On edge opposite the cuff edge, on the RS, with Lagoon, pick up and K 30 sts evenly spaced along that edge.

TOE DECREASE ROW 1 AND ALL ODD TOE DECREASE ROWS: P across, turn.

TOE DECREASE ROW 2: *K3, K2 tog*, rep across, turn. (24 sts rem)

TOE DECREASE ROW 4: *K2, K2 tog*, rep across, turn. (18 sts rem)

TOE DECREASE ROW 6: *K1, K2 tog*, rep across, turn. (12 sts rem)

FINISHING Cut yarn, leaving a 12-in. tail. Thread tail in a large-eye needle and sew through the remaining loops. Tighten and knot. Fold sock in half lengthwise, and with Mattress st, (see Glossary for instructions) sew the back seam. Tie off and weave all loose ends in on the inside of the sock. Wash and block the socks.

Popcorn Stripes Sock

Ruffle Stripes Sock

Popcorn STRIPES SOCK

The narrow eyelet stripes look just like rows of popcorn on this easy-to-knit, comfy sock.

PATTERN DIFFICULTY: Beginner

YARN: Regia 4-Ply, Kaffe Fassett Collection, 75% superwash wool/25% polyamide, 50 g, 231 yd., #4250 Mirage Storm, 1 ball for Child/Youth sizes, 2 balls for Women's sizes; Regia 4-Ply, 75% superwash wool, 25% polyamide, 50 g, 231 yd., #600 White, 1 ball for all sizes

YARN WEIGHT: Fingering

NEEDLES: Size 1 (U.S.)/ 2.50 mm, or size needed to obtain gauge 1 or 2 circulars or 4 or 5 dpns, as desired

TOOLS: Large-eye blunt needle, stitch markers

PATTERN SIZES: Child (10–11, 12–13), Youth (1–2, 3–4), Women's Average, Women's Wide (5–6, 7–8, 9–10)

MEASUREMENTS: Cuff/Foot Width: Child: 3¼ in., Youth: 3½ in., Women's Average: 3¾ in., Women's Wide: 4 in.; Cuff Length from Top of Rolled Portion: Child: 5½ in., Youth: 6 in., Women's: 6½ in.; Heel-to-Toe Length: Child Shoe Size 10–11: 6¼ in., Child Shoe Size 12–13: 6½ in., Youth Shoe Size 1–2: 7 in., Youth Shoe Size 3–4: 7½ in., Women's Shoe Size 5–6: 8 in., Women's Shoe Size 7–8: 9 in., Women's Shoe Size 9–10: 10 in.

HEEL STYLE: Short Row

GAUGE: 9 sts = 1 in., 12 rnds = 1 in. in Stockinette st

*N*ote: **Women's Narrow** may fit **Youth** sizes; adjust cuff and foot length for shoe size.

*N*ote: When the Popcorn Stripes are divided by less than 5 rnds of Mirage Storm, you can omit cutting the White yarn between the stripes.

With Mirage Storm and size 1 needles, CO 54 (60, 66, 72) sts. Distribute on 1 or 2 circulars or 3 or 4 dpns, as desired. Without twisting the sts, join.

ROLL TOP K 12 rnds.

POPCORN STRIPE (PS) **PS RND 1:** Tie on White, leaving at least a 3-in. tail (do not cut Mirage Storm). K.

PS RND 2: *K2 tog, YO*, rep around.

PS RND 3: K. Cut White, leaving at least a 3-in. tail. Work the cuff in the following sequence of stripes: PS, 13 rnds Mirage Storm, PS, 5 rnds Mirage Storm, PS, 10 rnds Mirage Storm, PS, 3 rnds Mirage Storm, PS, 6 rnds Mirage Storm, PS.

Work even in Mirage Storm until the cuff measures from the naturally rolled top 5½ in. (6 in., 6½ in.).

HEEL SETUP K 13 (15, 16, 18) sts for heel, place next 28 (30, 34, 36) sts on a separate needle or holder for the instep, place the remaining 13 (15, 16, 18) sts with the first for the heel. (26, 30, 32, 36 heel sts)

HEEL Work a 26 (30, 32, 36)-st Short-Row Heel as instructed on pages 173–175.

FOOT SETUP Sl 1, K12 (14, 15, 17). Begin new rnd at center of heel. Redistribute sts on needles.

FOOT Work the Popcorn Stripe sequence, knitting the White stripes on the sole stitches and working the Popcorn Stripe Pattern on the instep, until foot measures: Child Shoe Size 10–11: 3½ in., Child Shoe Size 12–13: 3¾ in., Youth Shoe Size 1–2: 4¼ in., Youth Shoe Size 3–4: 4½ in., Women's Shoe Size 5–6: 4¾ in., Women's Shoe Size 7–8: 5¾ in., Women's Shoe Size 9–10: 6¼ in. Not all of the Popcorn Stripes will be worked on the smaller sizes.

*N*ote: Omit the final Popcorn Stripe if the stripe will not be fully completed before reaching the desired foot length.

TOE Work and finish a 54 (60, 66, 72)-st Star Toe as instructed on pages 176–177.

FINISHING Weave all loose ends in on the inside of the sock. Wash and block the socks.

Ruffle STRIPES SOCK

These ruffled stripes are sure to please any little girl. You work the cuff with two needles, then join for the heel and foot. A Seed stitch border keeps the ruffles from rolling.

PATTERN DIFFICULTY: Intermediate

YARN: Knit Picks Risata, 42% cotton/39% superwash Merino wool/13% polyamide, 6% Elite elastic, 50 g, 196 yd., #24127 Woodland Sage 1 (2) balls, #24108 Dusk, 1 ball for all sizes.

YARN WEIGHT: Fingering

NEEDLES: 1 pair 10-in. size 2 (U.S.)/2.75 mm straight needles, or size needed to obtain gauge Size 2 (U.S.)/2.75 mm, 1 or 2 circulars or 4 or 5 dpns, as desired, or size needed to obtain gauge 1 size 3 (U.S.)/3.25 mm needle for casting on

TOOLS: Large-eye blunt needle

PATTERN SIZES: Child (10–11, 12–13), Youth (1–2, 3–4)

MEASUREMENTS: Approx Foot Width: Child: 2¾ in., Youth: 3¼ in.; Cuff Length: Child: 4½ in., Youth: 5½ in.; Heel-to-Toe Length: Child Shoe Size 10–11: 5¾ in., Child Shoe Size 12–13: 6¼ in., Youth Shoe Size 1–2: 6½ in., Youth Shoe Size 3–4: 6¾ in.

HEEL STYLE: Short Row

GAUGE: 8.5 sts = 1 in., 11 rnds = 1 in. in Stockinette st

With size 3 needle and Woodland Sage, CO 48 (56) sts. Transfer sts to 10-in. size 2 straight needle. Work 10 rows in K1, P1 ribbing.

CUFF **CUFF ROW 1 (RS):** K.

CUFF ROW 2 (WS): K.

CUFF ROW 3 K.

CUFF ROW 4 P.

CUFF ROWS 5–13: Work in Stockinette st (K on RS, P on WS), end with RS row.

Work Cuff Rows 2–13 twice more. Place all sts on waste yarn.

RUFFLE With Dusk, beginning at the RS edge, with the sock ribbing up, pick up and P 48 sts along the first purl ridge on the RS of the cuff. (48, 56 sts)

ROW 1: K.

ROW 2: *P1, inc 1*, rep across. (96, 112 sts)

ROWS 3–5: Work Stockinette st.

ROW 6: *K1, P1* across.

ROW 7: *P1, K1* across.

BO in K.

Rep above sequence with the remaining 2 purl ridges.

REMAINDER OF CUFF Place the cuff sts on 1 or 2 circulars or 3 or 4 dpns, as desired. Join, with the beginning of the rnd at the center back of the sock.

With Woodland Sage, work in Stockinette st until cuff measures 4½ (5½) in.

HEEL SETUP K12 (14), place the next 24 (28) sts on a separate needle or holder for the instep, place the rem 12 (14) sts with the first for the heel.

HEEL Using Dusk, work a 24 (28)-st Short-Row Heel as instructed on page 175.

FOOT SETUP Sl 1, K11 (13), begin new rnd at center of heel. Redistribute sts on needles as desired. Change to Woodland Sage at center of heel.

FOOT Work in Stockinette st until foot measures: Child Shoe Size 10–11: 3 in., Child Shoe Size 12–13: 3½ in., Youth Shoe Size 1–2: 4 in., Youth Shoe Size 3–4: 4½ in. Change to Dusk. Work ½ in. even.

2ND TO THE LAST FOOT RND, YOUTH SIZE ONLY:

Dec 2 sts evenly spaced in rnd. (54 sts)

TOE Work a 48 (54)-st Star Toe (see page 177).

FINISHING With Woodland Sage in a large-eye needle, using a Mattress st (see Glossary for instructions), sew the back cuff seam. With Dusk in a large-eye needle, using a Mattress st, sew each ruffle back seam. Weave all loose ends in on the inside of the sock or the underside of the ruffle. Wash and block the socks.

Jester STRIPES SOCK

What child wouldn't love these whimsical socks with their garter stitch points and colorful stripes?

PATTERN DIFFICULTY: Intermediate

YARN: Knit Picks Swish DK™, 100% superwash wool, 50 g, 123 yd., #24062 Maple Leaf 1 (1, 2) balls; 1 ball each of #24059 Pale Lemon and #24053 Dusk for all sizes

YARN WEIGHT: DK

NEEDLES: Size 3 (U.S.)/ 3.25 mm, or size needed to obtain gauge 1 or 2 circulars or 4 or 5 dpns, as desired 1 pair size 3 (U.S.)/ 3.25 mm straight needles

TOOLS: Large-eye blunt needle, stitch markers

PATTERN SIZES: Toddler (6–8), Child (10–11, 12–13), Youth (1–2, 3–4)

MEASUREMENTS: Approx Foot Width: Toddler: 3 in., Child: 3¼ in., Youth: 3½ in.; Cuff Length from Jester Point Tip: Toddler: 5¾ in., Child: 6¾ in., Youth: 7¾ in.; Heel-to-Toe Length: Toddler: 5½ in., Child Shoe Size 10–11: 5¾ in., Child Shoe Size 12–13: 6¼ in., Youth Shoe Size 1–2: 6½ in., Youth Shoe Size 3–4: 6¾ in.

HEEL STYLE: Flap and Gusset

GAUGE: 7 sts = 1 in., 9.5 rnds = 1 in. in Stockinette st

Note: Only small amounts of colored yarn are needed for these socks; this pattern would be a great use for leftover yarns.

JESTER POINTS With Pale Lemon and a straight size 3 needle, CO 1.

ROW 1: K.

ROW 2: Inc 1 at the beg of the row. (1 st inc) Rep Row 2 until 6 sts are on the needle. Rep Row 1. Cut yarn.

Leave those sts on the needle. With the other needle, CO 1 st with Dusk, and rep sequence.

TODDLER SIZE: Work as above, alternating Pale Lemon and Dusk Jester Points until there are 36 sts on the needle.

CHILD SIZE: Work as above, alternating Pale Lemon and Dusk Jester Points until there are 42 sts on the needle. **Note:** Points will begin and end with Pale Lemon.

YOUTH SIZE: Work as above, alternating Pale Lemon and Dusk Jester Points until there are 48 sts on the needle.

NEXT ROW: With Maple Leaf, K across.

Divide sts on 1 or 2 circulars or 3 or 4 dpns, as desired, without twisting sts, join.

CUFF **CUFF RND 1:** P.

CUFF RND 2: K.

CUFF RND 3: P.

CUFF RND 4: K.

CUFF RNDS 5–10: Change to Pale Lemon, K.

CUFF RND 11: Change to Maple Leaf, K.

CUFF RND 12: P.

CUFF RND 13: P.

ALL SIZES: Rep Cuff Rnds 5–13 with Dusk and Maple Leaf.

TODDLER SIZE ONLY: Work 5 stripes total, ending with a Maple Leaf purl ridge.

CHILD SIZE ONLY: Work 6 stripes total, ending with a Maple Leaf purl ridge.

YOUTH SIZE ONLY: Work 7 stripes total, ending with a Maple Leaf purl ridge.

NEXT RND, ALL SIZES: K.

HEEL SETUP K 9 (10, 12) sts, place next 18 (22, 24) sts on a separate needle or holder for the instep, place rem 9 (10, 12) sts on needle with first sts for the heel. (18, 20, 24 heel sts)

HEEL FLAP ROW 1: Sl 1, P across, turn.

HEEL FLAP ROW 2 AND ALL EVEN HEEL FLAP ROWS: *Sl 1, K1*, rep across, turn.

HEEL FLAP ROW 3: Tie on Pale Yellow, Sl 1, P across, turn.

HEEL FLAP ROW 5: Cut Pale Yellow. With Maple Leaf, Sl 1, P across, turn.

Rep sequence, alternating Pale Lemon and Dusk stripes with Maple Leaf, for a total of 14 (16, 18) rows. End with a P row. Work heel with Maple Leaf.

HEEL Work an 18 (20, 24)-st Flap and Gusset Heel as instructed on page 172–173.

GUSSET **GUSSET RND 1:** With Maple Leaf, K 5 (6, 7) sts, pick up, twist, and K 7 (9, 10) sts along heel flap edge, place marker, K across instep sts, place marker, pick up, twist, and K 7 (9, 10) sts along other heel flap edge, K 5 (6, 7) sts.

GUSSET RND 2: K to within 2 sts of marker, SSK, move marker, K across instep sts, move marker, K2 tog, K to end. (2 sts dec)

GUSSET RND 3: K.

Rep Gusset Rnds 2–3 until 36 (42, 48) sts rem. Work foot in Stockinette st and Maple Leaf until foot measures from gusset edge: Toddler: 2½ in., Child Shoe Size 10–11: 3 in., Child Shoe Size 12–13: 3½ in., Youth Shoe Size 1–2: 4 in., Youth Shoe Size 3–4: 4½ in. On the last foot rnd, K 9 (10, 12) sts, place marker, K 18 (21, 24) sts, place marker, K 9 (11, 12) sts.

𝓝ote: If using 1 or 2 circulars, you may divide the sts so half are on one needle and half are on the other, making sure that the division lines up properly with the heel.

TOE **WEDGE TOE DECREASE RND 1:** K to within 2 sts of first marker, K2 tog, move marker, SSK, K to within 2 sts of second marker, K2 tog, move marker, SSK, K to end. (4 sts dec)

WEDGE TOE DECREASE RND 2: K.

Rep Wedge Toe Decrease Rnds 1–2, alternating 2 rnds of Maple Leaf with 2 rnds of Pale Lemon and Dusk, until 16 (18, 20) sts rem. You may need to K to a marker or side. Cut yarn, leaving a 12-in. tail. Close the remaining sts with Kitchener st (see Glossary for instructions).

FINISHING Weave all loose ends in on the inside of the sock. Wash and block the socks.

Watermelon STRIPES SOCK

If you're intimidated by stranding (see chapter 6), you can omit the alternating rows and work two more rounds of the original color. You can embroider in the black seeds after finishing the sock using Duplicate stitch.

PATTERN DIFFICULTY:
Beginner/Intermediate

YARN: Knit Picks Palette™, 100% Peruvian highland wool, 50 g, 231 yd., #24007 Tidepool Heather, #23717 Petal, #23718 Blush, #23728 White, #23729 Black, 1 ball each for all sizes. (**Note:** Less than 20 yd. of Black is needed for all sizes.)

YARN WEIGHT: Fingering

NEEDLES: Size 1 (U.S.)/ 2.50 mm, or size needed to obtain gauge 1 or 2 circular or 4 or 5 dpns, as desired

1 size 3 (U.S.)/3.25 mm needle for casting on

TOOLS: Large-eye blunt needle, stitch markers

PATTERN SIZES: Toddler (6–8), Child (10–11, 12–13), Youth (1–2, 3–4), Women's (5–6, 7–8, 9 10)

MEASUREMENTS: Cuff Length: Toddler: 4 in., Child: 5½ in., Youth: 6½ in., Women's: 7 in.; Approx Cuff Width: Toddler: 2¾ in., Child:

3 in., Youth: 3¼ in., Women's: 3¾ in.; Heel-to-Toe Length: Toddler: 5½ in., Child Shoe Size 10–11: 5¾ in., Child Shoe Size 12–13: 6¼ in., Youth Shoe Size 1–2: 6½ in., Youth Shoe Size 3–4: 6¾ in., Women's Shoe Size 5–6: 7¼ in., Women's Shoe Size 7–8: 8¼ in., Women's Shoe Size 9–10: 9¼ in.

HEEL STYLE: Flap and Gusset

GAUGE: 9.5 sts = 1 in., 10 rnds = 1 in. in Stockinette st

WATERMELON STRIPE PATTERN
(41-rnd repeat)

RNDS 1–4: K with White.

RND 5: Tie on Blush. *K1 White, K1 Blush*, rep around.

RND 6: *K1 Blush, K1 White*, rep around. Cut White.

RNDS 7–10: K with Blush.

RND 11: Tie on Petal. *K1 Blush, K1 Petal*, rep around.

RND 12: *K1 Petal, K1 Blush*, rep around. Cut Blush.

RNDS 13–16: K with Petal.

RND 17: Tie on Black. *K3 Petal, K1 Black*, rep around. Cut Black.

RNDS 18–21: K with Petal.

RND 22: Tie on Blush. *K1 Petal, K1 Blush*, rep around.

RND 23: *K1 Blush, K1 Petal*, rep around. Cut Petal.

RNDS 24–27: K with Blush.

RND 28: Tie on White. *K1 Blush, K1 White*, rep around.

RND 29: *K1 White, K1 Blush*, rep around. Cut Blush.

RNDS 30–33: K with White.

RND 34: Tie on Tidepool Heather. *K1 White, K1

Tidepool Heather*, rep around.

RND 35: *K1 Tidepool Heather, K1 White*, rep around. Cut White.

RNDS 36–39: K with Tidepool Heather.

RND 40: Tie on White. *K1 Tidepool Heather, K1 White*, rep around.

RND 41: *K1 White, K1 Tidepool Heather*, rep around. Cut Tidepool Heather.

Note: When stranding yarns, carry the unused color loosely on the back of the work. Leave at least a 3-in. tail when tying on or cutting colors.

With size 3 needle, and Tidepool Heather, CO 48 (56, 64, 72) sts. Divide on size 1 needles, 1 or 2 circulars or 3 or 4 dpns, as desired. Without twisting sts, join. Work 12 (12, 16, 16) rnds in K2, P2 ribbing.

RND 1: K.

RND 2: Tie on White. *K1 Tidepool Heather, K1 White*, rep around.

RND 3: *K1 White, K1 Tidepool Heather*, rep around. Cut Tidepool Heather.

Work Watermelon Stripe Pattern until cuff measures 4 in. (5½ in., 6½ in., 7 in.).

HEEL SETUP Work 12 (14, 16, 18) sts in established patt. Place the next 24 (28, 32, 36) sts on a separate needle or holder for the instep, place the rem 12 (14, 16, 18) sts with the first sts for the heel.

HEEL FLAP ROW 1: With Tidepool Heather, turn, Sl 1, P across, turn.

HEEL FLAP ROW 2: *Sl 1, K1*, rep across, turn.

Rep Heel Flap Rows 1–2, 9 (11, 13, 15) more times, end with a P row.

HEEL Work 24 (28, 32, 36)-st Flap and Gusset Heel as directed on pages 171–172. (14 (16, 20, 20) sts rem.)

GUSSET Sl 1, K 6 (7, 9, 9) sts. New rnd begins at center of heel. Cut Tidepool Heather (unless Tidepool Heather is the color you need to continue the established instep patt). Tie on the color you need to continue the established instep patt.

GUSSET RND 1: K 7 (8, 10, 10) sts, pick up, twist, and K 11 (13, 16, 17) sts along flap edge, place marker, K across instep sts in the established instep patt (that may include tying on another color and cutting it at the end of the instep), place marker, pick up, twist, and K 11 (13, 16, 17) sts along other flap edge, K 7 (8, 10, 10) sts.

GUSSET RND 2: Working in established Watermelon Stripe Pattern on the instep and the sole, K to within 2 sts of first marker, SSK, move marker, K across instep sts in established instep patt, move marker, K2 tog, K to end of rnd in established patt. (2 sts dec)

GUSSET RND 3: K, working in the established Watermelon Stripe Pattern.

Rep Gusset Rnds 2–3 until there are 48 (56, 64, 72) sts. Work in established Watermelon Stripe Pattern until foot measures: Toddler: 3½ in., Child Shoe Size 10–11: 3¾ in., Child Shoe Size 12–13: 4 in., Youth Shoe Size 1–2: 4½ in., Youth Shoe Size 3–4: 4¾ in., Women's Shoe Size 5–6: 5 in., Women's Shoe Size 7–8: 6 in., Women's Shoe Size 9–10: 6½ in.

2ND TO THE LAST FOOT ROW, CHILD: Dec 2 sts evenly spaced in rnd. (54 sts rem)

2ND TO THE LAST FOOT ROW, YOUTH: Dec 4 sts evenly spaced in rnd. (60 sts rem)

TOE Work a 48 (54, 60, 72)-st Star Toe as instructed on pages 176–177.

FINISHING Weave all loose ends in. Wash and block the socks.

Alpaca STRIPED KNEESOCK

Don't let the goofy shape of this toe-up sock fool you on the needles—
this wonderful alpaca yarn has little vertical stretch when knitted up, so it does
take 18 in. of sock cuff to cover 12 in. of leg.

PATTERN DIFFICULTY:
Beginner/Intermediate

YARN: Classic Elite Yarns Alpaca
Sox, 60% alpaca/20% Merino
wool/20% nylon, 100 g, 450 yd.,
Stripe Pattern 1: #1816 Oatmeal,
#1855 Russet; Stripe Pattern 2:
#1854 Amethyst, #1876 Coffee,
1 skein each for all sizes

YARN WEIGHT: Fingering

NEEDLES: Size 2 (U.S.)/2.75mm,
or size needed to obtain gauge
1 or 2 circulars or 4 or 5 dpns,
as desired

1 size 3 (U.S.)/3.25 mm needle for
binding off

TOOLS: Large-eye blunt needle

PATTERN SIZES: Child
(10–11, 12–13), Youth (1–2, 3–4),
Women's Average, Women's Wide
(5–6, 7–8, 9–10)

MEASUREMENTS: Foot Width,
Unstretched: Child: 1¼ in., Youth:
1½ in., Women's Average:
1¾ in., Women's Wide: 2 in.; Cuff
Length: Child: 12 in., Youth:
14 in., Women's: 17½ in.;
Heel-to-Toe Length: Child Shoe

Size 10–11: 5¾ in., Child Shoe
Size 12–13: 6¼ in., Youth Shoe
Size 1–2: 6½ in., Youth Shoe Size
3–4: 6¾ in., Women's Shoe Size
5–6: 7¼ in., Women's Shoe Size
7–8: 8¼ in., Women's Shoe Size
9–10: 9¼ in.

HEEL STYLE: Short Row

GAUGE: 8 sts = 1 in., 10 sts =
1 in. in Stockinette st
17 sts = 1 in., 10 sts = 1 in. in
Knit and Purl Rib (unstretched)

Note: **Youth** may fit **Women's Narrow**; adjust length
according to shoe size.

STRIPE PATTERN 1

2 Rnds Russet

2 Rnds Oatmeal

2 Rnds Russet

2 Rnds Oatmeal

10 Rnds Russet

10 Rnds Oatmeal

STRIPE PATTERN 2

2 Rnds Amethyst

2 Rnds Coffee

2 Rnds Amethyst

2 Rnds Coffee

10 Rnds Amethyst

10 Rnds Coffee

KNIT AND PURL RIB INCREASES

Work these increase rnds where indicated in the cuff
pattern for your size. Work all the calf-shaping incs

in the purl ribs. The number of sts in the knit ribs does not change throughout the sock. Each size has a different knit rib width.

INCREASE RND 1: Pick up and P 1 st at the beginning of each purl rib. (6 sts inc in rnd)

INCREASE RND 2: Pick up and P 1 st at the end of each purl rib. (6 sts inc in rnd)

With Oatmeal/Amethyst and a size 2 needle, CO 12 sts, distribute on 1 or 2 circulars or 3 or 4 dpns, as desired. Without twisting sts, join.

RND 1: K.

RND 2: *K2, inc 1*, rep around. (18 sts)

RND 3: *K3, inc 1*, rep around. (24 sts)

RND 4 AND ALL EVEN RNDS: K.

RND 5: *K4, inc 1*, rep around. (30 sts)

RND 7: *K5, inc 1*, rep around. (36 sts)

RND 9: *K6, inc 1*, rep around. (42 sts)

RND 11: *K7, inc 1*, rep around. (48 sts—for Child size, go to Foot)

RND 13: *K8, inc 1*, rep around. (54 sts—for Youth size, go to Foot)

RND 15: *K9, inc 1*, rep around. (60 sts—for Women's Average size, go to Foot)

RND 17: *K10, inc 1*, rep around. (66 sts—for Women's Wide size, go to Foot)

F O O T Work 5 rnds in the Knit and Purl Rib for your size, with Oatmeal/Amethyst). Begin Stripe Pattern.

KNIT AND PURL RIB **CHILD SIZE:** Work *K5, P3* ribbing through foot.

YOUTH SIZE: Work *K6, P3* ribbing through foot.

WOMEN'S AVERAGE SIZE: Work *K6, P4* ribbing through foot.

WOMEN'S WIDE SIZE: Work *K7, P4* ribbing through foot.

Work until foot measures from the end of the toe incs: Child Shoe Size 10–11: 3¾ in., Child Shoe Size 12–13: 4 in., Youth Shoe Size 1–2: 4½ in., Youth Shoe Size 3–4: 4¾ in., Women's Shoe Size 5–6: 5 in., Women's Shoe Size 7–8: 6 in., Women's Shoe Size 9–10: 6½ in.

H E E L   S E T U P K 12 (14, 15, 16) heel sts, place the next 24 (26, 30, 34) sts on a separate needle or holder for the instep. Place the rem 12 (14, 15, 16) sts with the first for the heel.

H E E L Work a 24 (28, 30, 32)-st Short-Row Heel as instructed on pages 174–175.

C U F F Redistribute sts on needles as desired, and work even in established stripe and ribbing patts until cuff reaches 6 in.

CHILD SIZE: Work Increase Rnd 1 at 6 in. (54 sts). Work even in established patt until cuff is 12 in.

YOUTH SIZE: Work Increase Rnd 1 at 6 in. (60 sts). Work Increase Rnd 2 at 10 in. (66 sts). Work even in established patt until cuff is 14 in.

WOMEN'S AVERAGE SIZE: Work Increase Rnd 1 at 6 in. (66 sts). Work Increase Rnd 2 at 10 in. (72 sts). Work Increase Rnd 1 at 14 in. (78 sts). Work even until cuff measures 17½ in.

WOMEN'S WIDE SIZE: Work Increase Rnd 1 at 6 in. (72 sts). Work Increase Rnd 2 at 10 in. (78 sts). Work Increase Rnd 1 at 14 in. (84 sts). Work even until cuff measures 17½ in.

B I N D O F F For a stretchier bind-off, use a size 3 needle. Loosely, K 1 st, slip that st back on the left needle, K2 tog, *slip that st back on the left needle, loosely K2 tog*. Work around the sock.

F I N I S H I N G Weave all loose ends in. Wash and block the socks.

Two-Needle Garter Stitch
VERTICAL STRIPE SOCK

These easy two-needle socks are worked flat, with self-striping worsted weight yarn, and then seamed. Garter stitch provides an extremely elastic fabric, and self-patterning yarn makes the striping a snap.

PATTERN DIFFICULTY:
Beginner

YARN: Yarn Treehouse Wool Slub, 100% Wool, 100 g, 174 yd., #CK15 Daisy, 1 ball for Child Shoe Sizes 6–11, 2 balls for all other sizes ◆

YARN WEIGHT: Worsted

NEEDLES: 1 pair 10-in. size 5 (U.S.)/3.75 mm straight needles, or size needed to obtain gauge 1 size 6 (U.S.)/4.0 mm needle for binding off

TOOLS: Large-eye blunt needle, stitch markers

PATTERN SIZES: Child (6–8, 10–11, 12–13), and Youth (1–2, 3–4), Women's (5–6, 7–8, 9–10), Men's (9, 10–11, 12–13)

MEASUREMENTS: Cuff Length without Ribbing: Child/Youth: 3½ in., Women's: 4 in., Men's: 4½ in.; Cuff Length with Ribbing: Child/Youth: 5 in., Women's: 6 in., Men's: 7 in.; Cuff Width Sewn: Child/Youth: 3 in., Women's: 3½ in., Men's: 4 in.; Heel-to-Toe Length:

Child Shoe Size 6–8: 3¼ in., Child Shoe Size 10–11: 4 in., Child Shoe Size 12–13: 4½ in., Child Shoe Size 1–2: 5 in., Child Shoe Size 3–4: 5½ in., Women's Shoe Size 5–6: 6¾ in., Women's Shoe Size 7–8: 7¼ in., Women's Shoe Size 9–10: 7¾ in., Men's Shoe Size 8–9: 7¾ in., Men's Shoe Size 11–12: 8¼ in., Men's Shoe Size 12–13: 8¾ in.

HEEL STYLE: Afterthought

GAUGE: 5.5 sts = 1 in., 9 rows = 1 in. in Garter st

CUFF AND INSTEP With size 5 needles, CO as follows:

For Child Shoe Size 6–8: 32, Size 10–11: 34, Size 12–13: 36 sts. Size 1–2: 38, Size 3–4: 40 sts.

For Women's Shoe Size 5–6: 42, Size 7–8: 44, Size 9–10: 47 sts.

For Men's Shoe Size 8–9: 50, Size 10–11: 55, Size 12–13: 60 sts.

Work in Garter st (K every row) for 3 in. (3½ in., 4 in.).
BACK OF CUFF K 20 (22, 25) sts, turn. You may place the rem sts for the sole on a holder. Work the 20 (22, 25) cuff sts in Garter st for 3 in. (3½ in., 4 in.). BO loosely.
SOLE Work the sole sts in Garter st for 4 in. BO loosely.

AFTERTHOUGHT HEEL Pick up and K 16 (20, 24) sts evenly spaced along one heel edge, place marker, pick up and K 16 (20, 24) sts evenly spaced along rem heel edge. Turn. (32, 40, 48 sts)

AFTERTHOUGHT HEEL ROW 1: K2 tog, K to within 2 sts of marker, K2 tog, move marker, K2 tog, K to within 2 sts of the end, K2 tog, turn. (4 sts dec)

AFTERTHOUGHT HEEL ROW 2: K, turn.

Rep Afterthought Heel Rows 1–2 until 16 (20, 24) sts rem. BO.

RIBBING Beginning on WS of upper cuff edge, pick up and K 40 (48, 54) sts. Work 12 (16, 18) rnds in K2, P2 ribbing. BO loosely in pattern, using a size larger needle if needed.

TOE On lower foot edge, pick up and K 42 (48, 48) sts. Work a 42 (48, 48)-st Star Toe as instructed on page 177.

FINISHING Fold heel in half, RS out. Using yarn in a large-eye needle, sew the heel bottom and side seam using a Mattress st (see Glossary for instructions). Fold the sock in half lengthwise, and sew the side seam using a Mattress st, from the ribbing to the toe. Weave all loose ends in on the inside of the sock. Wash and block the socks.

4

Textured

~ AND ~

CABLED

SOCKS

Whether you're working simple knit and purl variations or going all-out with twisted and cabled stitches, textured socks often look best when worked with solid or softly mottled yarns. You want your gorgeous (and painstaking) stitchwork to take center stage.

That said, don't let my color suggestions deter you from trying out other yarns and colorways. It's true, many think that textured knitting means classic knitting. But experimentation is half the fun when working with texture. You'll see that there is plenty here that goes beyond cables. You can choose from waves to worms to seeds to macaroni. For example, the Macaroni Sock on page 89, with its raised pasta-like bobbles, looks great knitted up in a highly variegated yarn.

Alpaca TEXTURE SOCK

You cannot beat the pure luxury of this superfine alpaca, silk, and Merino wool blend. Warm, soft, and durable, these socks will keep ladies' toes toasty on the coldest of days.

PATTERN DIFFICULTY: Intermediate

YARN: Knit Picks Andean Silk™, 55% superfine alpaca/23% silk/22% Merino wool, 50 g, 96 yd., #23778 Cornflower, 3 balls (4 balls for Women's Wide Shoe Size 9–10 only)

YARN WEIGHT: Worsted

NEEDLES: Size 5 (U.S.)/ 3.75 mm, or size needed to obtain gauge 1 or 2 circulars or 4 or 5 dpns, as desired

TOOLS: Large-eye blunt needle

PATTERN SIZES: Women's Narrow, Women's Average, Women's Wide (5–6, 7–8, 9–10)

MEASUREMENTS: Cuff Length, All Sizes: 7 in.; Cuff Width: Women's Narrow: 3¼ in., Women's Average: 3⅔ in., Women's Wide: 4 in.; Heel-to-Toe Length: Shoe Size 5–6: 9 in., Shoe Size 7–8: 9½ in., Shoe Size 9–10: 10 in.

HEEL STYLE: Flap and Gusset, Eye of Partridge Heel Flap

GAUGE: 6 sts = 1 in., 8 rnds = 1 in. in Stockinette st 6.5 sts = 1 in., 10 rnds = 1 in. in Pattern

PATTERN (3-st, 11-rnd repeat)

RND 1: *P1, K2*, rep around.

RNDS 2–3: *K1, P2*, rep around.

RND 4: *P1, K2*, rep around.

RNDS 5–7: K.

RND 8: P.

RNDS 9–11: K.

With size 5 needles, CO 40 (48, 52) sts. Distribute on 1 or 2 circulars or 3 or 4 dpns, as desired, make sure that the stitches aren't twisted, and join.

RND 1: *K2, P2*, rep around.

RND 2: P1, *K2, P2*, rep around, end P1.

RND 3: *P2, K2*, rep around.

RND 4: K1, P2, *K2, P2*, rep around, end K1.

Rep Rnds 1–4 twice more.

NEXT RND, WOMEN'S NARROW ONLY: K, inc 2 sts evenly spaced in rnd. (42 sts)

NEXT RND, WOMEN'S AVERAGE ONLY: K.

NEXT RND, WOMEN'S WIDE ONLY: K, inc 2 sts evenly spaced in rnd. (54 sts)

NEXT 2 RNDS, ALL SIZES: K.

Work from chart, or follow Pattern rep, until cuff measures 7 in. for all sizes.

HEEL SETUP K 20 (24, 28) sts for heel, place rem 22 (24, 28) sts on a separate needle or holder for instep.

EYE OF PARTRIDGE HEEL FLAP ROW 1: Turn, Sl 1, P across, turn.

EYE OF PARTRIDGE HEEL FLAP ROW 2: *Sl 1, K1* across, turn.

EYE OF PARTRIDGE HEEL FLAP ROW 3: Sl 1, P across, turn.

EYE OF PARTRIDGE HEEL FLAP ROW 4: Sl 2, K1, *Sl 1, K1* across, end with K2.

Rep Eye of Partridge Heel Flap Rows 1–4 for a total of 16 (18, 20) rows (last RS row will not necessarily be Row 4). End with a P row.

HEEL Work a 20 (24, 28)-st Flap and Gusset Heel as instructed on pages 172–173.

GUSSET **GUSSET RND 1, ALL SIZES:** K 6 (7, 8) sts, pick up, twist, and K 10 (11, 12) sts along edge of heel flap, place marker, work across instep sts in established patt, place marker, pick up, twist, and K 10 (11, 12) sts along other edge of heel flap, K 6 (7, 8) sts.

GUSSET RND 2, ALL SIZES: K to within 2 sts of marker, SSK, move marker, work across instep sts, move marker, K2 tog, K to end. (2 sts dec)

GUSSET RND 3, ALL SIZES: K.

Rep Gusset Rnds 2–3 until 42 (48, 52) sts rem. Redistribute sts on needles if desired.

Work sole sts in Stockinette st and instep sts in established patt until foot measures from the beginning of the gusset: Shoe Size 5–6: 4½ in., Shoe Size 7–8: 5½ in., Shoe Size 9–10: 6 in.

LAST FOOT RND: K 10 (12, 13) sts, place marker, K 21 (24, 27) sts, place marker, K 11 (12, 14) sts.

TOE WEDGE TOE DECREASE RND 1: K to within 2 sts of marker, SSK, move marker, K2 tog, K to within 2 sts of marker, SSK, move marker, K2 tog, K to end. (4 sts dec)

WEDGE TOE DECREASE RND 2: K.

Rep Wedge Toe Decrease Rnds 1–2 until 22 (24, 26) sts rem. K to the next marker.

FINISHING Close rem sts with Kitchener st (see Glossary for instructions). Weave all ends in on the inside of the sock. Wash and block the socks.

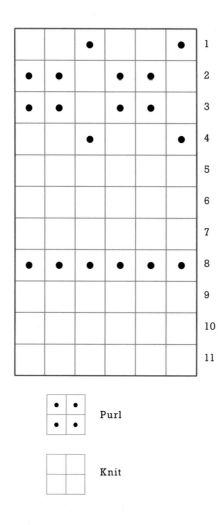

ALPACA TEXTURE SOCK CHART

$\mathcal{S}eedy$ SQUARES SOCK

Dress up an otherwise simple sock with Seed stitch squares and a Seed stitch gusset and toe.
Adapt this sock for boys and men by working a ribbed cuff.

PATTERN DIFFICULTY:
Beginner
YARN: Blue Moon Fiber Arts
Seduction, 50% Merino wool/
50% Tencel, 113 g, 400 yd.,
Hoofle Foofle, 1 skein for all sizes
through Women's Wide, 2 skeins
for Men's sizes
YARN WEIGHT: Fingering
NEEDLES: Size 2 (U.S.)/
2.75 mm, or size needed to obtain
gauge 1 or 2 circulars or 4 or
5 dpns, as desired
1 size 3 needle for casting on
Boys' and Men's socks

TOOLS: Large-eye blunt needle,
stitch markers
PATTERN SIZES: Child
(10–13), Youth (1–2, 3–4),
Women's Average, Women's Wide
(5–6, 7–8, 9–10), Men's Average
(9, 10–11, 12–13)
MEASUREMENTS: Cuff Length:
Child/Youth: 5 in., Women's
Average and Wide: 6½ in., Men's:
7 in.; Cuff Width: Child: 2¾ in.,
Youth/Women's Narrow: 3¼ in.,
Women's Average: 3½ in., Women's
Wide: 3¾ in., Men's: 4¼ in.; Heel-
to-Toe Length: Child Shoe Size

10–11: 5¾ in., Child Shoe Size
12–13: 6¼ in., Youth Shoe Size
1–2: 6½ in., Youth Shoe Size 3–4:
7 in., Women's Shoe Size 5–6:
7¼ in., Women's Shoe Size 7–8:
8¼ in., Women's Shoe Size 9–10:
9¼ in., Men's Shoe Size 9–10:
9½ in., Men's Shoe Size 11–12:
10 in., Men's Shoe Size 13: 11 in.
HEEL STYLE: Flap and Gusset
GAUGE: 7.5 sts = 1 in., 12 rnds
= 1 in. in Stockinette st

Note: Work **Women's Narrow** as for **Youth**; adjust the cuff
and foot length for shoe size.

SEED STITCH PATTERN (2-st, 2-row repeat)
RND 1: *K1, P1*, rep.
RND 2: *P1, K 1*, rep.
SEEDY SQUARES PATTERN FOR CHILD,
WOMEN'S AVERAGE, MEN'S AVERAGE
SIZES **RND 1:** K1, P1, K1, P1, K1, P1, K6.
RND 2: P1, K1, P1, K1, P1, K1, K6.
RNDS 3–10: Rep Rnds 1–2, 4 more times.
RND 11: K6, K1, P1, K1, P1, K1, P1.
RND 12: K6, P1, K1, P1, K1, P1, K1.
RNDS 13–20: Rep Rnds 11–12, 4 more times.
SEEDY SQUARES PATTERN FOR
YOUTH, WOMEN'S WIDE SIZES **RND 1:** K3,
K1, P1, K1, P1, K1, P1, K6, rep around, end with K3
(rather than K6).
RND 2: K3, *P1, K1, P1, K1, P1, K1, K6*, rep around, end
with K3 (rather than K6).

RNDS 3–10: Rep Rnds 1–2, 4 more times.
RND 11: K1, P1, K1, *K6, K1, P1, K1, P1, K1, P1*, rep
around, end with P1, K1, P1 (rather than the entire 6-st
Seed st sequence).
RND 12: P1, K1, P1, *K6, P1, K1, P1, K1, P1, K1*, rep
around, end with K1, P1, K1 (rather than the entire 6-st
Seed st sequence).
RNDS 13–20: Rep Rnds 11–12, 4 more times.
WOMEN'S AND GIRLS' PICOT HEM
SOCKS With a size 2 needle, CO 48 (54, 60, 66,
72) sts. Divide on 1 or 2 circulars or 3 or 4 dpns, as
desired. Without twisting the sts, join.
K 12 rnds.
PICOT RND 1: *K2 tog, YO*, rep around.
PICOT RND 2: K, knitting each YO as a st.
SEED ST BORDER: Work 10 rnds Seed st.
MEN'S AND BOYS' RIB TOP SOCKS
With a size 3 needle, CO 48 (54, 60, 66, 72) sts. Divide
on size 2 needles, 1 or 2 circulars or 3 or 4 dpns, as
desired. Without twisting the sts, join.

Work 10 (12, 14, 16, 18) rnds in K3, P3 ribbing.

CUFF Work the Seedy Squares Pattern for your size until cuff measures 5 in. (6½ in., 7 in.) from Picot Rnd on Women's/Girls' sizes.

HEEL SETUP K 12 (14, 15, 16, 18) sts. Place the next 24 (26, 30, 34, 36) sts on a separate holder or needle for the instep. Place the remaining 12 (14, 15, 16, 18) sts with the first sts for the heel. (24, 28, 30, 32, 36 heel sts)

HEEL FLAP ROW 1: Sl 1, P across, turn.

HEEL FLAP ROW 2: *Sl 1, K 1*, rep across, turn.

Rep Heel Flap Rows 1–2 until heel measures 1¼ in. (1½ in., 1¾ in., 2 in., 2½ in.), end with P row.

HEEL Work a 24 (28, 30, 32, 36)-st Flap and Gusset Heel as instructed on pages 171–172.

GUSSET Sl 1, K 6 (7, 8, 9, 9) sts. New rnd begins at center of heel.

GUSSET RND 1: K 7 (8, 9, 10, 10), pick up, twist, and K 9 (10, 11, 12, 13) sts along flap edge, place a marker, K across instep sts in established pattern, place a marker, pick up, twist, and K 9 (10, 11, 12, 13) sts along other flap edge, K 7 (8, 9, 10, 10) sts.

GUSSET RND 2: K 12 (14, 15, 16, 18) sts, place marker, work Seed st to within 2 sts of next marker, K2 tog, move marker, work across instep in established patt, move marker, SSK, work Seed st until 12 (14, 15, 16, 18) sts rem, place marker, K to end of rnd.

GUSSET RND 3: K to first marker, move marker, work Seed st to within 2 sts of next marker, K2, move marker, work across instep in established patt, move marker, K2, work Seed st to the next marker, move marker, K to end of rnd.

Rep Gusset Rnds 2–3 until 48 (54, 60, 66, 72) sts rem (you will have to remove the first marker for the last dec). Leave instep markers in place.

FOOT Work foot until it measures from gusset edge: Child: 3 in., Youth Shoe Size 1–2: 3½ in., Youth Shoe Size 3–4: 4 in., Women's Shoe Size 5–6: 4½ in., Women's Shoe Size 7–8: 5½ in., Women's Shoe Size 9–10: 6 in., Men's Shoe Size 9: 5½ in., Men's Shoe Size 10–11: 6 in., Men's Shoe Size 12–13: 6½ in.

TOE **WEDGE TOE RND** 1: K to within 2 sts of marker, K2 tog, move marker, SSK, K to within 2 sts of next marker, K2 tog, move marker, SSK, K to end.

WEDGE TOE RND 2: Work Seed st to within 2 sts of marker, K2, move marker, K2, work Seed st to within 2 sts of next marker, K2, move marker, K2, work Seed st to end.

WEDGE TOE RND 3: Work Seed st to within 2 sts of marker, K2 tog, move marker, SSK, work Seed st to within 2 sts of next marker, K2 tog, move marker, SSK, work Seed st to end.

Rep Wedge Toe Rnds 2–3 until 24 (26, 28, 30, 32) sts rem. Work in patt to next marker.

FINISHING Divide sts on 2 needles and close the toe with Kitchener st (see Glossary for instructions). Weave all loose ends in on the inside of the sock. Wash and block the socks.

PICOT HEM: Using yarn in a large-eye needle, fold the hem down at the Picot Rnd and sew in place. Weave loose end in on the inside of the hem.

Sampler Texture Sock

Seedy Squares Sock

$\mathcal{S}$ampler TEXTURE SOCK

I've combined some simple knit and purl borders for this elegant pattern,
sized for children through adult men.

PATTERN DIFFICULTY:
Intermediate
YARN: Rio De La Plata Sock,
100% superwash Merino wool,
100 g, 437 yd., #SC20 Fall Leaf/
Garden Green, 1 ball for Child
through Women's Average Width,
2 balls for Women's Wide and all
Men's sizes
YARN WEIGHT: Fingering
NEEDLES: Size 2 (U.S.)/
2.75 mm, or size needed to obtain
gauge 1 or 2 circulars or 4 or
5 dpns, as desired
1 size 3 (U.S.)/3.25 mm for
casting on

TOOLS: Large-eye blunt needle,
2 stitch markers
PATTERN SIZES: Child
(10–11, 12–13), Youth (1–2, 3–4),
Women's Narrow, Women's Average,
Women's Wide (5–6, 7–8, 9–10),
Men's Average, Men's Wide (9,
10–11, 12–13)
MEASUREMENTS: Cuff Length:
Child/Youth: 5¼ in., All Adult
Sizes: 6⅝ in.; Cuff Width at Border
3: Child: 2¾ in., Youth/Women's
Narrow: 3¼ in., Women's Average:
3½ in., Women's Wide/Men's
Average: 3¾ in., Men's Wide: 4¼ in.;
Heel-to-Toe Length: Child Shoe

Size 10–11: 5¾ in., Child Shoe
Size 12–13: 6¼ in., Youth Shoe
Size 1–2: 6½ in., Youth Shoe Size
3–4: 6 in., Women's Shoe Size
5–6: 7¼ in., Women's Shoe Size
7–8: 8¼ in., Women's Shoe Size
9–10: 9¼ in., Men's Shoe Size
9–10: 9½ in., Men's Shoe Size
11–12: 10 in., Men's Shoe Size
13: 11 in.
HEEL STYLE: Flap and Gusset,
Eye of Partridge Heel Flap
GAUGE: 7.5 sts = 1 in., 12 rnds
= 1 in. in Stockinette st
8.5 sts = 1 in., 12 rnds = 1 in.
over Border 3 Pattern

$\mathcal{N}$ote: Work **Women's Narrow** as for **Youth**; adjust cuff and
foot length for shoe size. Work **Women's Wide** as for **Men's
Average**; adjust cuff and foot length for shoe size.

BORDER 1 PATTERN **RND 1: K.**
RND 2: *P1, K4*, rep around.
RND 3: *P2, K3*, rep around.
RND 4: *P3, K2*, rep around.
RND 5: *P4, K1*, rep around.
BORDER 2 PATTERN **RND 1:** *K1, P1*, rep around.
RND 2: *P1, K1*, rep around.
BORDER 3 PATTERN **RNDS 1–4:** *K3, P3*, rep
around.
RNDS 5–8: *P3, K3*, rep around.
BORDER 4 PATTERN **RND 1:** *K3, P1*, rep around.
RND 2: K.
PURL BORDER (**Note:** Do not work the first
K rnd if the preceding border ended with a

K rnd; do not work the last K rnd if the following
border begins with a K rnd.)
RND 1: K.
RNDS 2–3: P.
RND 4: K.
EYE OF PARTRIDGE HEEL FLAP
ROW 1: *Sl 1, K1* across, end with K1, turn.
ROW 2: Sl 1, P across, turn.
ROW 3: Sl 2, *K1, Sl 1* across, end with K2, turn.
ROW 4: Sl 1, P across, turn.
INCREASE AND DECREASE RNDS
BORDER 1, CHILD: Inc 2 sts evenly spaced in the first
rnd (50 sts). Dec 2 sts evenly spaced in the last rnd
(48 sts).
BORDER 1, YOUTH: Inc 1 st in the first rnd (55 sts).
Dec 1 st in the last rnd (54 sts).
BORDER 1, MEN'S AVERAGE: Dec 1 st in the first rnd
(65 sts). Inc 1 st in the last rnd (66 sts).

continued

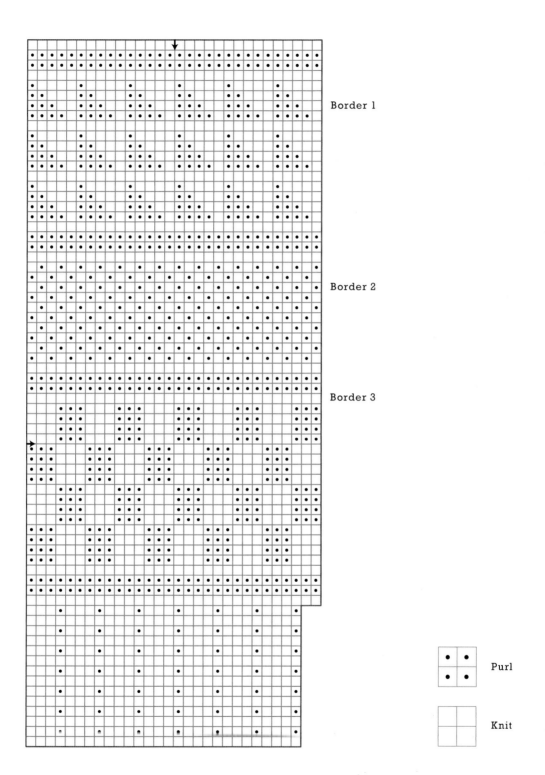

Border 1

Border 2

Border 3

| • | • |
| • | • |

Purl

| | |
| | |

Knit

SAMPLER TEXTURE SOCK CHART

continued from page 86

BORDER 1, MEN'S WIDE: Inc 3 sts evenly spaced in the first rnd (75 sts). Dec 3 sts evenly spaced in the last rnd (72 sts).

BORDER 4, YOUTH: Dec 2 sts evenly spaced in the first rnd (52 sts). Inc 2 sts evenly spaced in the last rnd (54 sts).

BORDER 4, MEN'S AVERAGE: Dec 2 sts evenly spaced in the first rnd (64 sts). Inc 2 sts evenly spaced in the last rnd (66 sts).

With size 3 needle, CO 48 (56, 60, 64, 72) sts. Distribute sts on size 2 needles, 1 or 2 circulars or 3 or 4 dpns, as desired. Without twisting sts, join.

C U F F Work 20 rnds in K2, P2 ribbing.

NEXT RND, YOUTH ONLY: Dec 2 sts evenly spaced in rnd. (54 sts)

NEXT RND, MEN'S AVERAGE ONLY: Inc 2 sts evenly spaced in rnd. (66 sts)

CHILD/YOUTH SIZES: Work the chart as indicated, beginning at the top of the chart, or work the border patts as follows: 3 reps of Border 1, 5 reps of Border 2, 2 reps of Border 3, with a Purl Border between each numbered border and at the beginning and end of the entire 4-border patt. Be sure to inc and dec sts as indicated above.

ALL ADULT SIZES: Work the chart as indicated, beginning at the top of the chart, or work the border patts as follows: 3 reps of Border 1, 5 reps of Border 2, 2 reps of Border 3, 7 reps of Border 4, with a Purl Border between each numbered border and at the beginning and end of the entire 4-border patt. Be sure to inc and dec sts as indicated above.

H E E L   S E T U P   K 12 (14, 15, 17, 18) sts, place next 24 (26, 30, 30, 36) sts on separate needle or holder for instep. Place rem 12 (14, 15, 17, 18) sts on the first needle for heel.

HEEL FLAP ROW 1: Sl 1, P across, turn.

Work the Eye of Partridge Heel Flap until heel measures 1½ in. (1¾ in., 2 in., 2½ in.), end with a P row.

H E E L   Work 24 (28, 30, 34, 36)-st Flap and Gusset Heel as instructed on pages 171–172.

G U S S E T   **GUSSET RND 1:** K 7 (8, 9, 10, 10) sts, pick up and twist loop and K 9 (10, 11, 12, 13) sts along flap edge, place marker, K across instep sts in established patt (do not inc or dec sts for borders according to size, just work the established patt over the instep sts), place marker, pick up and twist loop and K 9 (10, 11, 12, 13) sts along other flap edge, K 7 (8, 9, 10, 10) sts.

GUSSET RND 2: K to within 2 sts of first marker, SSK, move marker, K across instep sts, move marker, K2 tog, K to end of rnd. (2 sts dec)

GUSSET RND 3: K.

Rep Gusset Rnds 2–3 until 48 (54, 60, 66, 72) sts rem.

F O O T   Work even, continuing to work the established border patt over instep and Stockinette st on sole.

CHILD/YOUTH SIZES: Work Borders 1–3.

ALL ADULT SIZES: Work Borders 1–4.

If necessary, work even in Stockinette st until foot measures from gusset edge: Child: 3½ in., Youth Shoe Size 1–2: 4 in., Youth Shoe Size 3–4: 4½ in., Women's Shoe Size 5–6: 5 in., Women's Shoe Size 7–8: 6 in., Women's Shoe Size 9–10: 6½ in., Men's Shoe Size 9: 6 in., Men's Shoe Size 10–11: 6½ in., Men's Shoe Size 12–13: 7 in.

T O E   Work a 48 (54, 60, 66, 72)-st Star Toe as instructed on pages 176–177.

F I N I S H I N G   Weave all loose ends in on the inside of the sock. Wash and block the socks.

$\mathcal{M}$acaroni SOCK

Have some fun making pasta-shaped bobbles on these ankle socks, sized to fit toddlers through women. The purled heel flap adds even more texture to this great pattern.

PATTERN DIFFICULTY:
Intermediate
YARN: Blue Moon Fiber Arts
Socks That Rock Mediumweight,
100% superwash Merino wool,
155 g, 380 yd., Rooster Rock,
1 skein for all sizes
YARN WEIGHT: Heavy fingering
NEEDLES: Size 2 (U.S.)/
2.75 mm, or size needed to obtain
gauge 1 or 2 circulars or 4 or
5 dpns, as desired

1 size 3 (U.S.)/3.25 mm needle for
casting on
TOOLS: Large-eye blunt needle,
stitch markers
PATTERN SIZES: Toddler (6–8),
Child (10–11, 12–13), Youth (1–2,
3–4), Women's Average (5–6,
7–8, 9)
MEASUREMENTS: Cuff Length
All Sizes: 4¼ in.; Approx Width:
Toddler: 2¼ in., Child: 2⅝ in.,
Youth: 3 in., Women's Average:

3⅜ in.; Heel-to-Toe Length:
Toddler: 5½ in., Child Shoe Size
10–11: 5¾ in., Child Shoe Size
12–13: 6¼ in., Youth Shoe Size
1–2: 6½ in., Youth Shoe Size 3–4:
6¾ in. Women's Shoe Size 5–6:
7¼ in., Women's Shoe Size 7–8:
8¼ in., Women's Shoe Size 9–10:
9¼ in.
HEEL STYLE: Flap and Gusset
GAUGE: 8 sts = 1 in., 11 rnds =
1 in. in Stockinette st

$\mathcal{N}$ote: Work **Women's Narrow** as for **Youth**; adjust foot length for shoe size.

MACARONI BOBBLE STITCH (MS)
ROW 1: K2, turn.
ROW 2: P2, turn.
Rep Rows 1–2, 5 more times.
NEXT ROW: Pick up loop from first st to the right of Macaroni Bobble, knit that loop and the first Macaroni st together, K1, pick up loop from the base of the Macaroni Bobble, knit that loop with the next st on the needle.

With a size 3 needle, CO 36 (42, 48, 54) sts. Arrange sts on size 2 needles, 1 or 2 circulars or 3 or 4 dpns, as desired. Make sure sts are not twisted, and join.
Work cuff for all sizes as follows:
RND 1: *K1, P1*, rep around.
RND 2: *P1, K1*, rep around.
Rep Rnds 1–2 once.
RND 3: K.
RND 4: *K4, MS*, rep around.
RND 5: K.

RND 6: *K2, MS, K2*, rep around.
RND 7: K.
RND 8: *MS, K4*, rep around.
RNDS 9–12: K.
RND 13: *K1, P1*, rep around.
RND 14: *P1, K1*, rep around.
Rep Rnds 3–14 once.
Work even in Stockinette st until cuff measures 4¼ in.
HEEL SETUP K 18 (20, 24, 26) sts for heel. Place rem 18 (22, 24, 28) sts on a separate needle or holder for the instep.
HEEL FLAP ROW 1: Sl 1, P across, turn.
HEEL FLAP ROW 2: *Sl 1, P1, put yarn behind work*, rep across.
Rep Heel Flap Rows 1–2, 6 (7, 9, 11) times more, end with Row 1.
HEEL Work an 18 (20, 24, 26)-st Flap and Gusset Heel as instructed on pages 172–173.
GUSSET **GUSSET RND 1:** K 5 (6, 7, 7) sts, pick up, twist, and K 8 (9, 10, 11) sts along the heel flap edge, place marker, K across instep sts, place marker, pick up, twist, and K 8 (9, 10, 11) sts along the other heel

flap edge, K 5 (6, 7, 7) sts.

GUSSET RND 2: K to within 2 sts of first marker, SSK, move marker, K across instep sts, move marker, K2 tog, K to end of rnd. (2 sts dec)

GUSSET RND 3: K.

Rep Gusset Rnds 2–3 until there are 9 (10, 12, 13) sts before the first marker and after the last marker. You will have the same number of sts as on the cuff. (36, 42, 48, 54 sts)

Work even for Toddler: 3½ in., Child Shoe Size 10–11: 3¾ in., Child Shoe Size 12–13: 4 in.; Youth Shoe Size 1–2: 4½ in., Youth Shoe Size 3–4: 4¾ in., Women's Shoe Size 5–6: 5 in., Women's Shoe Size 7–8: 6 in., Women's Shoe Size 9: 6½ in.

T O E Work a 36 (42, 48, 54)-st Star Toe as instructed on page 177.

F I N I S H I N G Weave all loose ends in on the inside of the sock. Wash and block the socks.

Classic Worsted CABLE SOCK

There is nothing more elegant than white-on-white cablework.
This worsted weight sock is not only lovely, it's quick to knit as well.

PATTERN DIFFICULTY:
Intermediate

YARN: Henry's Attic Kona DK, 100% superwash Merino wool, 225 g, 560 yd., Natural, 1 skein for all sizes

YARN WEIGHT: DK

NEEDLES: Size 3 (US)/3.25 mm and 4 (U.S.)/3.50 mm, or size needed to obtain gauge 1 or 2 circulars or 4 or 5 dpns, as desired
Cable needle

TOOLS: Large-eye blunt needle, stitch markers

PATTERN SIZES: Child (6–8, 10–11, 12–13) and Youth (1–2, 3–4), Women's (5–6, 7–8, 9–10) (**Note:** Child and Youth sizes are worked with the same number of sts. Adjust foot length for shoe size.)

MEASUREMENTS: Cuff Length: Child/Youth: 5 in., Women's: 6 in.; Cuff Width: Child/Youth: 2¾ in., Women's: 3½ in.; Heel-to-Toe Length: Child Shoe Size 6–8: 5½ in., Child Shoe Size 10–11: 5¾ in., Child Shoe Size 12–13:

6¼ in., Youth Shoe Size 1–2: 6½ in., Youth Shoe Size 3–4: 6¾ in., Women's Shoe Size 5–6: 9 in., Women's Shoe Size 7–8: 9½ in., Women's Shoe Size 9–10: 10 in.

HEEL STYLE: Flap and Gusset, Eye of Partridge Heel Flap

GAUGE: 6.5 sts = 1 in., 8 rnds = 1 in. with size 4 needle in Stockinette st
8.5 sts = 1 in., 8 rnds = 1 in. with size 4 needle in Cable Pattern

CABLE STITCHES **4LT: LEFT TWIST OVER 4 STS:** Place 2 sts on cable needle, hold in front of work, K the next 2 sts, place the sts from the cable needle on the left needle, K those 2 sts.

2LT: LEFT TWIST OVER 2 STS: Place K st on cable needle, hold in front of work, P the next st, place the st from the cable needle on the left needle, K that st.

2RT: RIGHT TWIST OVER 2 STS: Place P st on cable needle, hold in back of work, K the next st, place the st from the cable needle on the left needle, P that st.

CABLE PATTERN (10-st, 6-rnd repeat)

RND 1: *P1, 4LT, P2, K2, P1*, rep around.

RND 2: *P1, K4, P2, K2, P1*, rep around.

RND 3: *P1, K4, P1, 2LT, 2RT*, rep around.

RND 4: *P1, K4, P1, 2RT, 2LT*, rep around.

RND 5: *P1, K4, P2, K2, P1*, rep around.

RND 6: *P1, K4, P2, K2, P1*, rep around.

𝒩ote: Foot stitch count is less than the cuff stitch count.

With size 3 needles, CO 50 (60) sts. Divide on 1 or 2 circular needles or 3 or 4 dpns, as desired, making sure that the sts aren't twisted, and join.

RIBBING RND 1: *K4, P2, K2, P2*, rep around.

RIBBING RNDS 2–8: Rep Rnd 1.

CUFF Change to size 4 needles. Work Cable Pattern instructions, Rnds 1–6, until cuff measures 5 in.(6 in.), ending with Rnd 2, 5, or 6.

HEEL SETUP, CHILD: P1, K next 24 sts for heel. Place rem 26 sts (including the first st worked) on a separate needle or holder for the instep.

HEEL SETUP, WOMEN'S: P1, K4, P2, K1, K next 30 sts for heel. Place rem 30 sts (including the first 8 sts worked) on a separate needle or holder for the instep.

continued

continued from page 91

EYE OF PARTRIDGE HEEL FLAP

ROW 1: Turn, Sl 1, P across, turn.

ROW 2: *Sl 1, K1*, rep across, turn.

ROW 3: Sl 1, P across, turn.

ROW 4: Sl 2, K1, *Sl 1, K1*, across, end with K2, turn.

Rep Eye of Partridge Heel Flap Rows 1–4 until flap measures 1¼ in. (1½ in.), end with a P row.

HEEL Work a 24 (30)-st Flap and Gusset Heel as instructed on page 172.

GUSSET **GUSSET RND** 1: K 7 (9) sts, pick up, twist, and K 11 (13) sts along edge of heel flap, place marker, work across instep sts in established patt following chart, place marker, pick up, twist, and K 11 (13) sts along other edge of heel flap, K 7 (9) sts.

GUSSET RND 2: K to within 2 sts of marker, SSK, move marker, work across instep sts in established patt following chart, move marker, K2 tog, K to end. (2 sts dec)

GUSSET RND 3: K.

Rep Gusset Rnds 2–3 until 48 (54) sts rem. Redistribute sts on needles as desired.

FOOT Work foot, Stockinette st on the sole, established patt on the instep, until it measures: Child Shoe Size 6–8: 3 in., Child Shoe Size 10–11: 3½ in., Child Shoe Size 12–13: 4 in., Youth Shoe Size 1–2: 4½ in., Youth Shoe Size 3–4: 4¾ in., Women's Average and Women's Wide Shoe Size 5–6: 5¼ in., Women's Average and Women's Wide Shoe Size 7–8: 6½ in., Women's Average and Women's Wide Shoe Size 9–10: 6½ in., from the edge of the gusset.

TOE Work a 48 (54)-st Star Toe as instructed on page 177.

FINISHING Weave all loose ends in on the inside of the sock. Wash and block the socks.

Gentle WAVES SOCK

Cable designs are usually very orderly—geometrically placed and precisely aligned. The texture of this lovely sock is much more organic. The overall effect is of gentle, rolling waves.

PATTERN DIFFICULTY:
Intermediate
YARN: Alpaca with a Twist, 100%
baby alpaca, 50 g, 110 yd., #4001
Seasprite Green, 3 (3, 4) balls
YARN WEIGHT: Worsted
NEEDLES: Size 5 (U.S.)/3.75
mm, or size needed to obtain gauge
1 or 2 circulars or 4 or 5 dpns, as
desired
Cable needle

TOOLS: Large-eye blunt needle,
stitch markers
PATTERN SIZES: Youth (1–2,
3–4), Women's Average, (5–6, 7–8,
9–10), Women's Wide
MEASUREMENTS: Cuff Length:
Youth: 5 in., Women's Sizes: 6 in.;
Cuff Width: Youth: 3 in., Women's
Average: 3¼ in., Women's Wide:
3½ in.; Heel-to-Toe Length: Youth

Shoe Size 1–2: 7½ in., Youth Shoe
Size 3–4: 8 in., Women's Shoe Size
5–6: 9 in., Women's Shoe Size
7–8: 9½ in., Women's Shoe Size
9–10: 10 in.
HEEL STYLE: Short Row
GAUGE: 7 sts = 1 in., 8 rnds =
1 in. in Stockinette st
Approx 9 sts = 1 in., 8 rnds = 1 in.
in Gentle Waves Pattern

CABLE STITCHES 4LT: LEFT TWIST OVER 4 STS:
Place 2 sts on cable needle, hold in front of work,
K the next 2 sts, place the sts from the cable needle
on the left needle, K those 2 sts.

4RT: RIGHT TWIST OVER 4 STS: Place 2 sts on cable
needle, hold in back of work, K the next 2 sts, place
the sts from the cable needle on the left needle,
K those 2 sts.

GENTLE WAVES PATTERN (6 sts, 6 rnds):
RND 1: K.
RND 2: 4LT, K2.
RNDS 3–4: K.
RND 5: K1, 4RT, K1.
RND 6: K.

CO 42 (48, 54) sts. Distribute on 1 or 2 circulars or
3 or 4 dpns, as desired. Without twisting the sts, join.
Work 11 (15) rnds in K3, P3 ribbing.
NEXT RND, ALL SIZES: K, inc 12 sts evenly spaced in
rnd. (54, 60, 66 sts)
Work the Gentle Waves Pattern, using the chart or the
written instructions, until the cuff measures 5 in. (6 in.,
6 in.).
HEEL SETUP K 12 (12, 12) sts, place next 30

(30, 36) sts on a separate needle or holder for the
instep, place the rem 12 (18, 18) sts with the first sts
for the heel. (24, 30, 30 sts)
HEEL Work a 24 (30, 30)-st Short-Row Heel as
instructed on pages 174–175.
FOOT Work the sole in Stockinette st, the instep in
the established Gentle Waves Pattern, until the foot
measures from the heel: Youth Shoe Size 1–2: 3½ in.,
Youth Shoe Size 3–4: 4 in., Women's Shoe Size 5–6:
4½ in., Women's Shoe Size 7–8: 5 in., Women's Shoe
Size 9–10: 5½ in.
TOE Work a 54 (60, 66)-st Star Toe, as instructed on
page 177.
FINISHING Weave all loose ends in on the inside
of the sock. Wash and block the socks.

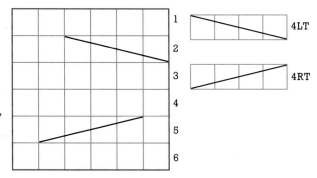

Wiggle Worm
Sandal Sock

Gentle Waves Sock

𝒲𝒾𝑔𝑔𝓁𝑒 𝒲𝑜𝓇𝓂 SANDAL SOCK

These sturdy socks are perfect for sandals or clogs. I've worked the wiggly cable all the way down the heel for added interest.

PATTERN DIFFICULTY: Intermediate

YARN: Cascade 220 Quatro, 100% Peruvian highland wool, 100 g, 220 yd., #5010 yellow, 2 skeins

YARN WEIGHT: Worsted

NEEDLES: Size 5 (U.S.)/ 3.75 mm, or size needed to obtain gauge 1 or 2 circulars or 4 or 5 dpns, as desired

Cable needle

TOOLS: Large-eye blunt needle, stitch markers

PATTERN SIZES: Women's Narrow, Women's Average, Women's Wide (5–6, 7–8, 9–10)

MEASUREMENTS: Cuff Length: 6 in.; Cuff Width: Women's Narrow: 2¾ in.; Women's Average: 3 in., Women's Wide: 3¼ in.; Heel-to-Toe

Length: Women's Shoe Size 5–6: 8 in., Shoe Size 7–8: 9 in., Shoe Size 9–10: 10 in.

HEEL STYLE: Flap and Gusset

GAUGE: 6.5 sts = 1 in., 9 rnds = 1 in. in Stockinette st
11 sts = 1 in. over 2 Wiggle Worm Cable Pattern repeats

CABLE STITCHES 4LT: LEFT TWIST OVER 4 STS: Place 2 sts on cable needle, hold in front of work, K the next 2 sts, place the sts from the cable needle on the left needle, K those 2 sts.

4RT: RIGHT TWIST OVER 4 STS: Place 2 sts on cable needle, hold in back of work, K the next 2 sts, place the sts from the cable needle on the left needle, K those 2 sts.

WIGGLE WORM CABLE PATTERN (8 rnds)

RND 1: *P1, K4, P1*, rep around.

RND 2: *P1, K4, P1*, rep around.

RND 3: *P1, K4, P1*, rep around.

RND 4: *P1, 4LT, P1*, rep around.

RND 5: *P1, K4, P1*, rep around.

RND 6: *P1, K4, P1*, rep around.

RND 7: *P1, K4, P1*, rep around.

RND 8: *P1, 4RT, P1*, rep around.

With size 5 needles, CO 48 (52, 56) sts. Divide on 1 or 2 circulars or 3 or 4 dpns, as desired. Without twisting the sts, join.

RIBBING RND 1: *K2, P2*, rep around.

Repeat Ribbing Rnd 1 for a total of 16 rnds.

NEXT RND: K, inc 12 (14, 16) sts evenly in rnd. (60, 66, 72 sts)

Work Rnds 7–8 of Cable Pattern chart, or Rnds 7–8 of Cable Pattern instructions.

Work Rnds 1–8 of Cable Pattern chart, or Rnds 1–8 of Cable Pattern instructions, until cuff reaches 6 in., or desired length. End with a cable rnd.

HEEL SETUP Work 30 sts in established patt for the heel sts. Place the remaining sts (the instep) on a single needle or holder while the heel is being worked.

HEEL FLAP ROW 1 (WS): Sl 1, work across in established patt (K the K sts, P the P sts). Turn.

HEEL FLAP ROW 2 (RS): Sl 1, work across in established patt (K the K sts, P the P sts). Turn.

Work the heel flap in the established Cable Pattern until the flap measures 2¼ in. (2½ in., 2¾ in.). End with a WS row.

HEEL Work a 30-st Flap and Gusset Heel as instructed on page 172.

GUSSET GUSSET RND 1: K 9 sts, pick up, twist, and K 11 (13, 15) sts along edge of heel flap, place marker, work across instep sts in established patt, place marker, pick up, twist, and K 11 (13, 15) sts along other edge of heel flap, K 9 sts.

GUSSET RND 2: K to within 2 sts of marker, SSK, move marker, work across instep sts, move marker, K2 tog, K to end. (2 sts dec)

GUSSET RND 3: K.

Rep Gusset Rnds 2–3 until 60 (66, 72) sts rem. Redistribute sts on needles if desired. Work foot in established patt (cable on the instep, Stockinette on the sole), until the foot measures 5 in. (6 in., 7 in.).

T O E   **TOE DECREASE RND 1:** (**Note:** Do not work 4LT or 4RT in the toe.)

K 15 (16, 18) sts, place marker, work in established patt (omitting Rnds 4 and 8) until there are 15 (17, 18) sts left, place marker, K to end of rnd.

TOE DECREASE RND 2: K to within 3 sts of marker, K2 tog, K1, move marker, K1, SSK, K to within 3 sts of 2nd marker, K2 tog, K1, move marker, K1, SSK, K to end of rnd.

TOE DECREASE RND 3: Work in established patt.

Rep Toe Decrease Rnds 2–3 until 36 (38, 40) sts rem.

F I N I S H I N G   Work to the end of one needle in the established patt. Close the remaining sts with Kitchener st (see Glossary for instructions). Weave all loose ends in. Wash and block the socks.

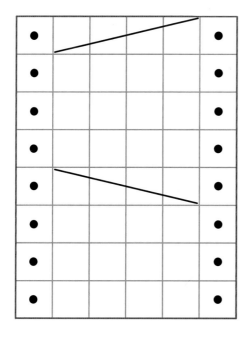

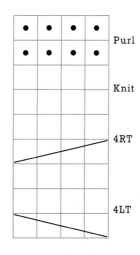

Purl

Knit

4RT

4LT

WIGGLE WORM SANDAL SOCK CABLE CHART

Two-Needle CABLED KNEESOCK

These elegant kneesocks, with their flat construction and
two-color cables, work up quickly with worsted weight yarn.

PATTERN DIFFICULTY:
Intermediate

YARN: Classic Elite Renaissance, 100% wool, 50 g, 110 yd., #7168 Vatican Gold and #7118 Basil, 1 skein each for all Child sizes, 2 skeins each for all Youth sizes and Women's sizes through 7–8, 3 skeins each for Women's size 9–10 and all Men's sizes

YARN WEIGHT: Worsted

NEEDLES: 1 pair 10-in. size 5 (U.S.)/3.75 mm straight needles, or size needed to obtain gauge

5 size 5 (U.S.)/3.75 mm dpns
Cable needle

TOOLS: Large-eye blunt needle

PATTERN SIZES: Child (10–11, 12–13), Youth (1–2, 3–4), Women's (5–6, 7–8, 9–10), Men's (8–9, 10–11, 12–13)

MEASUREMENTS: Cuff Length: Child: 7 in., Youth: 10 in., Women's: 12 in., Men's: 15 in.; Approx Cuff Width at Widest Point (unsewn, unstretched): Child: 6 in., Youth: 8 in., Women's: 10 in.,

Men's: 12 in.; Heel-to-Toe Length: Child Shoe Size 10–11: 5½ in., Child Shoe Size 12–13: 6¼ in., Youth Shoe Size 1–2: 7 in., Youth Shoe Size 3–4: 7½, Women Shoe Size 5–6: 9 in., Women's Shoe Size 7–8: 9½ in., Women's Shoe Size 9–10: 10 in., Men's Shoe Size 8–9: 10½ in., Men's Shoe Size 10–11: 11 in., Men's Shoe Size 12–13: 12 in.

HEEL STYLE: Afterthought

GAUGE: 6.5 sts = 1 in., 7 rows = 1 in. in Stockinette st

Note: I knitted Women's Shoe Size 7–8 and had just a few yards of Vatican Gold left. You may need to purchase an additional skein of that color if you knit loosely.

Note: Twist the new yarn around the old yarn on the wrong side of the work when changing colors.

Note: YB = move the yarn to the back of the work

With size 5 straight needle and Vatican Gold, CO 42 (48, 60, 72) sts.

Work 1 in. (1½ in., 1¾ in., 2 in.) in K2, P2 ribbing. End on RS.

CUFF **CUFF ROW 1 (WS):** P across, increasing 0 (6, 6, 6) sts evenly spaced across the row. (42, 54, 66, 78 sts)

CUFF ROW 2 (CABLE SETUP ROW—RS): Cut Vatican Gold. Tie on Basil. K6 (9, 13, 15), P2, K2, tie on Vatican Gold, K2, P2, K14 (20, 24, 32), P2, K2, tie on another ball of Basil, P2, K2, K6 (9, 13, 15).

CUFF ROW 3 (WS): Work across, working the Basil sts with Basil, and the Vatican Gold sts with Vatican Gold, K the K sts, P the P sts.

CUFF ROW 4 (CABLE 1): K6 (9, 13, 15), P2, YB, place 2 Basil K sts on cable needle (CN) and hold in front of work, K2 Vatican Gold sts, K the 2 Basil sts from the CN, P2 Vatican Gold, K14 (20, 24, 32), P2, YB, place 2 Vatican Gold K sts on CN and hold in front of work, K2 Basil sts, K the 2 Vatican Gold sts from the CN, P2 Basil, K6 (9, 13, 15). Turn.

CUFF ROW 5: Work across, working the Basil sts with Basil, and the Vatican Gold sts with Vatican Gold, K the K sts, P the P sts.

CUFF ROWS 6–9: Rep Cuff Row 5.

CUFF ROW 10 (CABLE 2): K6 (9, 13, 15), P2, YB, place 2 Vatican Gold K sts on CN and hold in front of work, K2 Basil sts, K the 2 Vatican Gold sts from the CN, P2 Vatican Gold, K14 (20, 24, 32) sts, P2, YB, place 2 Basil K sts on CN and hold in front of work, K2 Vatican Gold, K the 2 Basil sts from the CN, P2 Basil, K6 (9, 13, 15).

CUFF ROWS 11–15: Rep Cuff Row 5.

Rep Cuff Rows 4–15 until cuff measures 3 in. (4 in., 5 in., 6 in.), end with WS row.

CUFF DECREASE ROW (RS): Working the Basil sts with Basil, and the Vatican Gold sts with Vatican Gold, K2 tog, K to within 2 sts of first P st, K2 tog, work across P sts, cable, and P sts, K2 tog, K to within 2 sts of 2nd P row, K2 tog, work across P sts, cable, and P sts, K2 tog, K to within 2 sts of the end, K2 tog. (6 sts dec; 36, 48, 60, 72 sts rem)

CHILD AND YOUTH SIZES: Work even in established patt on 36 (48) sts until cuff measures 7 in. (10 in.). End with WS row. Go to Heel Opening Rows.

WOMEN'S AND MEN'S SIZES: Work even in established patt until cuff measures 7 in. (8 in.). End with WS row. Work Cuff Decrease Row (54, 66 sts rem). Work even in established patt until cuff measures 12 in. (15 in.). End with WS row.

HEEL OPENING ROW 1: BO 8 (10, 11, 12) sts, work across row in established patt.

HEEL OPENING ROW 2: BO 8 (10, 11, 12) sts, work across row in established patt, CO 8 (10, 11, 12) sts.

HEEL OPENING ROW 3: Work across row in established patt, CO 8 (10, 11, 12) sts.

HEEL OPENING ROW 4: Work across row in established patt.

Work even in established patt until foot measures: Child Shoe Size 10–11: 3¼ in., Child Shoe Size 12–13: 3¾ in., Youth Shoe Size 1–2: 4¼ in., Youth Shoe Size 3–4: 4½ in., Women's Shoe Size 5–6: 5¼ in., Women's Shoe Size 7–8: 5¾ in., Women's Shoe Size 9–10: 6¼ in., Men's Shoe Size 8–9: 6½ in., Men's Shoe Size 10–11: 6¾ in., Men's Shoe Size 12–13: 7¼ in., end with RS row.

NEXT ROW: Cut yarns, P across with Vatican Gold.

T O E With Vatican Gold, work a 36 (42, 54, 66)-st Star Toe as instructed on page 177.

S E A M Cut a 12-in. tail, thread tail in a large-eye needle, sew through remaining loops, and tie off. Weave all loose ends in on the inside of the sock. With matching yarns and Mattress st (see Glossary for instructions), sew the back cuff and foot seam.

H E E L With Basil and size 5 dpns, beginning at the cable edge of the foot opening, pick up and K 18 (21, 24, 27) sts evenly spaced along that foot opening, place marker. With another needle, pick up another 18 (21, 24, 27) sts along the other foot opening, place marker. Divide the sts on dpns as desired.

AFTERTHOUGHT HEEL DECREASE RND 1: K to within 2 sts of the first marker, K2 tog, move marker, SSK, K to within 2 sts of the 2nd marker, K2 tog, move marker, SSK, K to end. (4 sts dec)

AFTERTHOUGHT HEEL DECREASE RND 2: K.

Rep Toe Decrease Rnds 1–2 until there are 16 (20, 24, 26) sts left. If the sts are not already divided in half, divide them on 2 needles, so that the decs are at either side of each needle. You may need to knit to the end of one needle.

F I N I S H I N G Close the toe with Kitchener st (see Glossary for instructions). Wash and block the socks.

Diamond Tracings SOCK

The beautiful tracings of the diamond-shaped cables of this pattern are worth the work, especially in Blue Moon Fiber Art's Silkie, a fantastic wool-and-silk-blend sock yarn. Working the cable down the heel makes the socks perfect for wearing with sandals or clogs.

PATTERN DIFFICULTY: Advanced

YARN: Blue Moon Fiber Arts Silkie Socks That Rock, 81% superwash Merino wool/19% silk, 100 g, 360 yd., Stonewash, 1 skein for Women's Average Shoe Sizes 5–6, 7–8; 2 skeins for Women's Average Shoe Sizes 9–10 and all Women's Wide Shoe Sizes.

YARN WEIGHT: Fingering

NEEDLES: Size 1 (U.S.)/ 2.25 mm, or size needed to obtain gauge 1 or 2 circulars or 4 or 5 dpns, as desired 1 size 3 (U.S.)/3.25 mm needle for casting on Cable needle

TOOLS: Large-eye blunt needle, stitch markers

PATTERN SIZES: Women's Average, Women's Wide (5–6, 7–8, 9–10)

MEASUREMENTS: Cuff Length: All sizes: 6¼ in.; Cuff Width: Women's Average: 3 in., Women's Wide: 3½ in.; Foot Width: Women's Average: 3½ in., Women's Wide: 4 in.; Heel-to-Toe Length: Women's Shoe Size 5–6: 7½ in., Shoe Size 7–8: 8½ in., Shoe Size 9–10: 9½ in.

HEEL STYLE: Flap and Gusset

GAUGE: 9 sts = 1 in., 12 rnds = 1 in. in Stockinette st 3 repeats (27 sts) = 2 in and 2 repeats (28 rnds) = 2¼ in. in Diamond Tracings Pattern

CABLE STITCHES RT: RIGHT TWIST: Place K st on cable needle, hold in back of work, K the next st, place the st from the cable needle on the left needle, K that st.

2RT: RIGHT TWIST OVER 2 STS: Place P st on cable needle, hold in back of work, K the next st, place the st from the cable needle on the left needle, P that st.

2LT: LEFT TWIST OVER 2 STS: Place K st on cable needle, hold in front of work, P the next st, place the st from the cable needle on the left needle, K that st.

DIAMOND TRACINGS PATTERN FOR CUFF AND INSTEP (9-st, 14-row repeat)

ROW 1: K1, P3, RT, P3.

ROW 2: K1, P3, K2, P3.

ROW 3: K1, P2, 2RT, 2LT, P2.

ROW 4: K1, P2, K1, P2, K1, P2.

ROW 5: K1, P1, 2RT, P2, 2LT, P1.

ROW 6: K1, P1, K1, P4, K1, P1.

ROW 7: K1, 2RT, P4, 2LT.

ROW 8: P1, K1, P6, K1.

ROW 9: K1, 2LT, P4, 2RT.

ROW 10: K1, P1, K1, P4, K1, P1.

ROW 11: K1, P1, 2LT, P2, 2RT, P1.

ROW 12: K1, P2, K1, P2, K1, P2.

ROW 13: K1, P2, 2LT, 2RT, P2.

ROW 14: K1, P3, K2, P3.

DIAMOND TRACINGS PATTERN FOR HEEL FLAP Work as for the Cuff and Instep Pattern, but on the WS rows, K the K sts, P the P sts, with the exception of Row 8. Work a P st on st 1 of the rep on the RS of the heel flap, work a K st on st 1 of the rep on the WS of the heel flap.

With size 3 needle, CO 81 (90) sts. Redistribute on size 1 needles, 1 or 2 circular needles or 3 or 4 dpns, as desired. Without twisting sts, join.

SETUP RND 1: *K1, P3, K2, P3*, rep around. Place markers after each rep if desired.

Work Rnds 1–14 of the rep as written and charted until cuff measures 6¼ in.

HEEL SETUP RND: Work 37 sts in established patt. Set

the rem sts on a separate needle or holder for the instep.

Work the heel flap in the established patt, as noted above, for 2 in. (all sizes), Sl the first st of each row. End with a WS row.

LAST HEEL FLAP ROW: Dec 1 st in row. (36 sts rem)

HEEL Work a 36-st Flap and Gusset Heel as instructed on page 171.

GUSSET **GUSSET RND 1:** K 10 sts, pick up, twist, and K 14 sts along heel flap edge, place marker, pick up, twist, and K 1 st, which becomes the first st of the established patt repeat, work across instep in established patt, pick up, twist, and K 1 st at the end of the instep, which becomes the outside rib (to be worked as for st 1 of the pattern/chart), place marker, pick up, twist, and K 14 sts along the other heel flap edge, K 10 sts.

GUSSET RND 2: K to within 2 sts of marker, SSK, move marker, work instep sts in established patt, move marker, K2 tog, K to end.

GUSSET RND 3: K to marker, move marker, work instep sts in established patt, move marker, K to end.

Rep Gusset Rnds 2–3 until 18 sts rem before first marker and after 2nd marker. (82, 91 sts)

Work foot in established patt until it measures:

Women's Average: 4½ in. (5½ in., 6½ in.) from gusset edge, Women's Wide: 4¼ in. (5¼ in., 6¼ in.) from gusset edge.

NEXT RND: K, dec 4 (1) sts evenly spaced in rnd. (78, 90 sts rem)

TOE **WOMEN'S AVERAGE TOE DECREASE RND 1:** *K11, K2 tog*, rep around. (72 sts rem)

WOMEN'S WIDE TOE DECREASE RND 1: *K13, K2 tog*, rep around. (84 sts rem)

WOMEN'S WIDE TOE DECREASE RND 2, AND ALL EVEN RNDS UNTIL OTHERWISE NOTED: K.

WOMEN'S WIDE TOE DECREASE RND 3: *K12, K2 tog*, rep around. (78 sts rem)

WOMEN'S WIDE TOE DECREASE RND 5: *K11, K2 tog*, rep around. (72 sts rem)

TOE Work 72-st Star Toe as instructed on pages 176–177

FINISHING Weave all loose ends in on the inside of the sock. Wash and block the socks.

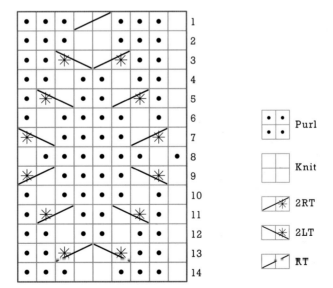

DIAMOND TRACINGS SOCK CHART

5

Lace SOCKS

It spooked me at first, this whole notion of putting holes in my knitting on purpose. But the beauty of knitted lace won me over. A pair of lace socks is an instant heirloom. The delicate patterns combined with the gorgeous array of sock yarns that are available today make lace socks some of the most popular socks to knit.

And the ease—lace looks so much more complex than it actually is, just a simple series of decreases and yarn overs. Once you've knitted your first pair, you'll be thinking about the next.

In this chapter, there are easy lace patterns and more complicated ones. Try one or try them all; you, and everyone on your sock gift list, will be happy that you did.

Many of the patterns also have charts for those who are comfortable using lace charts. All of the patterns also have complete written instructions for those who would rather read along.

Easy LACE SOCK

This easy four-stitch, four-round lace repeat works up elegantly in a simple lace pattern. It's especially well suited for mottled or lightly variegated yarns.

PATTERN DIFFICULTY: Beginner/Intermediate

YARN: Yarn Treehouse Multi-Color Variegated Color Print, 100% wool, 50 g, 220 yd., #Y23 orange/yellow green, 1 (1, 2, 2, 2) balls

YARN WEIGHT: Fingering

NEEDLES: Size 2 (U.S.)/ 2.75 mm, or size needed to obtain gauge 1 or 2 circulars or 4 or 5 dpns, as desired 1 size 3 (U.S.)/3.25 mm needle for casting on

TOOLS: Large-eye blunt needle

PATTERN SIZES: Toddler (6–8), Child (10–11, 12–13), Youth (1–2, 3–4), Women's Average, Women's Wide (5–6, 7–8, 9–10)

MEASUREMENTS: Cuff Length: Toddler: 4½ in., Child: 4½ in., Youth: 5½ in., Women's: 6 in.; Approx Width: Toddler: 2½ in., Child: 2¾ in., Youth: 3 in.; Women's Average: 3¼ in., Women's Wide: 3½ in.; Heel-to-Toe Length: Toddler: 5½ in., Child Shoe Size 10–11: 5¾ in., Child Shoe Size

12–13: 6¼ in., Youth Shoe Size 1–2: 6½ in., Youth Shoe Size 3–4: 6¾ in., Women's Shoe Size 5–6: 7¼ in., Women's Shoe Size 7–8: 8¼ in., Women's Shoe Size 9–10: 9¼ in.

HEEL STYLE: Short Row

GAUGE: 8.5 sts = 1 in., 11 rnds = 1 in. in Stockinette st 9.25 sts = 1 in. over Easy Lace Pattern

---

EASY LACE PATTERN (4-st, 4-rnd repeat):
RND 1: *K2 tog, YO, P2*.
RND 2: *K2 P2*.
RND 3: *YO, K2 tog, P2*.
RND 4: *K2 P2*.

Note: Work **Women's Narrow** as for **Youth**; adjust cuff and foot length for shoe size.

With size 3 needle, CO 48 (52, 56, 60, 64) sts. Divide on size 2 needles, 1 or 2 circular needles or 3 or 4 dpns, as desired. Without twisting the sts, join. Work 15 rnds in K2, P2 ribbing.

NEXT RND: K. Work Easy Lace Pattern until cuff measures 4½ in. (4½ in., 5½ in., 6 in., 6 in.).

HEEL SETUP K 24 (26, 28, 30, 32) sts for heel. In order to make sure that the instep sts begin and end with a P1 or P2, you may need to rearrange the heel sts by beginning the heel on the 2nd st of the rnd. Set rem 24 (26, 28, 30, 32) sts on a separate needle or holder for the instep.

HEEL Work a 24 (26, 28, 30, 32)-st Short-Row Heel as instructed on pages 174–175.

FOOT Work instep in established Easy Lace Pattern, sole in Stockinette st, for Toddler: 3 in., Child Shoe Size 10–11: 3¼ in., Child Shoe Size 12–13: 3½ in., Youth Shoe Size 1–2: 4 in., Youth Shoe Size 3–4: 4¼ in., Women's Shoe Size 5–6: 4½ in., Women's Shoe Size 7–8: 5½ in., Women's Shoe Size 9–10: 6 in.

ALL SIZES: Work ½ in. in Stockinette st.

2ND TO THE LAST FOOT ROW, YOUTH: Dec 2 sts evenly spaced in rnd. (54 sts rem)

2ND TO THE LAST FOOT ROW, CHILD: Dec 4 sts evenly spaced in rnd. (48 sts rem)

2ND TO THE LAST FOOT ROW, WOMEN'S WIDE: Dec 4 sts evenly spaced in rnd. (60 sts rem)

TOE Work a 48 (48, 54, 60, 60)-st Star Toe as instructed on page 177.

FINISHING Weave all loose ends in on the inside of the sock. Wash and block the socks.

Ridge and
Eyelet Sock

Easy Lace Sock

Ridge and Eyelet SOCK

I've paired a simple yarn-over combination with purl rows to make a lovely
and quick-to-knit textured lace pattern.

PATTERN DIFFICULTY:
Beginner/Intermediate

YARN: Knit Picks Bare Superwash
Merino, Nylon, Donegal Sock Yarn,
65% superwash Merino wool/
25% nylon/10% Donegal tweed,
100 g, 462 yd., #23853 Natural,
1 skein for all sizes

YARN WEIGHT: Fingering

NEEDLES: Size 2 (U.S.)/
2.75 mm, or size needed to obtain
gauge 1 or 2 circulars or 4 or
5 dpns, as desired

1 size 3 (U.S.)/3.25 mm needle for
casting on

TOOLS: Large-eye blunt needle

PATTERN SIZES: Toddler (6–8),
Child (10–11, 12–13), Youth (1–2,
3–4), Women's Average, Women's
Wide (5–6, 7–8, 9–10)

MEASUREMENTS: Cuff Length:
Toddler: 4½ in., Child: 4½ in.,
Youth: 5½ in., Women's: 7¼ in.;
Approx Width: Toddler: 2½ in.,
Child: 2¾ in., Youth: 3 in.,
Women's Average: 3¼ in., Women's

Wide: 3½ in.; Heel-to-Toe Length:
Toddler: 5½ in., Child Shoe Size
10–11: 5¾ in., Child Shoe Size
12–13: 6¼ in., Youth Shoe Size
1–2: 6½ in., Youth Shoe Size 3–4:
6¾ in. Women's Shoe Size 5–6:
7¼ in., Women's Shoe Size 7–8:
8¼ in., Women's Shoe Size 9–10:
9¼ in.

HEEL STYLE: Short Row

GAUGE: 9 sts = 1 in., 12 rnds =
1 in. in Stockinette st

RIDGE & EYELET PATTERN (12-rnd repeat)

RND 1: P.

RND 2: K.

RND 3: *K2 tog, YO*.

RND 4: K, working each YO as a st.

RND 5: K.

RND 6: P.

RNDS 7–12: K.

Note: **Women's Narrow** is knit as for **Youth**; adjust cuff
and foot length for shoe size.

With size 3 needle, CO 48 (52, 56, 60, 64) sts. Divide
on size 2 needles, 1 or 2 circulars or 3 or 4 dpns, as
desired. Without twisting the sts, join.
Work 15 rnds in K2, P2 ribbing.
K 6 rnds.
Work Ridge and Eyelet Pattern 3 (3, 4, 5, 5) times.
Work even in Stockinette st until cuff measures 4½ in.
(4½ in., 5½ in., 7¼ in., 7¼ in.).

HEEL SETUP K 24 (26, 28, 30, 32) sts for heel.

Set rem 24 (26, 28, 30, 32) sts on a separate needle or
holder for the instep.

HEEL Work a 24 (26, 28, 30, 32)-st Short-Row Heel
as instructed on pages 174–175.

FOOT Work even in Stockinette st for: Toddler:
3½ in., Child Shoe Size 10–11: 3¾ in., Child Shoe
Size 12–13: 4 in., Youth Shoe Size 1–2: 4½ in., Youth
Shoe Size 3–4: 4¾ in. Women's Shoe Size 5–6: 5 in.,
Women's Shoe Size 7–8: 6 in., Women's Shoe Size
9–10: 6½ in.

2ND TO THE LAST FOOT ROW, YOUTH:

Dec 2 sts evenly spaced in rnd. (54 sts rem)

2ND TO THE LAST FOOT ROW, CHILD:

Dec 4 st evenly spaced in rnd. (48 sts rem)

2ND TO THE LAST FOOT ROW, WOMEN'S WIDE:

Dec 4 sts evenly spaced in rnd. (60 sts rem)

TOE Work a 48 (48, 54, 60, 60)-st Star Toe as
instructed on page 177.

FINISHING Weave all loose ends in on the inside
of the sock. Wash and block the socks.

$\mathcal{L}$ace TUBE BOOTIE

This little lace bootie with the picot hem is adorable and will fit growing babies for quite a while. You can run a ribbon or chained drawstring through the top row of eyelets, but be sure to anchor the tie firmly to the fabric of the sock for safety. If you have any doubt, leave it out.

PATTERN DIFFICULTY: Advanced Beginner

YARN: Crystal Palace Panda Silk, 52% bamboo/43% superwash Merino wool/5% combed silk, 50 g, 204 yd., #3003 Strawberry Cream, 1 ball for all sizes

YARN WEIGHT: Fingering

NEEDLES: Size 1 (U.S.)/ 2.25 mm, or size needed to obtain gauge 1 or 2 circulars or 4 or 5 dpns, as desired

TOOLS: Large-eye blunt needle

PATTERN SIZES: Infant 0–3 months, 3–6 months, 6–12 months

MEASUREMENTS: Width: 0–3 months: 1¾ in., 3–6 months: 2¼ in., 6–12 months: 2⅜ in.; Length: 0–3 months: 5½ in., 3–6 months: 6½ in., 6–12 months: 7½ in.

HEEL STYLE: None

GAUGE: 10 sts = 1 in., 12 rnds = 1 in. in Stockinette st

LACE PATTERN (3-st, 5-rnd repeat)

RND 1: *YO, P3 tog, YO*, rep around.

RND 2: K, knitting the first YO in each pair, then knitting the 2nd YO TBL (through the back of the loop) in each pair.

RNDS 3–5: K.

Note: This lace repeat is adaptable to any pattern with a st count that is a multiple of 3.

With size 1 needles, CO 36 (42, 48) sts. Distribute on 1 or 2 circulars or 4 or 5 dpns, as desired. Without twisting, join.

RNDS 1–8: K.

PICOT RND 9: *K2 tog, YO*, rep around.

PICOT RND 10: K, knitting each YO as a st.

RNDS 11–18: K.

EYELET RNDS 19–20: Rep Picot Rnds 9–10.

RNDS 21–23: K.

Work Lace Bootie Pattern 4 times for all sizes.

FOOT Work even in Stockinette st until sock measures 2¼ in., (3¼ in., 4¼ in.) from last Lace Pattern Rnd.

TOE Work a 36 (42, 48)-st Star Toe as instructed on page 177.

FINISHING Fold the upper hem down and in, and stitch in place. Weave loose end in on the inside of the hem. Wash and block the socks.

$\mathcal{K}$notwork SPIRAL SOCK

This toe-up, Star Toe sock pattern is perfect for variegated yarns. The simple
Knotwork Spiral fold-down cuff highlights the color changes in the yarn.

PATTERN DIFFICULTY:
Intermediate
YARN: Fly Designs Boo Fly Sock,
60% superwash Merino wool/
30% bamboo/10% nylon, 113 g,
435 yd., Raspberry Latte, 1 skein
for all sizes
YARN WEIGHT: Fingering
NEEDLES: Size 2 (U.S.)/
2.75 mm, or size needed to obtain
gauge 1 or 2 circulars or 4 or
5 dpns, as desired

1 size 3 (U.S.)/3.25 mm needle
for BO
TOOLS: Large-eye blunt needle
PATTERN SIZES: Child
(10–11, 12–13), Youth (1–2, 3–4),
Women's Average, Women's Wide
(5–6, 7–8, 9–10)
MEASUREMENTS: Fold-Down
Cuff Length: Child: 2¼ in., Youth:
2½ In., Women's: 2¾ in.; Approx
Foot Width: Child: 2½ in., Youth:
2¾ in., Women's Average:

3¼ in., Women's Wide: 3½ in.;
Heel-to-Toe Length: Child Shoe
Size 10–11: 5¾ in., Child Shoe
Size 12–13: 6¼ in., Youth Shoe
Size 1–2: 6½ in., Youth Shoe Size
3–4: 6¾ in., Women's Shoe Size
5–6: 7½ in., Women's Shoe Size
7–8: 8½ in., Women's Shoe Size
9–10: 9½ in.
HEEL STYLE: Short Row
GAUGE: 9.5 sts = 1 in., 11 rnds
= 1 in. in Stockinette st

$\mathcal{N}$ote: Youth size may fit **Women's Narrow**; adjust foot
length accordingly.

With size 2 needle, CO 12 sts, leaving at least an 8-in.
tail. Divide as desired, without twisting sts, join.

TOE **TOE INCREASE RND 1:** K.

TOE INCREASE RND 2: *K2, inc 1*, rep around. (18 sts)

**TOE INCREASE RND 3 AND ALL ODD TOE INCREASE
RNDS UNTIL OTHERWISE NOTED:** K.

TOE INCREASE RND 4: *K3, inc 1*, rep around. (24 sts)

TOE INCREASE RND 6: *K4, inc 1*, rep around. (30 sts)

TOE INCREASE RND 8: *K5, inc 1*, rep around. (36 sts)

TOE INCREASE RND 10: *K6, inc 1*, rep around. (42 sts)

TOE INCREASE RND 12: *K7, inc 1*, rep around.
(48 sts—for Child Size, go to Foot)

TOE INCREASE RND 14: *K8, inc 1*, rep around.
(54 sts—for Youth Size, go to Foot)

TOE INCREASE RND 16: *K9, inc 1*, rep around.
(60 sts—for Women's Average Size, go to Foot)

TOE INCREASE RND 18: *K10, inc 1*, rep around.
(66 sts—for Women's Wide Size, go to Foot)

FOOT Distribute the 48 (54, 60, 66) sts as desired
on your needles. Work in Stockinette st until foot

measures, from end of Toe Increases: Child Shoe Size
10–11: 3¾ in., Child Shoe Size 12–13: 4 in., Youth Shoe
Size 1–2: 4¼ in., Youth Shoe Size 3–4: 4½ in. Women's
Shoe Size 5–6: 5 in., Women's Shoe Size 7–8: 6 in.,
Women's Shoe Size 9–10: 6½ in.

HEEL SETUP K 24 (28, 30, 32) sts for heel. Place
rem 24 (26, 30, 34) sts on a separate needle or holder
for the instep.

HEEL Work a 24 (28, 30, 32)-st Short-Row Heel as
instructed on pages 174–175.

CUFF Redistribute sts as desired on needles, and
work 1 in. (1 in., 1½ in., 1½ in.) in Stockinette st.

INNER RIBBING: Work K3, P3 ribbing for 2¼ in.
(2½ in., 2¾ in., 2¾ in.).

KNOTWORK SPIRAL CUFF While still on the
needles, turn the sock inside out.

CUFF RND 1: Pick up a loop from the last st on the
previous needle, and K together with the first st on
the new needle, K around.

CUFF RNDS 2–4: K.

KNOTWORK SPIRAL CUFF RND 1: *YO, K3, using the
point of your needle, lift the first K st up and over the

next 2 K sts, and off the needle*, rep around.

KNOTWORK SPIRAL CUFF RND 2: K.

Rep Knotwork Spiral Cuff Rnds 1–2 until cuff measures 2¼ in. (2½ in., 2¾ in.) from beginning of Knotwork Spiral section.

NEXT RND: K.

FINISHING With a size 3 needle, BO loosely. Weave loose end in. Turn sock right side out, fold cuff down. Thread the CO tail in a large-eye needle and sew through the CO loops. Tighten and tie the toe closed, weave the loose end in on the inside of the sock. Wash and block the socks.

Women's LACY FOOTLET

Slip into lacy luxury with this pair of wonderful footlets worked with a traditional Eyelet Twig design on the instep and heel flap. The lace fabric is quite elastic, so one width will fit almost all women.

PATTERN DIFFICULTY: Intermediate

YARN: ShibuiKnits Sock, 100% superwash Merino wool, 50 g, 191 yd., #S3001 Pebble, 1 skein for all sizes

YARN WEIGHT: Fingering

NEEDLES: Size 2 (U.S.)/ 2.75 mm, or size needed to obtain gauge 1 or 2 circulars or 4 or 5 dpns, as desired 1 size 3 (U.S.)/3.25 mm needle for casting on

TOOLS: Large-eye blunt needle, stitch markers

PATTERN SIZES: Women's Average (5–6, 7–8, 9–10)

MEASUREMENTS: Width across Foot: 3½ in.; Heel-to-Toe Length: Women's Shoe Size 5–6: 7¼ in., Women's Shoe Size 7–8: 8¼ in., Women's Shoe Size 9–10: 9¼ in.

HEEL STYLE: Flap and Gusset

GAUGE: 8.5 sts = 1 in., 11 rnds = 1 in. in Stockinette st 1 rep (14 sts) = 1⅝ in., 1 rep (12 rnds) = 1⅛ in. in Eyelet Twig Pattern

EYELET TWIG PATTERN
(14-st, 12-rnd repeat)

ROW 1: K1, YO, K3 tog, YO, K3, YO, Sl 1, K2 tog, PSSO, YO, K4.

ROW 2 AND ALL EVEN ROWS: K.

ROW 3: YO, K3 tog, YO, K5, YO, Sl 1, K2 tog, PSSO, YO, K3.

ROW 5: K5, YO, K3 tog, YO, K1, YO, Sl 1, K2 tog, PSSO, YO, K2.

ROW 7: K4, YO, K3 tog, YO, K3, YO, Sl 1, K2 tog, PSSO, YO, K1.

ROW 9: K3, YO, K3tog, YO, K5, YO, Sl 1, K2 tog, PSSO, YO.

ROW 11: K2, YO, K3 tog, YO, K1, YO, Sl 1, K2 tog, PSSO, YO, K5.

With size 3 needles, CO 56 sts. Arrange on size 2 needles, 1 or 2 circulars or 3 or 4 dpns, as desired. Without twisting sts, join.

Work 6 rnds in K2, P2 ribbing.

NEXT RND: K.

HEEL SETUP K 28 sts for heel. Set rem 28 sts on a separate needle or holder for the instep.

HEEL FLAP ROW 1: Turn, Sl 1, P across, turn.

HEEL FLAP ROW (RS): Work Eyelet Twig Pattern as follows: Sl 1, K6, work 1 Eyelet Twig Pattern rep, K7, turn.

HEEL FLAP ROW (WS): Sl 1, P across, turn.

Work Heel Flap in Eyelet Twig Pattern for 2 in., end with a WS row.

HEEL Work a 28-st Flap and Gusset Heel as instructed on page 172.

GUSSET **GUSSET RND 1:** K8, pick up, twist, and K 14 sts along edge of heel flap, place marker, work across the instep sts beginning with Rnd 1 of the Eyelet Twig Pattern, place marker, pick up, twist, and K 14 sts along other edge of heel flap, K 8 sts.

GUSSET RND 2: K to within 2 sts of marked spot, SSK, work across instep sts in established patt, K2 tog, K to end.

GUSSET RND 3: K.

Rep Gusset Rnds 2–3 until 56 sts rem.

Work foot as established, Stockinette st on sole, Eyelet Twig Pattern on instep, until foot measures: Shoe Size 5–6: 4½ in., Shoe Size 7–8: 5½ in., Shoe Size 9–10: 6 in.

ALL SHOE SIZES: Work ½ in. in Stockinette st.

LAST RND STOCKINETTE ST: Dec 2 sts evenly spaced in rnd. (54 sts)

T O E Work a 54-st Star Toe as instructed on page 177.

F I N I S H I N G Weave all loose ends in on the inside of the sock. Wash and block the socks.

Women's Lacy Footlet

Candelabra Lace Sock

Candelabra LACE SOCK

This toe-up sock is sized for young girls and preteens, though women
with narrow feet may be able to wear them as well. The 14-stitch pattern
repeat is based on a traditional Candelabra design.

PATTERN DIFFICULTY:
Intermediate

YARN: Crystal Palace Panda
Wool, 51% bamboo/39% wool/
10% nylon, 50 g, 186 yd.,
#2303 Vanilla Cream, 2 balls

YARN WEIGHT: Fingering

NEEDLES: Size 2 (U.S.)/2.75 mm,
or size needed to obtain gauge

1 or 2 circulars or 4 or 5 dpns,
as desired

1 size 3 (U.S.)/3.25 mm needle for
binding off

TOOLS: Large-eye blunt needle,
stitch markers

PATTERN SIZES:
Youth (1–2, 3–4)

MEASUREMENTS: Cuff Length:
5¾ in.; Cuff Width: 3 in. (after

blocking); Heel-to-Toe Length:
Youth Shoe Size 1–2: 7¼ in.,
Youth Shoe Size 3–4: 7½ in.

HEEL STYLE: Short Row

GAUGE: 9.25 sts = 1 in.,
11 rnds = 1 in. in Stockinette st
9.25 sts = 1 in., 11 rnds = 1 in.
in Candelabra Lace Pattern
(after blocking)

CANDELABRA LACE PATTERN
(14-st, 14-row repeat)

RNDS 1–4: K.

RND 5: K5, K2 tog, YO, K1, Sl 1, K1, PSSO, K4.

RND 6 AND ALL EVEN RNDS: K.

RND 7: K4, K2 tog, YO, K3, YO, Sl 1, K1, PSSO, K3.

RND 9: K3, K2 tog, YO, K2 tog, YO, K1, YO, Sl 1, K1, PSSO,
YO, Sl 1, K1, PSSO, K2.

RND 11: K2, K2 tog, YO, K2 tog, YO, K3, YO, Sl 1, K1,
PSSO, YO, Sl 1, K1, PSSO, K1.

RND 13: K1, K2 tog, YO, K2 tog, YO, K2 tog, YO, K1, YO,
Sl 1, K1, PSSO, YO, Sl 1, K1, PSSO, YO, Sl 1, K1, PSSO.

RND 14: K.

With size 2 needles and Vanilla Cream, CO 12, leaving at least an 8-in. tail. Divide as desired on 1 or
2 circulars or 3 or 4 dpns, as desired. Without twisting
sts, join.

RND 1: K.

RND 2: *K2, inc 1*, rep around. (18 sts)

RND 3: *K3, inc 1*, rep around. (24 sts)

RND 4 AND ALL EVEN RNDS: K.

RND 5: *K4, inc 1*, rep around. (30 sts)

RND 7: *K5, inc 1*, rep around. (36 sts)

RND 9: *K6, inc 1*, rep around. (42 sts)

RND 11: *K7, inc 1*, rep around. (48 sts)

RND 13: *K8, inc 1*, rep around. (54 sts)

RND 15: Inc 2 sts evenly spaced in rnd. (56 sts)

Work even in Stockinette st until foot measures
4½ (4¾ in.) from the end of the incs.

HEEL SETUP K 28 sts, place the rem 28 sts on a
separate needle or holder for the instep.

HEEL Work a 28-st Short-Row Heel as instructed on
page 175.

CUFF K 6 rnds.

Work Rnds 1–14 of the Candelabra Lace Pattern
3 times, placing markers between the 14-st reps,
if desired.

K 3 rnds.

Work 10 rnds in K2, P2 ribbing.

FINISHING With a size 3 needle, BO loosely in
patt. Thread the CO tail in a large-eye needle. Sew
through the CO loops, tighten, and tie off on the
inside of the sock to close the toe. Weave all ends in
on the inside of the sock. Wash and block the socks.

Diamond Rib LACE SOCK

This pattern will fit children with shoe sizes from 10 to 13. The simple open ribs separate the four diamond motifs and run down the instep for a gorgeous sock.

PATTERN DIFFICULTY: Intermediate

YARN: Knit Picks Essential, 75% superwash wool/25% nylon, 50 g, 231 yd., #23699 Pumpkin, 1 ball

YARN WEIGHT: Fingering

NEEDLES: Size 2 (U.S.)/ 2.75 mm, or size needed to obtain gauge 1 or 2 circulars or 4 or 5 dpns, as desired 1 size 3 (U.S.)/3.25 mm needle for casting on

TOOLS: Large-eye blunt needle, stitch markers

PATTERN SIZES: Child (10–11, 12–13)

MEASUREMENTS: Cuff Length (unblocked): 4½ in.; Width: 2¾ in.; Heel-to-Toe Length: Child Shoe Size 10–11: 5¾ in., Child Shoe Size 12–13: 6¼ in.

HEEL STYLE: Short Row

GAUGE: 8.5 sts = 1 in., 11 rnds = 1 in. in Stockinette st

DIAMOND RIB LACE PATTERN (12-st, 24-row repeat)

RND 1: YO, Sl 1, K 1, PSSO, K3, K2 tog, YO, YO, Sl 1, K 1, PSSO, K3.

RND 2: K7, K YO TBL, K4.

RND 3: K2 tog, YO, K2, K2 tog, YO, K2, YO, Sl 1, K1, PSSO, K2.

RND 4: K.

RND 5: YO, Sl 1, K1, PSSO, K2, Sl 1, K1, PSSO, K2, K2 tog, YO, K2.

RND 6: K.

RND 7: K2 tog, YO, K3, YO, Sl 1, K1, PSSO, K2 tog, YO, K3.

RND 8: K.

RND 9: YO, Sl 1, K1, PSSO, K4, YO, Sl 1, K1, PSSO, K4.

RND 10: K.

RND 11: K2 tog, YO, K4, K2 tog, YO, K4.

RND 12: K.

RND 13: YO, Sl 1, K1, PSSO, K3, K2 tog, YO, YO, Sl 1, K1, PSSO, K3.

RND 14: K7, K YO TBL, K4.

RND 15: K2 tog, YO, K2, K2 tog, YO, K2, YO, Sl 1, K1, PSSO, K2.

RND 16: K.

RND 17: YO, Sl 1, K1, PSSO, K2, YO, Sl 1, K1, PSSO, K2, K2 tog, YO, K2.

RND 18: K.

RND 19: K2 tog, YO, K3, YO, Sl 1, K1, PSSO, K2 tog, YO, K3.

RND 20: K.

RND 21: YO, Sl 1, K1, PSSO, K4, YO, Sl 1, K1, PSSO, K4.

RND 22: K.

RND 23: K2 tog, YO, K4, K2 tog, YO, K4.

RND 24: K.

DIAMOND RIB LACE RIBBING
(4-st, 4-row repeat)

RND 1: YO, Sl 1, K1, PSSO, P2.

RND 2: K2, P2.

RND 3: K2 tog, YO, P2.

RND 4: K2, P2.

With size 3 needle, CO 48 sts. Divide on size 2 needles, 1 or 2 circulars or 3 or 4 dpns, as desired. Making sure not to twist the sts, join.

RND 1: K.

Work Diamond Rib Lace Ribbing rep 3 times, following chart or written instructions. Place markers between the reps, if desired. Work Diamond Rib Lace Pattern Rnds 1–24, following chart or written

instructions. Repeat Rnds 21–24 until cuff measures 4½ in. (unstretched).

HEEL SETUP Last rnd before heel, work to within 2 sts of the end of the rnd. Begin new needle with those 2 sts, and K the next 22 sts. Those 24 sts will be the heel sts. Place the remaining 24 sts on a separate needle or holder for the instep.

HEEL Work a 24-st Short-Row Heel as instructed on page 175.

FOOT Work even in Stockinette st on the sole, continuing the established patt on the instep, until foot measures 3 in. (3½ in.) from the heel. Work ½ in. in Stockinette st.

TOE Work a 48-st Star Toe as instructed on page 177.

FINISHING Weave all loose ends in on the inside of the sock. Wash and block the socks.

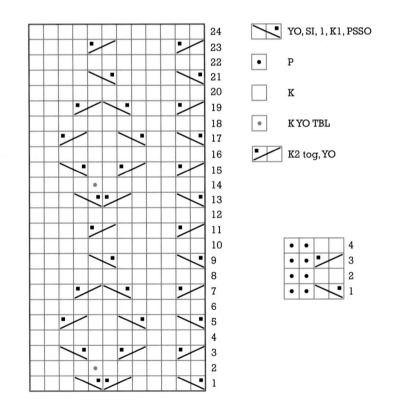

DIAMOND RIB LACE SOCK CHART

Mini Bobble LACE SOCK

The one-stitch mini bobbles add subtle texture to this simple lace sock, shown on page 182.

PATTERN DIFFICULTY:
Intermediate
YARN: Yarn Treehouse Melody
Multi-Color Fingering Weight,
100% wool, 50 g, 220 yd., #Y08,
2 balls for all sizes
YARN WEIGHT: Fingering
NEEDLES: Size 1 (U.S.)/
2.25 mm, or size needed to obtain
gauge 1 or 2 circulars or 4 or
5 dpns, as desired

1 size 3 (U.S.)/3.25 mm needle for
casting on
TOOLS: Large-eye blunt needle,
stitch markers
PATTERN SIZES: Women's
Average, Women's Wide (5–6, 7–8,
9–10)
MEASUREMENTS: Cuff Length:
Women's: 6½ in.; Approx Width:
Women's Average: 3¼ in., Women's

Wide: 3½ in.; Heel-to-Toe Length:
Women's Shoe Size 5–6: 7¼ in.,
Women's Shoe Size 7–8: 8¼ in.,
Women's Shoe Size 9–10: 9¼ in.
HEEL STYLE: Short Row
GAUGE: 10 sts = 1 in., 12 rnds
= 1 in. in Stockinette st
9.25 sts = 1 in., 14 rnds = 1 in. in
Mini Bobble Lace Pattern

MINI BOBBLE (MB) K st indicated on chart, slide that single st back onto the left needle. Rep 2 more times, knitting the single st.

MINI BOBBLE LACE PATTERN
(15–17-st, 4-rnd repeat)

RND 1: P1 (2), MB, K5, MB, K5, MB, P1 (2).

RND 2: P1 (2), K1, YO, K2 tog, K1, YO, K2 tog, K1, K2 tog, YO, K1, K2 tog, YO, K1, P1 (2).

RND 3: P1 (2), K13, P1 (2).

RND 4: P1 (2), K3, YO, K2 tog, K3, K2 tog, YO, K3, P1 (2). With size 3 needle, CO 60 (68) sts. Distribute on size 1 needles, 1 or 2 circulars or 3 or 4 dpns, as desired, without twisting sts, join.

RND 1: K.

RND 2: P.

RND 3: K.

CUFF Work chart or follow Mini Bobble Lace Pattern instructions, placing stitch markers between pattern reps if desired, until cuff is 6¼ in. long.

HEEL SETUP K 15 (16) sts, place next 30 (36) sts on a separate needle or holder for the instep, place the rem 15 (16) sts with the first for the heel.

HEEL Work a 30 (32)-st Short-Row Heel as instructed on pages 174–175.

FOOT Redistribute sts as desired, working 30 (34) sts for the sole in Stockinette st, and 30 (34) sts in 2 full reps of the Mini Bobble Lace Pattern for the instep until foot measures: Women's Shoe Size 5–6: 5 in., Women's Shoe Size 7–8: 6 in., Women's Shoe Size 9–10: 6½ in.

ALL SIZES: Work ¼ in. in Stockinette st.

2ND TO THE LAST FOOT RND, WOMEN'S WIDE ONLY:
Dec 2 sts evenly spaced in the rnd. (66 sts)

TOE Work a 60 (66)-st Star Toe as instructed on page 177.

FINISHING Weave all loose ends in on the inside of the sock. Wash and block the socks.

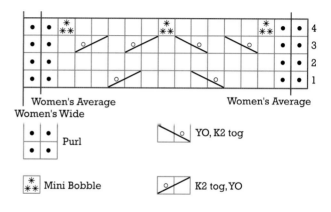

Women's Average
Women's Wide

• • Purl

✳✳ Mini Bobble

⟋₀ YO, K2 tog

₀⟋ K2 tog, YO

Alpaca Lace BED SOCK

The simple tube sock pattern is a great way to practice your yarn overs, and this cozy alpaca sock is super-warm, even though it's knitted in lace. These lounging socks, with their I-Cord ties, are not meant for wearing in shoes—or on rough floors without slippers.

PATTERN DIFFICULTY: Beginner/Intermediate

YARN: ShibuiKnits Baby Alpaca DK, 100% baby alpaca, 100 g, 255 yd., #BA1765 Blossom, 1 (2) skeins

YARN WEIGHT: DK

NEEDLES: Size 4 (U.S.)/3.5 mm, or size needed to obtain gauge

1 or 2 circulars or 4 or 5 dpns, as desired

2 size 4 dpns for I-Cord

TOOLS: Large-eye blunt needle, stitch markers

PATTERN SIZES: Child (Women's)

MEASUREMENTS BEFORE BLOCKING: Child: 3¼ in. wide, 10½ in. long, Women's: 4¼ in. wide, 13 in. long

MEASUREMENTS AFTER BLOCKING: Child: 2¼ in. wide, 12¾ in. long, Women's: 3¼ in. wide, 14¾ in. long

HEEL STYLE: None

GAUGE: 2 in. wide by 1¾ in. long over 1 Lace Pattern rep (before blocking)

LACE PATTERN (12-st, 16-rnd repeat)

RND 1: K2 tog, YO, K2, K2 tog, YO, YO, Sl 1, K1, PSSO, K2, YO, Sl 1, K1, PSSO.

RND 2: K6, K YO TBL, K5.

RND 3: K3, K2 tog, YO, K2, YO, Sl 1, K 1, PSSO, K3.

RND 4: K.

RND 5: K2, K2 tog, YO, K4, YO, Sl 1, K 1, PSSO, K2.

RND 6: K4, K2 tog, YO, YO, Sl 1, K 1, PSSO, K 4.

RND 7: K1, K2 tog, YO, K3, K YO TBL, K2, YO, Sl 1, K1, PSSO, K1.

RND 8: K.

RND 9: K1, YO, Sl 1, K1, PSSO, K6, K2 tog, YO, K1.

RND 10: K4, YO, Sl 1, K1, PSSO, K2 tog, YO, K4.

RND 11: K2, YO, Sl 1, K1, PSSO, K4, K2 tog, YO, K2.

RND 12: K.

RND 13: K3, YO, Sl 1, K1, PSSO, K2, K2 tog, YO, K3.

RND 14: K.

RND 15: YO, Sl 1, K1, PSSO, K2, YO, Sl 1, K1, PSSO, K2 tog, YO, K2, K2 tog, YO.

RND 16: K YO TBL, K 11.

Note: This sock is quite stretchy and will fit a variety of foot sizes.

Note: TBL means "through the back of the loop" (twist the YO when you knit it).

With size 4 needles, CO 36 (48) sts. Arrange on 1 or 2 circulars or 3 or 4 dpns, as desired. Without twisting, join.

RND 1: *K1, P1* around.

RND 2: *P1, K1*, around.

Rep Rnds 1–2 once.

NEXT 4 RNDS: K.

PICOT RND 1: *K2, K2 tog, YO*, rep around.

PICOT RND 2: K, working each YO as a st.

NEXT 4 RNDS: K.

Work the Lace Pattern rep as written, or follow the chart, placing markers between the reps if desired. Work 4 (5) reps.

NEXT 4 RNDS: K.

TOE Work a 36 (48)-st Star Toe as instructed on page 177.

FINISHING Weave all loose ends in on the inside of the sock. Thread I-Cord through the Picot Eyelets and tie in a bow. Wash and block the socks.

I-CORD TIE (make 2) With size 4 dpn, CO 4.

ROW 1: K across. Do not turn.

ROW 2: Slide sts to the right side of the needle, bring the yarn around behind the work, and K across. Do not turn.

Rep Row 2 until I-Cord is 30 in. long.

FINISHING: Cut a 6-in. tail, thread the tail in a large-eye needle, and pull through the loops. Tighten and weave end inside the I-Cord. Weave the CO tail inside the I-Cord.

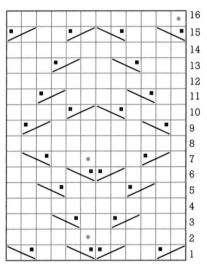

			YO, SI 1, K1, PSSO
			K
			K YO TBL
			K2 tog, YO

ALPACA LACE BED SOCK CHART

6

Colorwork
SOCKS

Colorwork is just knitting with more than one color. To carry the different yarns, I hold strands with my right hand, then pick up the color I need with the left needle. Others hold a strand in each hand. The important thing is to strand the unused yarn loosely from section to section.

It's important, too, to take color *dominance* into consideration with stranded knitting. Whether you hold both of your strands in one hand, or one in each hand, always hold and strand the motif color underneath the background color. That will cause your motif color to dominate the background color. If you're knitting a sock with many color changes, decide for each border which color will be dominant. If you're knitting socks with just two colors, such as our Mosaic Tile Sock, decide which color will be dominant and maintain that dominance consistently throughout, unless you want your socks to have very different looking stripes.

Intarsia knitting is often worked flat and involves using many colors per row, holding one strand at a time and switching colors (by twisting the strands around each other) at new sections. Each colored area of an intarsia design is worked with a separate length of yarn. Those lengths can be wound on cardboard bobbins. In all cases, you do colorwork by reading a chart (I like to make a color copy) that indicates which stitches to work in which colors.

Stripes and Stairsteps SOCK

This intermediate pattern, sized to fit children through adults, is a good introduction to intarsia work because it uses fairly short yarn lengths for the stairstep blocks. Just let the yarns hang free from the back of your needle instead of winding them on bobbins.

PATTERN DIFFICULTY: Intermediate

YARN: Knit Picks Telemark™, 100% Peruvian highland wool, 50 g, 103 yd., #23925 Aubergine, #23945 Rosemary, #24016 Royal Heather, #23940 Lichen, 1 ball each for sizes up through Women's Average (all shoe sizes), 2 balls each for Men's Average and Men's Wide (all shoe sizes)

YARN WEIGHT: Sport

NEEDLES: Size 4 (U.S.)/3.5 mm, or size needed to obtain gauge 10-in. straight or circular, as desired

TOOLS: Large-eye blunt needle, stitch markers

PATTERN SIZES: Child (10–11, 12–13), Youth (1–2, 3–4), Women's Average (5–6, 7–8, 9–10), Men's Average, Men's Wide (8–9, 10–11, 12–13)

MEASUREMENTS: Cuff Length: Child: 4 in., Youth: 5 in., Women's: 6 in., Men's: 7 in.; Cuff Width, Unsewn: Child: 5½ in., Youth: 6½ in., Women's Average: 7⅜ in., Men's Average: 8⅜ in., Men's Wide: 9⅜ in.; Heel-to-Toe Length: Child Shoe Size 10–11: 5½ in.,

Child Shoe Size 12–13: 6¼ in., Youth Shoe Size 1–2: 7 in., Youth Shoe Size 3–4: 7½ in., Women's Shoe Size 5–6: 9 in., Women's Shoe Size 7–8: 9½ in., Women's Shoe Size 9–10: 10 in., Men's Shoe Size 8–9: 10½ in., Men's Shoe Size 10–11: 11 in., Men's Shoe Size 12–13: 12 in.

HEEL STYLE: Two-Needle Afterthought

GAUGE: 6.5 sts = 1 in., 8 rows = 1 in. in Stockinette st

It takes approximately 42 in. of yarn to knit each individual intarsia square on this pattern. You may wind the loose yarn on bobbins, or you may leave the ends hanging. Tie on new colors as indicated on the chart, leaving at least a 3-in. tail. When changing colors, wrap the new color around the old color on the wrong side of the work before continuing.

Note: If you want your socks to be mirror images of each other, knit the right sock as directed. Knit the left sock by beginning at the opposite side of the chart.

Note: Work **Women's Wide** as for **Men's Average**; adjust length for shoe size. Work **Women's Narrow** as for **Youth**; adjust length for shoe size.

RIGHT SOCK With size 4 straight or circular needle and Aubergine, CO 36 (42, 48, 54, 60) sts. Work 4 rows in K3, P3 ribbing, working back and forth. Cut Aubergine and tie on Rosemary, and work 4 rows in K3, P3 ribbing. Rep with Royal Heather and Lichen.

FIRST CUFF RND: With Lichen, P across. Turn. Follow chart as indicated, beginning all sizes except Men's Average at the right upper corner of the chart. Begin Men's Average at the right upper corner of the chart, on the stitch indicated. Continue, repeating chart as needed, until cuff measures 4 in. (5 in., 6 in., 7 in., 7 in.). End with WS row at the bottom of a square.

RIGHT HEEL DIVISION ROW 1: With Aubergine, BO 18 (21, 24, 27, 30) sts, K remainder of row.

RIGHT HEEL DIVISION ROW 2: P 18 (21, 24, 27, 30) sts, CO 18 (21, 24, 27, 30) sts.

Continue working foot on 36 (42, 48, 54, 60) sts in Stockinette st, in 8-row stripes of Aubergine, Rosemary, Royal Heather, Lichen, repeating the stripe sequence if necessary, until foot measures: Child Shoe Size 10–11: 2½ in., Child Shoe Size 12–13: 4 in., Youth Shoe Size 1–2: 4½ in., Youth Shoe Size 3–4: 4¾ in., Women's Shoe Size 5–6: 5½ in., Women's Shoe Size 7–8: 6 in., Women's Shoe Size 9–10: 6½ in., Men's Shoe Size 8–9: 6½ in., Men's Shoe Size 10–12: 7 in., Men's Shoe Size 13: 7 in. End with a P row.

T O E Continuing in established stripe sequence, work a 36 (42, 48, 54, 60)-st Star Toe as instructed on page 177. Cut a 12-in. tail, and thread the yarn through a large-eye needle. Thread the needle through the remaining loops, tighten, and tie off. Do not weave loose end in.

L E F T S O C K Work ribbing and cuff as for Right Sock, end with a **Knit** row.

LEFT HEEL DIVISION ROW 1 (WS): BO 18 (21, 24, 27, 30) sts, **Purl** rem of row.

LEFT HEEL DIVISION ROW 2: Knit 18 (21, 24, 27, 30) sts, CO 18 (21, 24, 27, 30) sts.

Complete foot as for Right Sock.

Note: Work heel in 4-row stripes in the following order: Aubergine, Rosemary, Royal Heather, Lichen. Rep sequence if necessary.

B O T H S O C K S **AFTERTHOUGHT HEEL ROW 1:** With Aubergine, on the WS of the sock, pick up and P 18 (21, 24, 27, 30) sts along one edge of the heel opening, place marker, along the other edge of the heel opening, pick up and P 18 (21, 24, 27, 30) sts. (36, 42, 48, 54, 60 sts)

AFTERTHOUGHT HEEL ROW 2: SSK, K to within 2 sts of the marker, K2 tog, move marker, SSK, K to within 2 sts of the end of the row, K2 tog. (4 sts dec)

AFTERTHOUGHT HEEL ROW 3: P.

Rep Rows 2–3 until there are 16 (22, 24, 26, 30) sts left. Divide the rem sts on 2 needles so that the decs are at the beginning and the end of each needle. You may need to work half of the sts so that the yarn is at the working end of the needle. Close the heel with Kitchener st (see Glossary for instructions). Tighten and tie off.

F I N I S H I N G Line up the heel side seam and sew it with yarn threaded in a large-eye needle, using the Mattress st (see Glossary for instructions). Sew the sock side seam, lining up squares on the cuff and stripes on the foot. Tie off ends, and weave all loose ends in on the inside of the sock. Wash and block the socks.

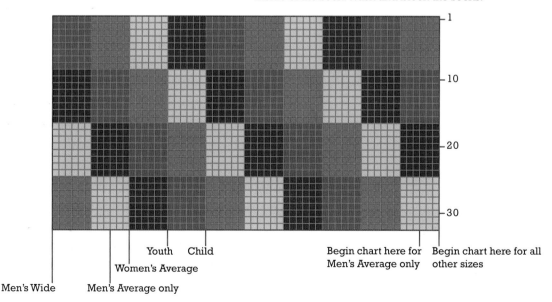

STRIPES AND STAIRSTEPS INTARSIA CHART

Argyle BORDER SOCK

Argyle styling and luxury yarns combine to make this classic sock a keeper.
Knit the cuff flat, and then join and knit the heel and foot in the round.

PATTERN DIFFICULTY:
Intermediate

YARN: Knit Picks Andean Silk,
55% superfine alpaca/23%
silk/22% Merino wool, 50 g,
96 yd., #23510 Lettuce, 2 balls
for all sizes through Women's Shoe
Size 9–10, 3 balls for all Men's
sizes; #23507 Cinnamon, 1 ball
for all sizes through Women's Shoe
Size 7–8, 2 balls for Women's
Shoe Size 9–10, all Men's sizes;
#23517 Navy, 1 ball for all sizes

YARN WEIGHT: Worsted

NEEDLES: 1 pair 10-in. straight
size 5 (U.S.)/3.75 mm needles, or
size needed to obtain gauge
1 or 2 circular needles or 4 or
5 dpns, as desired

TOOLS: Large-eye blunt needle,
stitch markers

PATTERN SIZES: Youth (1–2,
3–4), Women's (5–6, 7–8, 9–10),
Men's (8–9, 10–11, 12–13)

MEASUREMENTS: Cuff Length:
Youth: 6 in., Women's: 6½ in.,
Men's: 7 in.; Cuff Width: Youth:
3¼ in., Women's: 4 in., Men's:
5 in.; Foot Width: Youth: 3¼ in.,
Women's: 3¾ in., Men's: 4¾ in.;

Heel-to-Toe Length: Youth Shoe
Size 1–2: 6½ in., Youth Shoe
Size 3–4: 7 in., Women's Shoe
Size 5–6: 8½ in., Women's Shoe
Size 7–8: 9 in., Women's Shoe
Size 9–10: 10 in., Men's Shoe
Size 8–9: 10 in., Men's Shoe Size
10–11: 11 in., Men's Shoe Size
12–13: 12 in.

HEEL STYLE: Flap and Gusset

GAUGE: 6.5 sts = 1 in., 8 rnds =
1 in. in Stockinette st
6 sts = 1 in., 8 rows = 1 in. over
Argyle Pattern

Note: Tie on a new strand of yarn for each color section.
You may wind the loose yarn on bobbins, or you may leave
the ends hanging (this yarn is slick and doesn't tangle
easily). Tie on new colors as indicated on the chart, leaving
at least a 3-in. tail. When changing colors, wrap the new
color around the old color on the wrong side of the work
before continuing.

Note: Work **Women's Narrow** as for **Youth**; adjust cuff and
foot length for shoe size.

With Cinnamon and size 5 straight needles, CO 40
(50, 60) sts.

Work K1, P1 ribbing for 12 (15, 20) rows. End with
RS row.

CUFF SETUP (WS) P across.

CUFF Beginning at Row 1 as indicated, work the
chart, end with a WS row.

NEXT ROW: K with Lettuce.

NEXT ROW: P with Lettuce.

Transfer sts to 1 or 2 circulars or 3 or 4 dpns, as
desired, with the center back cuff opening the beginning of the new rnd.

RND 1, YOUTH: Inc 2 sts evenly spaced in rnd. (42 sts)

RND 1, WOMEN'S: Dec 2 sts evenly spaced in rnd.
(48 sts)

RND 1, MEN'S: K. (60 sts)

Work even in Lettuce until cuff measures 6 in. (6½ in.,
7 in.).

HEEL SETUP K 10 (12, 15) sts. Place the next 22
(24, 30) sts on a separate needle or holder for the
instep. Place the rem 10 (12, 15) sts with the first for
the heel. (20, 24, 30 heel sts)

HEEL FLAP ROW 1: Cut Lettuce. Tie on Cinnamon.
Turn. Sl 1, P across. Turn.

HEEL FLAP ROW 2: *Sl 1, K 1*, rep across. Turn.

Rep Heel Flap Rows 1–2 until heel flap measures
1½ in. (2 in., 2½ in.). End with a P row.

HEEL Work a 20 (24, 30)-st Flap and Gusset Heel as instructed on pages 172–173.

GUSSET SETUP Sl 1, K5 (6, 8). Cut Cinnamon. Tie on Lettuce.

GUSSET RND 1: K6 (7, 9), pick up, twist, and K 9 (11, 13) sts along the heel flap edge, place marker, K across the instep sts, place marker, pick up, twist, and K 9 (11, 13) sts along the other heel flap edge, K6 (7, 9).

GUSSET RND 2: K to within 2 sts of marker, K2 tog, move marker, K across instep to marker, move marker, SSK, K to end.

GUSSET RND 3: K.

Rep Gusset Rnds 2–3 until 42 (48, 60) sts rem.

FOOT Work even until foot measures from the gusset edge: Youth Shoe Size 1–2: 3½ in., Youth Shoe Size 3–4: 4 in., Women's Shoe Size 5–6: 4½ in., Women's Shoe Size 7–8: 5½ in., Women's Shoe Size 9–10: 6 in., Men's Shoe Size 8–9: 6½ in., Men's Shoe Size 10–11: 7 in., Men's Shoe Size 12–13: 7½ in.

LAST FOOT RND: K11 (12, 15), place marker, K21 (24, 30), place marker, K10 (12, 15).

TOE WEDGE TOE DECREASE RND 1: K to within 2 sts of first marker, K2 tog, move marker, SSK, K to within 2 sts of 2nd marker, K2 tog, move marker, SSK, K to end. (4 sts dec)

WEDGE TOE DECREASE RND 2: K.

Rep Wedge Toe Decrease Rnds 1–2 until 22 (24, 28) sts rem. You may need to K to a marker or side. Cut yarn, leaving a 12-in. tail. Close rem sts with Kitchener st (see Glossary for instructions).

FINISHING With matching yarn, using Mattress st (see Glossary for instructions), sew the back cuff seam. Weave all loose ends in on the inside of the sock. Wash and block the socks.

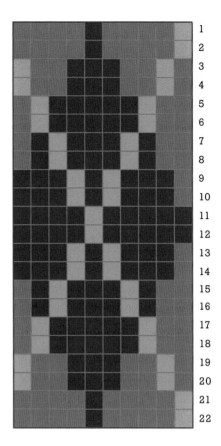

1
2
3
4
5
6
7
8
9
10
11
12
13
14
15
16
17
18
19
20
21
22

Navy #23517

Lettuce #23510

Cinnamon #23507

ARGYLE BORDER SOCK CHART

One-Skein CHECKERBOARD SOCK

The Noro Kureyon Sock Yarn seems to have been invented for this design, knitted with just one ball of yarn. Noro's long pattern repeats mean that you are unlikely to have the same color coming from the inside and the outside of the ball at the same time (and if you do, just snip one of the color strands and tie on again with the next color in the repeat).

PATTERN DIFFICULTY: Advanced

YARN: Noro Kureyon Sock Yarn, 70% wool/30% nylon, 100 g, 462 yd., #S180 pink/orange/purple, 1 ball for Youth through Women's Average, all shoe sizes; 2 balls for Women's Wide Shoe Size 9–10

YARN WEIGHT: Light fingering

NEEDLES: Size 2 (U.S.)/ 2.75 mm, or size needed to obtain gauge 1 or 2 circulars or 4 or 5 dpns, as desired 1 size 3 (U.S.)/3.25 mm needle for casting on

TOOLS: Large-eye blunt needle

PATTERN SIZES: Youth (1–2, 3–4), Women's Average, Women's Wide, (5–6, 7–8, 9–10)

MEASUREMENTS: Cuff Length: Youth: 5¼ in., Women's Average and Wide: 6¼ in.; Cuff Width: Youth: 3 in., Women's Average: 3¾ in., Women's Wide: 4¼ in.; Heel-to-Toe Length: Youth Shoe Size 1–2: 7½ in., Youth Shoe Size 3–4: 7¾ in., Women's Shoe Size 5–6: 8¼ in., Women's Shoe Size 7–8: 9¼ in., Women's Shoe Size 9–10: 10¼ in.

HEEL STYLE: Short Row

GAUGE: 10 sts = 1 in., 9 rnds = 1 in. over Checkerboard Pattern

---

CHECKERBOARD PATTERN (4-st, 4-rnd repeat) Wind the yarn into 2 balls or use 1 yarn strand from the outside of the ball and 1 from the center of the ball, knitting from the same ball throughout. The yarns will be designated OB (outside the ball) and IB (inside the ball). If using yarn from separate balls, designate one OB and one IB.

RNDS 1–2: *K 2 sts IB, K 2 sts OB*, rep around.

RNDS 3–4: *K 2 sts OB, K 2 sts IB*, rep around.

With a size 3 needle, and using the IB strand, CO 52 (60, 64) sts. Distribute on size 2 needles, 1 or 2 circulars or 3 or 4 dpns, as desired. Without twisting, join.

CUFF Work 12 (14, 16) rnds in K2, P2 ribbing.

NEXT RND: K, inc 8 (12, 20) sts evenly spaced in rnd. (60, 72, 84 sts)

Work Checkerboard Pattern until cuff measures 5¼ in. (6¼ in.) long, ending with either Rnd 2 or 4.

HEEL SETUP Work 15 sts in the established patt. Place the next 30 (42, 54) sts on a separate needle or holder for the instep. Place the rem 15 sts on the first needle for the heel. (30 heel sts)

HEEL Holding both the IB and OB strands together throughout, work a 30-st Short-Row Heel (see pages 174–175).

FOOT SETUP Sl 1, K14, begin new rnd at center of heel. Working again with just 1 strand of yarn at a time, begin established Checkerboard Pattern. Work established Checkerboard Pattern until foot measures: Youth Shoe Size 1–2: 3½ in., Youth Shoe Size 3–4: 4 in., Women's Shoe Size 5–6: 4½ in., Women's Shoe Size 7–8: 5¼ in., Women's Shoe Size 9–10: 5½ in.

TOE, WOMEN'S WIDE ONLY

TOE DECREASE RND 1: *K12, K2 tog*, rep around. (78 sts rem)

TOE DECREASE RND 2 AND ALL EVEN RNDS: K.

TOE DECREASE RND 3: *K11, K2 tog*, rep around. (72 sts rem)

TOE, ALL SIZES Work toe holding both the IB and OB strands together throughout. Work a 60 (72, 72)-st Star Toe as instructed on pages 176–177.

FINISHING Weave all ends in on the inside of the sock. Wash and block the socks.

Nordic Style
Adult Sock

Nordic Style
Child/Youth Sock

Nordic-Style ADULT SOCK

Traditional Nordic black-and-white patterning has been used for these strikingly beautiful socks, sized for men and women.

PATTERN DIFFICULTY: Advanced

YARN: Regia 4-Ply, 75% superwash wool/25% polyamide, 50 g, 230 yd., #2066 Black, 1 ball for all Women's Sizes, 2 balls for all Men's Sizes; #600 White, 1 ball for Women's Shoe Sizes 5–8, 2 balls for Women's Shoe Sizes 9–10 and all Men's Sizes

YARN WEIGHT: Fingering

NEEDLES: Size 2 (U.S.)/ 2.75 mm, or size needed to obtain gauge 1 or 2 circulars or 4 or 5 dpns, as desired 1 size 3 (U.S.)/3.25 mm needle for casting on

TOOLS: Large-eye blunt needle, stitch markers

PATTERN SIZES: Women's (5–6, 7–8, 9–10), Men's (9, 10–11, 12–13)

MEASUREMENTS: Cuff Length: Women's: 6¾ in., Men's: 7½ in.; Cuff Width: Women's: 4 in., Men's: 5 in.; Heel-to-Toe Length: Women's Shoe Size 5–6: 7¼ in., Women's Shoe Size 7–8: 8¼ in., Women's Shoe Size 9–10: 9¼ in., Men's Shoe Size 9–10: 9½ in., Men's Shoe Size 11–12: 10 in., Men's Shoe Size 13: 11 in.

HEEL STYLE: Flap and Gusset

GAUGE: 9.5 sts = 1 in., 10 sts = 1 in. over Stranded Knitting

Note: Hold the unused color on the inside of the sock, stranding it loosely behind the work. Do not strand more than 6 sts without winding the unused yarn around the active yarn. Leave at least a 3-in. tail when changing colors.

With White and size 3 needle, CO 76 (96) sts. Divide on size 2 needles, 1 or 2 circulars or 3 or 4 dpns, as desired. Without twisting sts, join.

RIBBING RNDS 1–2: *K2, P2*, rep around.

RIBBING RNDS 3–16: *K2 White, P2 Black*, rep around.

NEXT RND, WOMEN'S: K with White.

NEXT RND, MEN'S: K with White, dec 1 st in rnd. (95 sts)

CUFF Follow chart, beginning where indicated for your size, until cuff measures 6¾ in. (7½ in.).

HEEL SETUP Working *K1 White, K1 Black*, work 18 (20) sts. Place next 40 (55) sts on a separate holder or needle for the instep. Place the remaining 18 (20) sts with the first sts for the heel.

HEEL FLAP ROW 1: Turn. Sl 1, P across, working in alternate Black and White sts. Turn.

HEEL FLAP ROW 2: Sl 1, K across, working in alternate Black and White sts. Turn.

Work Heel Flap until it measures 1½ in. (2 in.), end with P row.

HEEL Cut Black. Work a 36 (40)-st Flap and Gusset heel with White, as instructed on page 171.

GUSSET With White, Sl 1, K9 (11). Begin new rnd at center of Heel.

GUSSET RND 1: With White, K10 (12), pick up, twist, and K 15 (20) sts along heel flap edge, picking up the sts on the 2nd st, not the Sl st edge. Place marker. Tie on Black, work across instep sts in established charted patt; work the extra sts on either side of the charted motif in alternate Black and White. Cut Black. Place marker. With White, pick up, twist, and K 15 (20) sts along heel flap edge, K the rem 10 (12) sts.

GUSSET RND 2: Tie on Black, work alternating Black and White sts, work to within 2 sts of marker, K2 tog, move marker, work across instep in established charted patt, move marker, SSK, work to end of rnd, alternating Black and White sts.

GUSSET RND 3: Work in alternating Black and White sts to marker, move marker, work instep in established charted patt, move marker, work alternating Black and White sts to end of rnd. Rep Gusset Rnds 2–3 until 76 (95) sts rem.

FOOT Work foot as established, charted patt on instep, alternating Black and White sts on sole, until 2 full reps have been worked for Women's, and 2½ reps have been worked for Men's. Work all sts in Black and White alternating sts, until foot measures: Women's Shoe Size 5–6: 4 in., Women's Shoe Size 7–8: 5 in., Women's Shoe Size 9–10: 5½ in., Men's Shoe Size 9: 5½ in., Men's Shoe Size 10–11: 6 in., Men's Shoe Size 12–13: 6½ in.

Note: Alternating sts may not match up perfectly at the instep when you begin the alternating Black and White patt across the instep. You may have to work 2 sts in the same color for the established patt to continue on the sole.

LAST FOOT RND, MEN'S SIZE: Dec 1 st in rnd. (94 sts rem)

TOE WEDGE TOE RND 1: Work 19 (24) sts in established alternating Black and White patt, place marker, work in established alternating Black and White patt until 19 (23) sts rem, place marker, finish rnd.

WEDGE TOE RND 2: Work in established alternating Black and White patt to within 2 sts of marker, K2, move marker, K2, work established alternating patt to within 2 sts of next marker, K2, move marker, K2, work established alternating patt to end.

WEDGE TOE RND 3: Work established alternating patt to within 2 sts of marker, K2 tog, move marker, SSK, work established alternating patt to within 2 sts of next marker, K2 tog, move marker, SSK, work established alternating patt to end.

Rep Wedge Toe Rnds 2–3 until 32 (38) sts rem. Work in patt to next marker.

FINISHING Divide sts on 2 needles and close the toe with Kitchener st (see Glossary for instructions). Weave all loose ends in on the inside of the sock. Wash and block the socks.

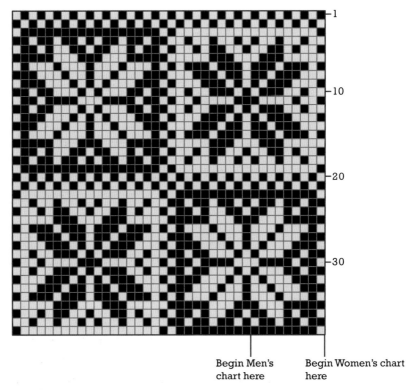

Begin Men's chart here

Begin Women's chart here

NORDIC-STYLE ADULT SOCK CHART

ℌordic-℟tyle CHILD/YOUTH SOCK

This smaller version of the two-color traditional Nordic sock is knit with Knit Picks Risata yarn, a comfy cotton/wool blend that is very stretchy.

PATTERN DIFFICULTY: Advanced

YARN: Knit Picks Risata, 42% cotton/39% superwash wool/13% polyamide/6% Elite elastic, 50 g, 196 yd., #24109 Buttermilk, #24106 Burgundy, 1 ball each for all sizes

YARN WEIGHT: Fingering

NEEDLES: Size 2 (U.S.)/ 2.75 mm, or size needed to obtain gauge
1 or 2 circulars, or 4 or 5 dpns as desired
1 size 3 (U.S.)/3.25 mm needle for casting on

TOOLS: Large-eye blunt needle, stitch markers

PATTERN SIZES: Child (10–11, 12–13), Youth (1–2, 3–4)

MEASUREMENTS: Cuff Length: Child: 4¼ in., Youth: 5¼ in.; Cuff Width: Child: 3 in., Youth: 3¾ in.; Heel-to-Toe Length: Child Shoe Size 10–11: 5¼ in., Child Shoe Size 12–13: 5¾ in., Youth Shoe Size 1–2: 6¾ in., Youth Shoe Size 3–4: 7 in.

HEEL STYLE: Flap and Gusset

GAUGE: 8.5 sts = 1 in., 9 rnds = 1 in. over Stranded Knitting

ℌote: Hold the unused color on the inside of the sock, stranding it loosely behind the work. Do not strand more than 6 sts without winding the unused yarn around the active yarn. Leave at least a 3-in. tail when changing colors.

ℌote: Knit Picks Risata yarn is quite stretchy. If you're substituting a yarn that does not have an elastic component, add ½ in. to the foot length before decreasing for the toe. You may need to work a size up for width as well. Swatch and measure before substituting yarns.

ℌote: Alternating sts may not match up perfectly at the instep when you begin the Buttermilk/Burgundy patterning across the instep. You may have to work 2 sts in the same color for the established stitch pattern to continue on the sole.

With Buttermilk and size 3 needle, CO 52 (64) sts. Distribute on size 2 needles, 1 or 2 circulars or 3 or 4 dpns, as desired. Without twisting sts, join.

RIBBING RNDS 1–2: *K2, P2*, rep around.

RIBBING RNDS 3–12: Tie on Burgundy. *K2 Buttermilk, P2 Burgundy*, rep around.

NEXT RND, CHILD: With Buttermilk, K.

NEXT RND, YOUTH: With Buttermilk, K, inc 1 st in rnd. (65 sts)

CUFF Follow chart, beginning rnd at st indicated on the chart for your size, until cuff measures 4¼ in. (5¼ in.).

HEEL SETUP Working *K1 Buttermilk, K1 Burgundy*, work 12 (15) sts. Place next 28 (35) sts on a separate holder or needle for the instep. Place the rem 12 (15) sts with the first sts for the heel. Work heel over 24 (30) sts.

HEEL FLAP ROW 1: Turn. Sl 1, P across, alternating Buttermilk and Burgundy sts. Turn.

HEEL FLAP ROW 2: Sl 1, K across, alternating Buttermilk and Burgundy sts. Turn.

Work Heel Flap until it measures 1 in. (1¼ in.), end with a P row.

HEEL Cut Burgundy. Work a 24 (30)-st Flap and Gusset Heel with Buttermilk, as instructed on page 172..

GUSSET With Burgundy, Sl 1, K6 (8). Begin new rnd at center of heel.

GUSSET RND 1: With Buttermilk, K7 (9), pick up, twist, and K 13 (14) sts along heel flap edge, picking up the sts on the 2nd st, not the Sl st edge. Place marker. Tie on Burgundy, work across instep sts in established charted patt; work extra sts on either side of the charted motif in solid Burgundy or Buttermillk. Cut Burgundy. Place marker. With Buttermilk, pick up, twist, and K 13 (14) sts along heel flap edge, K the rem 7 (9) sts.

GUSSET RND 2: Tie on Burgundy, work alternating Buttermilk and Burgundy sts to within 2 sts of marker, K2 tog, move marker, work across instep in established charted patt, move marker, SSK, work to end of rnd, alternating Buttermilk and Burgundy sts.

GUSSET RND 3: Work alternating Buttermilk and Burgundy sts to marker, move marker, work instep in established charted patt, move marker, work alternating Buttermilk and Burgundy sts to end of rnd.

Rep Gusset Rnds 2–3 until 52 (65) sts rem. Work 2 full charted patt reps for Child, work 2½ charted patt reps for Youth, and alternating color sts on the sole.

F O O T After completing the required charted patt reps, work the entire foot in alternating Buttermilk and Burgundy sts. Work foot as established, charted patt on instep, alternating Buttermilk and Burgundy sts on sole, until foot measures from heel: Child Shoe Size 10–11: 2½ in., Child Shoe Size 12–13: 3 in., Youth Shoe Size 1–2: 3½ in., Youth Shoe Size 3–4: 4 in.

LAST FOOT RND, YOUTH: Dec 1 st in rnd. (64 sts rem)

T O E **WEDGE TOE RND 1:** Work 13 (16) sts in established alternating Buttermilk/Burgundy patt, place marker, work in established alternating Buttermilk/Burgundy patt until 13 (16) sts rem, place marker, finish rnd.

WEDGE TOE RND 2: Work established alternating patt to within 2 sts of marker, K2 tog, move marker, SSK, work established alternating patt to within 2 sts of next marker, K2 tog, move marker, SSK, work established alternating patt to end.

WEDGE TOE RND 3: Rep Wedge Toe Rnds 2–3 until 28 (32) sts rem. Work in patt to next marker.

F I N I S H I N G Divide sts on 2 needles and close the toe with Kitchener st (see Glossary for instructions). Weave all loose ends in on the inside of the sock. Wash and block the socks.

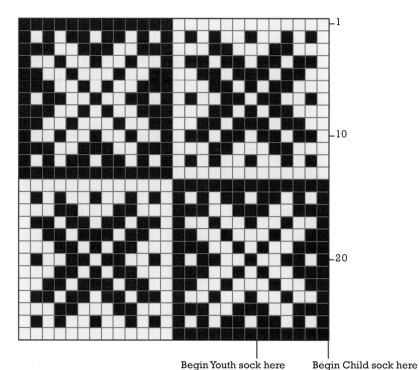

Begin Youth sock here   Begin Child sock here

NORDIC-STYLE CHILD/YOUTH SOCK CHART

$\mathcal{S}nowflake$ HOUSE SOCK

The picot hem and stranded toe and heel make this colorful sock design
a step outside the ordinary. One adult size fits most foot widths, and one child size
fits most child/youth foot widths.

PATTERN DIFFICULTY:
Advanced

YARN: Knit Picks Telemark,
100% Peruvian wool, 50 g, 103 yd.,
#23942 Northern Green 1 (2) balls;
#23932 Cream, #23947 Tangelo,
#24227 Cork, #23941 Skyline,
1 ball each for all sizes

YARN WEIGHT: Sport

NEEDLES: Size 4 (U.S.)3.5 mm,
or size needed to obtain gauge 1 or
2 circulars or 4 or 5 dpns, as desired

TOOLS: Large-eye blunt needle,
stitch markers

PATTERN SIZES: Child/Youth
(10–11, 12–13, 1–2, 3–4), Adult
(Women's 5–6, 7–8, 9–10, Men's
9, 10–11, 12–13)

MEASUREMENTS: Cuff Length
from Picot Rnd: Child: 5¾ in.,
Adult: 6½ in.; Cuff Width: Child:
3 in., Adult: 4¼ in.; Heel-to-Toe
Length: Child Shoe Size 10–11:
5¾ in., Child Shoe Size 12–13:

6¼ in., Youth Shoe Size 1–2:
6½ in., Youth Shoe Size 3–4:
6¾ in., Women's Shoe Size 5–6:
9 in., Women's Shoe Size 7–8:
9½ in., Women's Shoe Size 9–10:
10 in., Men's Shoe Size 9: 10½ in.,
Size 10–11: 11 in., Men's Shoe Size
12–13: 12 in.

HEEL STYLE: Flap and Gusset,
Stranded Flap

GAUGE: 6.5 sts = 1 in., 7.5 rnds
= 1 in. over Stranded Knitting

$\mathcal{N}ote$: Tie new colors on at the beginning of the round;
leave at least a 3-in. tail at each tie. Strand unused colors
loosely on the back of the work. Do not strand unused yarn
more than 5 stitches without twisting the yarn strands on
the back of the work.

With Tangelo and size 4 needles, CO 36 (48) sts.
Divide on 1 or 2 circulars or 3 or 4 dpns, as desired.
Without twisting sts, join.

RNDS 1–5: K.

RND 6, PICOT RND: *YO, K2 tog*, rep around.

RND 7: K, working each YO as a stitch.

RNDS 8–11: K.

CUFF Begin Cuff Chart from the top.

CUFF CHART RND 1: Inc 6 (8) sts evenly spaced in
rnd. (42, 56 sts)

Work cuff, following Cuff chart, repeating the lower
Cuff chart bands as needed, until cuff measures
5¾ in. (6½ in.) from Picot Rnd.

ADULT SIZE ONLY: End cuff on 2nd to last rnd of the
last Northern Green/Tangelo border.

HEEL SETUP K 10 (14) sts. Child Size Only:
Tie on Northern Green.

Place the next 22 (28) sts on a separate holder or
needle for the instep. Place the rem 10 (14) sts with
the heel sts.

HEEL FLAP: Work the heel flap as shown in the proper
size chart.

HEEL FLAP WS ROWS: Sl 1, P across according to the
chart, turn.

HEEL FLAP RS ROWS: Sl 1, K across according to the
chart, turn.

End with a WS row.

HEEL Work a 20 (24)-st Flap and Gusset Heel with
Northern Green, as instructed on pages 172–173.

GUSSET **GUSSET RND 1:** K6 (8), pick up, twist, and
K 10 (12) sts along heel flap edge, place marker,
K across instep sts following chart in established
manner, place marker, pick up, twist, and K 10 (12) sts
along other heel flap edge, K 6 (8) sts.

GUSSET RND 2: Work charted border, K to within

2 sts of marker, SSK, move marker, K across instep sts following chart in established manner, move marker, K2 tog, K to end. (2 sts dec)

GUSSET RND 3: K.

Rep Gusset Rnds 2–3 until 44 (56) sts rem. (**Note:** The Child Size will have 2 more sts on the foot than on the cuff.)

Work foot, following the charted borders, until foot measures from the beginning of the gusset: Child Shoe Size 10–11: 3 in., Child Shoe Size 12–13: 2½ in., Youth Shoe Size 1–2: 4 in., Youth Shoe Size 3–4: 4 in., Women's Shoe Size 5–6: 4 in., Women's Shoe Size 7–8: 5 in., Women's Shoe Size 9–10: 5½ in., Men's Shoe Size 9: 6 in., Men's Shoe Size 10–11: 6½ in., Men's Shoe Size 12–13: 7 in.

T O E Work Toe chart for your sock size, making sure that the toe lines up properly with the heel. SSK the decs on the right sides of the charts, and K2tog decs on the left sides of the charts. Close the opening with Kitchener st (see Glossary for instructions).

F I N I S H I N G Weave in all loose ends on the inside of the sock. Fold the Picot Hem in and stitch down with matching yarn. Wash and block the socks.

SNOWFLAKE HOUSE SOCK CHARTS

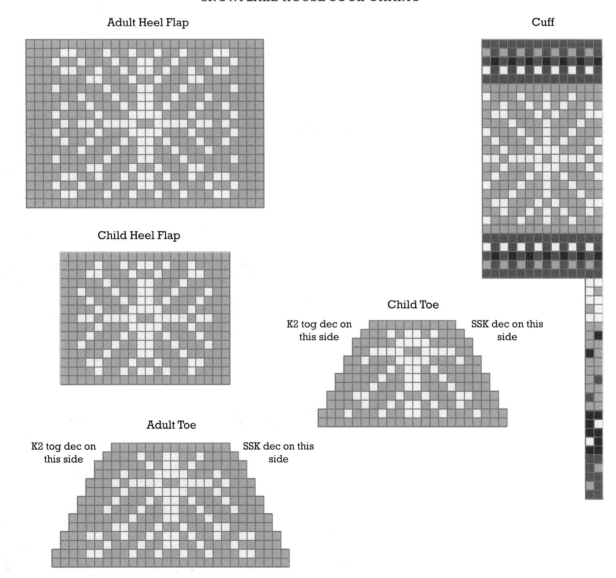

Adult Heel Flap

Cuff

Child Heel Flap

Child Toe

K2 tog dec on this side

SSK dec on this side

Adult Toe

K2 tog dec on this side

SSK dec on this side

Holiday Garland SOCK

Worked in red and green with embroidered golden highlights, these socks are perfect for the holidays—warm and cushy, with a lovely halo from the mohair content in the recommended yarn. Change up the colorway, and they're great for any fall or winter day.

PATTERN DIFFICULTY: Intermediate

YARN: ShibuiKnits Merino Kid, 55% kid mohair/45% Merino wool, 100 g, 218 yd., #MK7498 Seaweed, #MK1797 Chinese Red, 1 skein each for all sizes through Women's Wide, 2 skeins each for Men's sizes; a few yards of Knit Picks Wool of the Andes #23436 Daffodil, or any golden/yellow worsted weight yarn

YARN WEIGHT: Worsted

NEEDLES: Size 5 (U.S.)/3.75 mm, or size needed to obtain gauge

1 or 2 circulars or 4 or 5 dpns, as desired

TOOLS: Large-eye blunt needle

PATTERN SIZES: Child (10–11, 12–13), Youth (1–2, 3–4), Women's Average, Women's Wide (5–6, 7–8, 9–10), Men's Average (8–9, 10–11, 12–13)

MEASUREMENTS: Cuff Length: Child: 4½ in., Youth: 5½ in., Women's: 6½ in., Men's: 7½ in.; Cuff Width: Child: 2¾ in., Youth: 3¼ in., Women's Average: 3¾ in., Women's Wide: 4¼ in., Men's: 4¾ in.; Heel-to-Toe Length: Child

Shoe Size 10–11: 5½ in., Child Shoe Size 12–13: 6¼ in., Youth Shoe Size 1–2: 7 in., Youth Shoe Size 3–4: 7½ in., Women's Shoe Size 5–6: 9 in., Women's Shoe Size 7–8: 9½ in., Women's Shoe Size 9–10: 10 in., Men's Shoe Size 8–9: 10½ in., Men's Shoe Size 10–11: 11 in., Men's Shoe Size 12–13: 12 in.

HEEL STYLE: Short Row

GAUGE: 7 sts = 1 in., 7 rnds = 1 in. over Stranded Knitting

Note: Hold the unused color on the inside of the sock, stranding it loosely behind the work. Do not strand more than 5 sts without winding the unused yarn around the active yarn. Leave at least a 3-in. tail when changing colors.

Note: If you prefer not to Duplicate stitch the yellow highlights, you may knit with three strands for those rows. Be sure to strand the unused yarns loosely behind the work.

Note: Work **Women's Narrow** as for **Youth**; adjust foot and cuff length for shoe size.

With Chinese Red and size 5 needles, CO 40 (48, 52, 60, 66) sts. Distribute on 1 or 2 circulars or 3 or 4 dpns, as desired. Without twisting the sts, join.

RIBBING RND 1: *K2, P2* around.

RIBBING RNDS 2–3: Tie on Seaweed. *K2 Chinese Red, P2 Seaweed*, rep around.

RIBBING RNDS 4–5: *K2 Seaweed, P2 Chinese Red*, rep around.

Continue in established patt, alternating colors, until ribbing is 7 (9, 11, 11, 13) rnds long.

NEXT RND, ALL SIZES: Rep Ribbing Rnd 1 with Chinese Red.

NEXT RND, CHILD AND WOMEN'S AVERAGE SIZES ONLY: K with Chinese Red, inc 2 sts evenly spaced in rnd. (42, 54 sts)

NEXT RND, ALL OTHER SIZES: K with Chinese Red. Follow chart, beginning at Rnd 2 for first repeat, and then from Rnd 1 thereafter. You may work the Daffodil highlights by knitting with 3 strands, or you may work those squares with the background color and embroider the highlights with a Duplicate st after finishing the sock.

Work the cuff until it measures 4½ in. (5½ in., 6½ in., 6½ in., 7½ in.).

HEEL SETUP Work 10 (12, 13, 15, 16) sts in established charted patt. Place the next 22 (24, 28, 30, 34) sts on a separate needle or holder for the instep,

place the rem 10 (12, 13, 15, 16) sts with the first for
the heel. Cut Chinese Red, and knit the heel with
Seaweed.

HEEL Work a 20 (24, 26, 30, 32)-st Short-Row Heel
as instructed on pages 174–176.

FOOT SETUP Sl 1, K 9 (11, 12, 14, 15) sts. Tie on
Chinese Red, and begin new rnd at the center of
the heel.

FOOT Work the foot, continuing in the established
charted patt, until the foot measures: Child Shoe Size
10–11: 3 in., Child Shoe Size 12–13: 3¾ in., Youth Shoe
Size 1–2: 4¼ in., Youth Shoe Size 3–4: 4¾ in., Women's
Shoe Size 5–6: 5¼ in., Women's Shoe Size 7–8: 5¾ in.,
Women's Shoe Size 9–10: 6¼ in., Men's Shoe Size 8–9:
6¼ in., Men's Shoe Size 10–12: 6¾ in., Men's Shoe
Size 13: 7 in.

TOE Cut Chinese Red. Work a 42 (48, 54, 60, 66)-st
Star Toe with Seaweed, as instructed on page 177.

FINISHING If needed, thread Daffodil yarn in a
large eye needle and Duplicate st the highlights as
charted (see Glossary for instructions). Weave all
loose ends in on the inside of the sock. Wash and
block the socks.

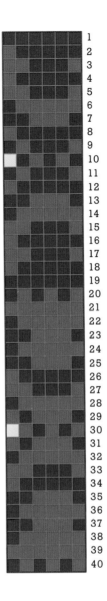

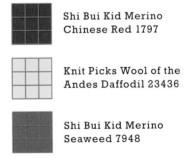

Shi Bui Kid Merino
Chinese Red 1797

Knit Picks Wool of the
Andes Daffodil 23436

Shi Bui Kid Merino
Seaweed 7948

HOLIDAY GARLAND SOCK CHART

Mosaic Tile SOCK

This design reminds me of mosaic tiles. I love the allover repeating pattern and the intricate two-color design. This chart has a short repeat and is much easier to knit than it looks, with very few ends to weave in when you're finished.

PATTERN DIFFICULTY: Advanced

YARN: ShibuiKnits Sock, 100% superwash Merino, 50 g, 191 yd., #S220 Peony, #S3115 Sky, 1 skein each for Child and Youth Sizes; 2 skeins Peony, 1 skein Sky for Women's Average Shoe Sizes 5–6, 7–8; 2 skeins each for Women's Average Shoe Size 9–10 and all Women's Wide Sizes

YARN WEIGHT: Fingering

NEEDLES: Size 2 (U.S.)/2.75 mm, or size needed to obtain gauge

1 or 2 circulars or 4 or 5 dpns, as desired

TOOLS: Large-eye blunt needle, stitch markers

PATTERN SIZES: Child (10–11, 12–13), Youth (1–2, 3–4), Women's Average, Women's Wide, (5–6, 7–8, 9–10)

MEASUREMENTS: Cuff Length: Child: 4¼ in., Youth: 5¼ in., Women's Average and Wide: 6¼ in.; Cuff Width: Child: 2½ in., Youth: 3 in., Women's Average: 3¾ in., Women's Wide: 4¼ in.;

Heel-to-Toe Foot Length: Child Shoe Size 10–11: 5¾ in., Child Shoe Size 12–13: 6¼ in., Youth Shoe Size 1–2: 7½ in., Youth Shoe Size 3–4: 7¾ in., Women's Shoe Size 5–6: 8¼ in., Women's Shoe Size 7–8: 9¼ in., Women's Shoe Size 9–10: 10¼ in.

HEEL STYLE: Flap and Gusset

GAUGE: 10 sts = 1 in., 9 rnds = 1 in. over Stranded Knitting

Note: Hold the unused color on the inside of the sock, stranding it loosely behind the work. Do not strand more than 6 sts without winding the unused yarn around the active yarn. Leave at least a 3-in. tail when changing colors.

With Peony and size 2 needles, CO 48 (60, 72, 84) sts. Without twisting the sts, join. Work 10 rnds in Stockinette st.

PICOT RND 1: Tie on Sky. K around.

PICOT RND 2: With Sky, *YO, K2 tog*, rep around.

PICOT RND 3: With Sky, K around, knitting each YO as a st.

PICOT RND 4: With Peony, K.

Work chart, beginning at Rnd 1, continue through Rnd 34. Rep Rnds 21–34 until otherwise noted. Continue until cuff measures from Picot Rnd 2: Child: 4¼ in., Youth: 5¼ in., Women's Average and Wide: 6¼ in.

HEEL SETUP Work the first 12 (15, 18, 20) sts in the established patt. Place the next 24 (30, 36, 44) sts on a separate needle or holder for the instep. Place the rem 12 (15, 18, 20) sts on the first needle for the heel (24, 30, 36, 40 heel sts).

HEEL FLAP ROW 1: Turn. Sl 1, P across, alternating Peony and Sky. Turn.

HEEL FLAP ROW 2: Sl 1, K across, alternating Peony and Sky in vertical rows. Turn.

Rep Heel Flap Rows 1–2, 10 (12, 14, 16) times more. End with a P row.

HEEL With Peony, work a 24 (30, 36, 40)-st Flap and Gusset Heel as shown on pages 171–172.

GUSSET Sl 1, K 6 (8, 9, 11) sts. Begin new rnd at center of heel.

GUSSET RND 1: With Peony, K 7 (9, 10, 12) sts, pick up, twist, and K 10 (12, 14, 16) sts along the heel flap edge (picking up the sts from the first K st, not the Sl st edge), place marker, tie on Sky, and work across the instep sts in the established patt following the chart, place marker. Cut Sky. With Peony, pick up, twist, and K 10 (12, 14, 16) sts along the other heel flap edge (picking up the sts from the first K st, not the Sl st edge), K7 (9, 10, 12).

GUSSET RND 2: Tie on Sky. K, alternating Peony and Sky, to within 2 sts of the marker, With Peony, K2 tog, move marker, work across instep sts in established patt, following the chart, move marker, SSK with Peony, work rem sts alternating Peony and Sky. (2 sts dec)

GUSSET RND 3: K, working the gusset and sole sts in established alternating Peony and Sky patt, work instep in established patt following the chart. Rep Gusset Rnds 2–3 until 48 (60, 72, 84) sts rem. Redistribute sts on needles if desired.

FOOT Work foot in established patt (alternating Peony and Sky on the sole, following the chart on the instep) until foot measures: Child Shoe Size 10–11: 2 in., Child Shoe Size 12–13: 2½ in., Youth Shoe Size 1–2: 3 in., Youth Shoe Size 3–4: 3½ in., Women's Shoe Size 5–6: 4 in., Women's Shoe Size 7–8: 5 in., Women's Shoe Size 9–10: 5½ in.

ALL SIZES: Work Charted Rnds 1–5. On last Charted Rnd, K 12 (15, 18, 21) sts in established patt, place marker, K 24 (30, 36, 42) sts in established patt, place marker, K rem 12 (15, 18, 21) sts.

TOE **TOE DECREASE RND 1:** K, alternating Peony and Sky, to within 2 sts of the first marker, K2 tog with Peony, move marker, SSK with Peony, K, alternating Peony and Sky, to within 2 sts of the 2nd marker, K2 tog with Peony, move marker, SSK with Peony, K to end, alternating Peony and Sky. (4 sts dec)

TOE DECREASE RND 2: K, alternating Peony and Sky as established, working the sts on either side of both markers with Peony.

Rep Toe Decrease Rnds 1–2 until 24 (32, 36, 40) sts rem, using Peony only on the last rnd. If the sts are not already divided in half, divide them on 2 needles, so that the decs are at either side of each needle. You may need to K to one marker. Close the toe with Kitchener st (see Glossary for instructions).

FINISHING Fold hem in at the picot edge, and stitch down on the inside of the sock. Weave all the loose ends in on the inside of the sock. Wash and block the socks.

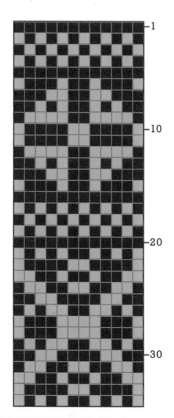

MOSAIC TILE SOCK CHART

Winter Blues SOCK

Stave off the winter blues—and cold feet—with these gorgeous stranded socks.

PATTERN DIFFICULTY:
Advanced

YARN: Knit Picks Palette,
100% Peruvian wool, 50 g, 231 yd.,
1 ball each of #23728 White,
#23733 Mist, #23734 Sky,
#23722 Blue, #24242 Suede,
#23731 Ash

YARN WEIGHT: Fingering

NEEDLES: Size 2 (U.S.)/
2.75 mm and size 3 (U.S.)/
3.25 mm, or size needed to obtain
gauge 1 or 2 circulars or 4 or
5 dpns as desired

TOOLS: Large-eye blunt needle,
stitch markers

PATTERN SIZES: Women's
Average, Women's Wide (5–6, 7–8,
9–10)

MEASUREMENTS: Cuff
Length: All Sizes: 7 in.; Cuff Width:
Women's Average: 3½ in., Women's
Wide: 4 in.; Heel-to-Toe Length:
Shoe Sizes 5–6: 7½ in., Shoe Size
7–8: 8 in., Shoe Size 9–10: 8½ in.

HEEL STYLE: Flap and Gusset

GAUGE: 9 sts = 1 in., 9 rows =
1 in. over Stranded Knitting with
size 3 needles

Note: Hold the unused color on the inside of the sock, stranding it loosely behind the work. Do not strand more than 6 sts without winding the unused yarn around the active yarn. Leave at least a 3-in. tail when changing colors.

With White and size 2 needles, CO 60 (64) sts. Divide on 1 or 2 circulars or 3 or 4 dpns, as desired. Without twisting the sts, join.

RNDS 1–3: K2, P2 around.

RND 4: Tie on Sky. Work in rib patt.

Rep Rnds 1–4 twice. End with 3 rnds White.

Change to size 3 dpns. Inc 4 (8) sts evenly spaced in rnd. (64, 72 sts)

Follow the chart. Begin at Rnd 1, as indicated on the chart. Work even until cuff measures 7 in.

HEEL SETUP With Sky, K15, place the next 34 (42) sts on a separate needle or holder for the instep. Place the rem 15 sts with the first for the heel. (30 heel sts)

HEEL FLAP ROW 1: Sl 1, P across, turn.

HEEL FLAP ROW 2: *Sl 1, K1*, rep across. Turn.

HEEL FLAP ROW 3: Sl, P across. Turn.

HEEL FLAP ROW 4: Tie on White. *Sl 1, K1*, rep across. Turn.

HEEL FLAP ROW 5: Sl 1, P across. Turn.

Rep Rows 2–5 until there are 6 White stripes. End with
a P row. Cut White.

H E E L With Sky, work a 30-st Flap and Gusset Heel
as instructed on page 172. You may work the heel
with 2 strands of Sky for extra reinforcement.

G U S S E T **GUSSET RND 1:** Tie on Mist. K9, pick up,
twist, and K 13 sts along the heel flap, place marker,
K the instep sts, place marker, pick up, twist, and
K 13 sts along the other heel flap, K9.

Follow the chart for the rest of the gusset and foot. Do
not worry if the color patt does not meet properly at
the bottom of the foot.

GUSSET RND 2: Work to within 2 sts of the first marker,
alternating sts in the colors used on that Rnd, K2 tog,
move marker, work the instep sts in the established
chart pattern, more marker, SSK, work to end of RND,
alternating stitch colors.

GUSSET RND 3: K, following chart on instep,
alternating colors on foot.

Rep Gusset Rnds 2–3 until 64 (72) sts rem. Redistribute sts on needles if desired.

Follow chart and work even until foot measures 4¾ in.
(5¼ in., 5¾ in.) from the heel. You may need to begin
the chart at the beginning for the largest shoe size.

LAST FOOT RND, WOMEN'S AVERAGE ONLY:
Dec 4 sts evenly spaced in rnd. (60 sts rem)

T O E Alternating 3 rnds White, 1 rnd Sky, work a
60 (72)-st Star Toe as instructed on page 177. Cut
Sky after 3 stripes have been knit, and finish toe with
White only.

F I N I S H I N G Weave all loose ends in on the inside
of the socks. Wash and block the socks.

23728 White		23722 Blue	
23733 Mist		24242 Suede	
23734 Sky		23731 Ash	

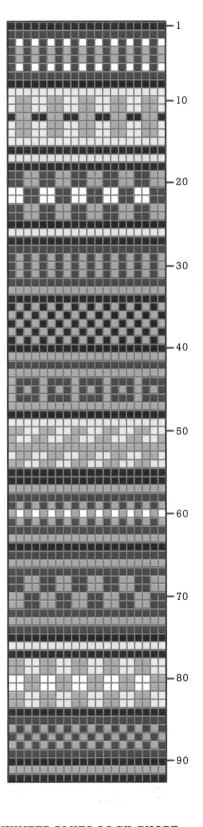

WINTER BLUES SOCK CHART

7

Just for

FUN
SOCKS

Here's an entire chapter's worth of socks that didn't fit into any of the other categories. Some have stripes but are not exactly striped, like the Bubble Stripe Sock, or they're worked from charts but aren't lace or stranded, like the Beaded Anklet, or they're just plain fun, like the Knees and Toes toe socks.

There's a bit of everything here, from the truly goofy Thrummed Slipper to the luxurious Silk Lounge Sock to the sparkly Bangle Sock. You'll also find complete instructions for the hand-dying process to make your own self-patterning yarns with the Spiral Dye Sock.

Whatever the technique, whatever the style, whatever the method, these socks are all about going beyond the basics and experimenting with new patterns for awesome yet timeless creations for your feet.

Thrummed SLIPPER

Thrums are tufts of unspun wool worked into knitted fabric. On the right side, the thrum look like contrasting stranded stitches. On the inside, they look like clouds. These are very easy to knit, worked flat with two needles and seamed after finishing.

PATTERN DIFFICULTY: Beginner

YARN: Decadent Fibers Crème Brulee, 50% Merino wool/ 30% silk/20% mohair, 227 g, 490 yd., Skittles, 1 skein (**Note:** You can knit more than one pair of Thrummed Slippers from 1 skein of Crème Brulee.)

YARN WEIGHT: Worsted

ROVING: Approx 2 oz. (57 g) Merino (or other feltable wool) unspun roving, dyed or undyed

NEEDLES: 10-in. size 5 (U.S.)/ 3.75 mm straight needles, or size needed to obtain gauge

TOOLS: Large-eye blunt needle

PATTERN SIZES: Child (Age 2–4), Youth (Age 5–10), Women's (Shoe Size 5–10), Men's Average (Shoe Size 8–10), Men's Large (Shoe Size 12–13)

MEASUREMENTS: Approx Width, seamed (socks will be thick and hard to measure flat): Child: 3¾ in., Youth: 4¼ in., Women's:

4¾ in., Men's Average: 5¼ in., Men's Large: 5¾ in.; Approx Length: Child: 11½ in., Youth: 12 in., Women's: 14½ in., Men's Average: 17 in., Men's Large: 18½ in.

HEEL STYLE: None

GAUGE: Approx 6 sts = 1 in., 7 rows = 1 in. in Stockinette st over thrummed section

PREPARING THE THRUMS Grab the end of the unspun roving with one hand. With the other, firmly grasp the roving about 3 in. from the end, and tug gently but repeatedly until the roving separates. If the roving won't pull apart easily, divide the roving lengthwise and then separate it into 3-in. sections. Gently separate each 3-in. section of roving into sections about ½ in. wide. Each section is a thrum.

THRUM PATTERN **THRUM ROW 1:** K4, *Work thrum by inserting the left needle in the next st; instead of wrapping the working yarn over the needle, wrap the roving section over the needle, and knit as usual. Don't pull the thrum all the way through the st; smooth it down, and strand the working yarn over the thrum, K5*, rep across, ending with K1.

ROW 2: P, working each thrum as a st. Hold the ends of the thrum together and tug gently after purling to tighten.

ROW 3: K.

ROW 4: P.

THRUM ROW 5: K2, *Work thrum as above, K5*, rep across, ending with K3.

ROW 6: P, working each thrum as a st. Hold the ends of the thrum together and tug gently after purling to tighten.

ROW 7: K.

ROW 8: P.

Note: The thrums will felt after wearing, which will reduce the bulk of the sock but not the softness or warmth. If the thrums are pulled free, the knitted stitches could ravel. However, it is unlikely for the thrums to pull free because they felt and mesh with the rest of the sock on the first wearing.

Note: If you want tighter thrummed socks for wearing with boots, omit the increases after the ribbing, and begin the toe decreases for the number of stitches you are using

Note: Continue working Thrum Pattern through toe decrease, only following decrease on non-thrum rows. Once the toe decrease start, the thrums will no longer line up as before.

continued

continued from page 149

With size 5 needles, and Crème Brulee, CO 36 (42, 48, 54, 60) sts.

CUFF RIBBING: Work K3, P3 ribbing for 12 (12, 16, 20, 20) rows.

NEXT ROW: P, increasing 6 sts evenly across. (42, 48, 54, 60, 66 sts)

NEXT ROW: K.

NEXT ROW: P.

Work Thrum Pattern Rows 1–8 until piece measures 10 in. (10 in., 12 in., 14 in., 15 in.), ending with any P row.

TOE DECREASE, MEN'S LARGE **ROW 1 (BEGIN ON ANY K ROW THAT IS NOT A THRUM ROW):** *K9, K2 tog*, rep across. (60 sts rem)

ROW 2 (WORK ON NEXT K ROW THAT IS NOT A THRUM ROW): *K8, K2 tog*, rep across. (54 sts rem)

ROW 3 (WORK ON NEXT K ROW THAT IS NOT A THRUM ROW): *K7, K2 tog*, rep across. (48 sts rem)

ROW 4 (WORK ON NEXT K ROW THAT IS NOT A THRUM ROW): *K6, K2 tog*, rep across. (42 sts rem)

ROW 5 (WORK ON NEXT K ROW THAT IS NOT A THRUM ROW): *K5, K2 tog*, rep across. (36 sts rem)

ROW 6 (WORK ON NEXT K ROW THAT IS NOT A THRUM ROW): *K4, K2 tog*, rep across. (30 sts rem)

ROW 7 (WORK ON NEXT K ROW THAT IS NOT A THRUM ROW): *K3, K2 tog*, rep across. (24 sts rem)

ROW 8 (WORK ON NEXT K ROW THAT IS NOT A THRUM ROW): *K2, K2 tog*, rep across. (18 sts rem)

ROW 9 (WORK ON NEXT K ROW THAT IS NOT A THRUM ROW): *K1, K2 tog*, rep across. (12 sts rem)

TOE DECREASE, MEN'S AVERAGE Work as for Men's Large, starting with Row 2.

TOE DECREASE, WOMEN'S Work as for Men's Large, starting with Row 3.

TOE DECREASE, YOUTH Work as for Men's Large, starting with Row 4.

TOE DECREASE, CHILD Work as for Men's Large, starting with Row 5.

FINISHING Cut yarn, leaving a 24-in. tail. Thread tail in a large-eye needle, and pull through the remaining loops. Tighten and tie off. Sew seam with Mattress st (see Glossary for instructions). Weave loose ends in on the inside of the sock. Wash and block the socks.

Bubble Stripe SOCK

The drape and sheen of Crystal Palace's Panda Silk yarn makes it perfect for these whimsical socks, sized for girls and women.

PATTERN DIFFICULTY: Intermediate

YARN: Crystal Palace Panda Silk, 52% Bamboo/43% superwash Merino wool/5% combed silk, 50 g, 204 yd., #3008 Mint Cream, 1 ball for Child to Women's Average, Shoe Size 5–6; 2 balls for Women's Average Shoe Size 7–10 and all Women's Wide sizes; #4008 Jade Tones, 1 ball for all sizes

YARN WEIGHT: Fingering

NEEDLES: Size 2 (U.S.)/ 2.75 mm, or size needed to obtain gauge 1 or 2 circulars or 4 or 5 dpns, as desired 1 size 3 (U.S.)/3.25 mm needle for casting on

TOOLS: Large-eye blunt needle, stitch markers

PATTERN SIZES: Child (10–11, 12–13), Youth (1–2, 3–4), Women's Average, Women's Wide (5–6, 7–8, 9–10)

MEASUREMENTS: Cuff Length: Child/Youth: 6 in., Women's: 8¼ in.; Foot Width: Child: 2¾ in., Youth: 3 in., Women's Average: 3¼ in. wide, Women's Wide: 3½ in.; Heel-to-Toe Length, Youth Shoe Size 1–2: 6½ in., Youth Shoe Size 3–4: 6¾ in. Women's Shoe Size 5–6: 7¼ in., Women's Shoe Size 7–8: 8¼ in., Women's Shoe Size 9–10: 9¼ in.

HEEL STYLE: Short Row

GAUGE: 9 sts = 1 in., 11 rnds = 1 in. in Stockinette st

Note: Work **Women's Narrow** as for **Youth**; adjust length for shoe size.

With size 3 needle and Mint Cream, CO 52 (56, 60, 64) sts. Distribute on size 2 needles, 1 or 2 circulars or 3 or 4 dpns, as desired. Being careful not to twist the sts, join.

Work 16 rnds in K1, P1 ribbing.

NEXT RND: K.

BUBBLE STRIPE RND 1: Cut Mint Cream. Tie on Jade Tones. K.

BUBBLE STRIPE RND 2: *K1, inc 1*, rep around. (104, 112, 120, 128 sts)

BUBBLE STRIPE RNDS 3–10: K.

BUBBLE STRIPE RND 11: *K2 tog, SSK*, rep around. (52, 56, 60, 64 sts)

BUBBLE STRIPE RND 12: K.

BUBBLE STRIPE RND 13: Cut Jade Tones. Tie on Mint Cream. K.

BUBBLE STRIPE RNDS 14–23: Work in K1, P1 ribbing.

BUBBLE STRIPE RND 24: K.

CHILD AND YOUTH SIZES ONLY: Rep Bubble Stripe Rnds 1–24 once more.

WOMEN'S SIZES ONLY: Rep Bubble Stripe Rnds 1–24 twice more.

ALL SIZES: K 8 rnds.

HEEL SETUP K 26 (28, 30, 32) sts. Set rem 26 (28, 30, 32) sts on a separate needle or holder for the instep.

HEEL Work a 26 (28, 30, 32)-st Short-Row Heel as instructed on pages 174–175.

FOOT Work even in Stockinette st for: Child Shoe Sizes 10–11: 3¾ in., Child Shoe Sizes 12–13: 4 in., Youth Shoe Sizes 1–2: 4½ in., Youth Shoe Sizes 3–4: 4¾ in., Women's Shoe Size 5–6: 5 in., Women's Shoe Size 7–8: 6 in., Women's Shoe Size 9–10: 6½ in.

2ND TO THE LAST FOOT ROW, CHILD: Dec 4 st evenly spaced in rnd. (48 sts rem)

2ND TO THE LAST FOOT ROW, YOUTH: Dec 2 sts evenly spaced in rnd. (54 sts rem)

2ND TO THE LAST FOOT ROW, WOMEN'S WIDE:
Dec 4 sts evenly spaced in rnd. (60 sts rem)

T O E Work a 48 (54, 60, 60)-st Star Toe as instructed on page 177.

FINISHING Cut yarn, leaving a 12-in. tail. Thread tail in a large-eye needle and weave needle through remaining loops. Tighten and tie off on the inside of the sock. Weave all loose ends in on the inside of the sock. Wash and block the socks.

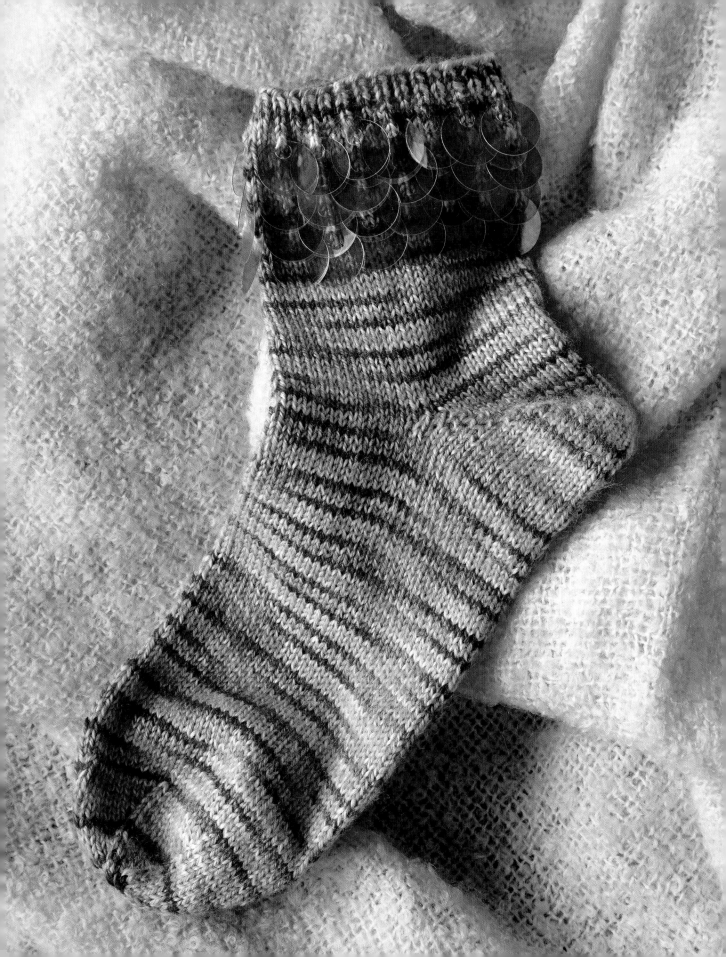

$Bangle$ SOCK

These adorable socks passed muster with both of my granddaughters, who each begged for a pair. The bangles are easily added with a crochet hook while knitting.

PATTERN DIFFICULTY: Intermediate

YARN: Blue Moon Fiber Arts Silkie Socks That Rock, 81% super-wash Merino wool/19% silk, 100 g, 360 yd., Chickabiddy, 1 skein for all sizes

YARN WEIGHT: Fingering

NEEDLES/HOOK: Size 2 (U.S.)/2.75 mm, or size needed to obtain gauge

1 or 2 circulars or 4 or 5 dpns, as desired

1 size 3 (U.S.)/3.25 mm needle for casting on

Size F/3.50 mm crochet hook or any size small enough to fit through the hole in the 20 mm large-hole paillette

TOOLS: Large-eye sharp needle

NOTIONS: Cartwright's Sequins, 20 mm Large-Hole Paillette, 1 package (approx 100 ct) each in Watermelon Sorbet and Sundrop

PATTERN SIZES: Toddler/Child (6–8, 10–11, 12–13), Youth/Women's Average (Youth Sizes 1–2, 3–4, Women's Sizes 5–6, 7–8, 9–10), Women's Wide

MEASUREMENTS: Cuff Length: Toddler/Child: 3 in., Youth: 3¼ in., Women's: 4¼ in.; Approx Width: Toddler/Child: 2¾ in., Youth/Women's Average: 3½ in., Women's Wide: 4¼ in.; Heel-to-Toe Length: Toddler Shoe Size 6–8: 5½ in., Child Shoe Size 10–11: 5¾ in., Child Shoe Size 12–13: 6¼ in., Youth Shoe Size 1–2: 6½ in., Youth Shoe Size 3–4: 6¾ in. Women's Shoe Size 5–6: 7¼ in., Women's Shoe Size 7–8: 8¼ in., Women's Shoe Size 9–10: 9¼ in.

HEEL STYLE: Short Row

GAUGE: 8.5 sts = 1 in., 11 rnds = 1 in. in Stockinette st

BANGLE STITCH When you come to a Bangle st, place a 20 mm large-hole paillette on the crochet hook. Insert the crochet hook through the next st on the left needle. Slide the st off the left needle and pull it through the bead with the crochet hook. Place the st back on the left needle, and knit as usual.

$Note$: Hand-wash and dry these socks flat.

With size 3 needle, CO 48 (56, 60) sts. Divide on size 2 needles, 1 or 2 circulars or 3 or 4 dpns, as desired. Without twisting the sts, join.

Work 4 rnds in K1, P1 ribbing.

K 2 rnds.

BANGLE RND 1: *Bangle st, K3*, rep around, alternating Watermelon Sorbet and Sundrop bangles.

BANGLE RNDS 2–4: K.

Rep Bangle Rnds 1–4, 3 more times (4 bangle rows total). Work even until cuff measures 3 in. (3½ in., 4¼ in.).

HEEL SETUP K 24 (28, 30) sts for the heel. Place rem 24 (28, 30) sts on a separate needle or holder for instep.

HEEL Work 24 (28, 30)-st Short-Row Heel as instructed on pages 174–175.

FOOT Work even in Stockinette st for: Toddler Shoe Size 6–8: 3½ in., Child Shoe Size 10–11: 3¾ in., Child Shoe Size 12–13: 4 in., Youth Shoe Size 1–2: 4½ in., Youth Shoe Size 3–4: 4¾ in., Women's Shoe Size 5–6: 5 in., Women's Shoe Size 7–8: 6 in., Women's Shoe Size 9–10: 6½ in.

2ND TO THE LAST FOOT ROW, YOUTH/WOMEN'S: Dec 2 sts evenly spaced in rnd. (54 sts rem)

TOE Work a 48 (54, 60)-st Star Toe as instructed on page 177.

FINISHING Cut yarn, leaving a 12-in. tail. Thread tail in a large-eye needle and weave needle through remaining loops. Tighten and tie off on the inside of the sock. Weave all loose ends in on the inside of the sock. Wash and block the socks.

Buttons and Bobbles SOCK

Who wouldn't love these adorable socks with the contrasting purl ridges, multicolored bobbles, and buttons sewn on for interest?

PATTERN DIFFICULTY: Intermediate

YARN: Blue Moon Fiber Arts Silkie Socks That Rock, 81% super-wash Merino wool/19% silk, 100 g, 360 yd., Chapman Springs, 1 skein for all sizes; Knit Picks Gloss™, 70% Merino wool/30% silk, 50 g, 220 yd., #23872 Woodland Sage, 1 skein for all sizes

YARN WEIGHT: Fingering

NEEDLES: Size 1 (U.S.)/ 2.50 mm, or size needed to obtain gauge 1 or 2 circulars or 4 or 5 dpns, as desired

TOOLS: Large-eye blunt needle

NOTIONS: Favorite Findings Mini Fun Buttons, #1196; sewing thread and needle

PATTERN SIZES: Child (10–11, 12–13), Youth (1–2, 3– 4), Women's Average, Women's Wide (5–6, 7–8, 9–10)

MEASUREMENTS: Cuff/Foot Width: Child: 3¼ in., Youth: 3½ in., Women's Average: 3¾ in., Women's Wide: 4 in.; Cuff Length: Child: 5½ in., Youth: 6 in., All Women's Sizes: 6½ in.; Heel-to-Toe Length: Child Shoe Size 10–11: 5¾ in., Child Shoe Size 12–13: 6¼ in., Youth Shoe Size 1–2: 6½ in., Youth Shoe Size 3–4: 6¾ in. Women's Shoe Size 5–6: 7¼ in., Women's Shoe Size 7–8: 8¼ in., Women's Shoe Size 9–10: 9¼ in.

HEEL STYLE: Short Row

GAUGE: 9 sts = 1 in., 12 rnds = 1 in. in Stockinette st

BOBBLES **BOBBLE ROW 1:** Tie on Bobble color, leaving a 3-in. tail. Pick up and K1, K1, pick up and K1. Turn. (3 Bobble sts)

BOBBLE ROW 2: Sl 1, P across. Turn.

BOBBLE ROW 3: Sl 1, pick up and K1, K1, pick up and K1, K1. Turn. (5 Bobble sts)

BOBBLE ROW 4: Sl 1, P across. Turn.

BOBBLE ROW 5: Sl 1, K2 tog twice. Turn.

BOBBLE ROW 6: Sl 1, P2 tog, PSSO. Turn.

Cut Bobble yarn, leaving a 3-in. tail. Tie the 2 Bobble tails together tightly. Leave the final Bobble st on left needle, and K that st with the band color.

Note: Though Blue Moon Fiber Arts Silkie Socks That Rock yarn is superwash, Knit Picks Gloss yarn is not. Hand-wash and dry these socks flat.

Note: **Women's Narrow** may fit **Youth** sizes; adjust length for shoe size.

With Woodland Sage and size 1 needles, CO 54 (60, 66, 72) sts. Distribute on 1 or 2 circulars or 3 or 4 dpns, as desired. Without twisting the sts, join. K 10 rnds with Woodland Sage.

BOBBLE RND: *K5, work Bobble with Chapman Springs*, rep around.

SOLID BAND: K 5 rnds with Woodland Sage.

MULTICOLOR BAND: Cut Woodland Sage. Tie on Chapman Springs, K 5 rnds.

RIDGE RND 1: Tie on Woodland Sage, K.

RIDGE RNDS 2–3: P. Cut Woodland Sage.

BUTTON BAND: K 6 (8, 10, 10) rnds with Chapman Springs.

Rep Ridge Rnds 1–3.

MULTICOLOR BAND: K 5 rnds with Chapman Springs. Cut Chapman Springs.

SOLID BAND: Tie on Woodland Sage. K 5 rnds.

Rep entire sequence from Bobble Rnd once.

Work even in Chapman Springs until cuff measures from first Bobble Rnd: 5½ in. (6 in., 6½ in., 6½ in.)

HEEL SETUP K 13 (15, 16, 18) sts for heel, place next 28 (30, 34, 36) sts on a separate needle or holder for the instep, place the rem 13 (15, 16, 18) sts with the first for the heel. (26, 30, 32, 36 heel sts)

HEEL Cut Chapman Springs. Tie on Woodland Sage. Work a 26 (30, 32, 36)-st Short-Row Heel as instructed on pages 173–175.

FOOT SETUP Sl 1, K12 (14, 15, 17). Cut Woodland Sage. Tie on Chapman Springs. Begin new rnd at center of heel. Redistribute sts on needles as desired.

FOOT Work even until foot measures: Child Shoe Size 10–11: 3½ in., Child Shoe Size 12–13: 3¾ in., Youth Shoe Size 1–2: 4¼ in., Youth Shoe Size 3–4: 4½ in., Women's Shoe Size 5–6: 4¾ in., Women's Shoe Size 7–8: 5¾ in., Women's Shoe Sizes 9–10: 6¼ in. Cut Chapman Springs. Tie on Woodland Sage. K 1 rnd. Work 54 (60 , 66, 72)-st Star Toe as instructed on pages 176–177.

FINISHING Fold hem down and in along the Bobble Rnd, and stitch in place loosely with yarn. Weave all loose ends in on the inside of the sock. With sewing thread, sew 6 buttons (green, blue, and purple), evenly spaced in each of the Button Bands. Wash and block the socks.

$\mathscr{Easy}$ BEADED SOCK

Here's a super-easy way to add beads to your socks without prestringing them:
Just add each bead to the proper stitch with a crochet hook before you knit it. The bead
stays perfectly in place on the front of the work, and you continue on without wrestling
with extra strands and stringing more beads.

PATTERN DIFFICULTY:
Intermediate

YARN: Blue Moon Fiber Arts
Socks That Rock Lightweight,
100% superwash Merino wool,
127 g, 360 yd., Watercolor
Colorway (pale green/pale pink/
rose tan), 1 skein

YARN WEIGHT: Fingering

NEEDLES/HOOK: Size 2
(U.S.)/2.75 mm, or size needed
to obtain gauge
1 or 2 circulars or 4 or 5 dpns,
as desired
1 size 3 (U.S.)/3.25 mm needle for
casting on

Size 10/1.30 mm steel crochet
hook, or any size small enough
to fit through the hole in a glass
E-bead

TOOLS: Large-eye blunt needle

NOTIONS: Mainstays Crafts
Glass E-Bead Mix, 28 g tube,
#80244-03 Opal Lined

PATTERN SIZES: Toddler/
Child (6–8, 10–11, 12–13), Youth/
Women's Average (Youth Sizes 1–2,
3–4, Women's Sizes 5–6, 7–8,
9–10), Women's Wide

MEASUREMENTS: Cuff Length:
Toddler/Child: 5½ in., Youth:
5½ in., Women's: 6½ in.; Approx

Width: Toddler/Child: 3 in., Youth/
Women's Average: 3½ in., Women's
Wide: 4 in.; Heel-to-Toe Length:
Toddler: 5½ in., Child Shoe Size
10–11: 5¾ in., Child Shoe Size
12–13: 6¼ in., Youth Shoe Size
1–2: 6½ in., Youth Shoe Size 3–4:
6¾ in., Women's Shoe Size 5–6:
7¼ in., Women's Shoe Size 7–8:
8¼ in., Women's Shoe Size 9–10:
9¼ in.

HEEL STYLE: Short Row

GAUGE: 8 sts = 1 in., 12 rnds =
1 in. in Stockinette st

BEAD STITCH As indicated on the chart, when
you come to a Bead st, place a glass E-bead on the
crochet hook. Insert the crochet hook through the st
on the left needle. Slide the st off the left needle and
pull it through the bead with the crochet hook. Place
the st back on the left needle, and knit as usual.

With size 3 needle, CO 48 (56, 64) sts. Divide on size
2 needles, 1 or 2 circular needles or 3 or 4 dpns, as
desired. Without twisting the sts, join.

Work 15 rnds in K2, P2 ribbing.

K 5 rnds.

Work 4 reps of the chart.

TODDLER/CHILD/YOUTH SIZES: Work even in
Stockinette st until cuff measures 5½ in.

YOUTH/WOMEN'S SIZES: Work even in Stockinette st
until cuff measures 6½ in.

HEEL SETUP K 24 (28, 32) sts for the heel. Place
rem 24 (28, 32) sts on a separate needle or holder for
instep.

HEEL Work a 24 (28, 32)-st Short-Row Heel as
instructed on pages 174–175.

FOOT Work even in Stockinette st for: Toddler:
3½ in., Child Shoe Size 10–11: 3¾ in., Child Shoe Size
12–13: 4 in., Youth Shoe Size 1–2: 4½ in., Youth Shoe
Size 3–4: 4¾ in. Women's Shoe Size 5–6: 5 in., Women's
Shoe Size 7–8: 6 in., Women's Shoe Size 9–10: 6½ in.

2ND TO THE LAST FOOT ROW, YOUTH/WOMEN:
Dec 2 sts evenly spaced in rnd. (54 sts rem)

2ND TO THE LAST FOOT ROW, WOMEN'S WIDE:
Dec 4 sts evenly spaced in rnd. (60 sts rem)

TOE Work a 48 (54, 60)-st Star Toe as instructed on
page 177.

FINISHING Cut yarn, leaving a 12-in. tail. Thread tail in a large-eye needle and weave needle through rem loops. Tighten and tie off on the inside of the sock. Weave all loose ends in on the inside of the sock. Wash and block the socks.

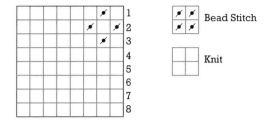

EASY BEADED SOCK CHART

Easy Beaded Sock

Beaded Anklet

Beaded ANKLET

This gorgeous beaded anklet, knitted with Blue Moon Fiber Arts luscious Seduction yarn, will delight little girls of all ages.

PATTERN DIFFICULTY: Intermediate

YARN: Blue Moon Fiber Arts Seduction, 50% Merino wool/ 50% Tencel, 113 g, 400 yd., Coral, 1 skein for all sizes

YARN WEIGHT: Fingering

NEEDLES/HOOK: Size 2 (U.S.)/2.75 mm, or size needed to obtain gauge 1 or 2 circulars or 4 or 5 dpns, as desired Size 10/1.30 mm steel crochet hook (or any hook small enough to fit through the hole of a glass E-bead)

TOOLS: Large-eye blunt needle

NOTIONS: Mainstays Crafts Glass E-Bead Mix, 28 g tube, 1 tube each of #80244-05 Vintage, #80244-02 Pink & Blue (includes pink transparent and blue-purple beads), #80244-14 Mardi Gras

PATTERN SIZES: Child (6–8, 10–11, 12–13), Youth (1–2, 3–4), Women's Average (5–6, 7–8, 9–10), Women's Wide

MEASUREMENTS: Cuff Length with Hem Sewn: Child/Youth: 3¼ in., Women's: 4¼ in.; Approx Foot Width: Child: 2¾ in., Youth: 3¼ in., Women's Average: 3½ in., Women's Wide: 3¾ in.; Heel-to-Toe Length: Child Shoe Size 6–8: 5½ in., Child Shoe Size 10–11: 5¾ in., Child Shoe Size 12–13: 6¼ in., Youth Shoe Size 1–2: 6½ in., Youth Shoe Size 3–4: 6¾ in., Women's Shoe Size 5–6: 7¼ in., Women's Shoe Size 7–8: 8¼ in., Women's Shoe Size 9–10: 9¼ in.

HEEL STYLE: Short Row

GAUGE: 8.5 sts = 1 in., 11 rnds = 1 in. in Stockinette st

BEAD STITCH As indicated on the chart, when you come to a Bead st, place a glass E-bead on the crochet hook. Insert the crochet hook through the st on the left needle. Slide the st off the left needle and pull it through the bead with the crochet hook. Place the st back on the left needle, and knit as usual.

Note: Work **Women's Narrow** as for **Youth**; adjust cuff and foot length for shoe size.

Note: The hole size in glass E-beads is variable. Some tubes of beads have a majority of beads with larger holes, others with holes too tight for even very small crochet hooks. You may need to purchase extra tubes in order to have sufficient beads to complete a pair of socks.

With size 2 needle, CO 48 (54, 60, 66) sts. Divide on 1 or 2 circulars or 3 or 4 dpns, as desired. Without twisting sts, join.

HEM K 8 rnds.

FOLD RND: P.

NEXT RND: K.

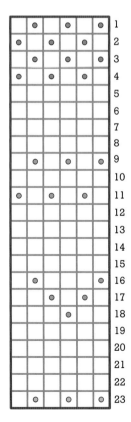

- ◉ Vintage Bead
- ◉ Pink Transparent
- ◉ Blue-Purple
- ◉ Mardi Gras

Work the Bead Chart as indicated, beginning at Rnd 1, using the bead colors as marked, or choose your own color combinations.

Work even until cuff measures 3½ in. (3½ in., 4½ in., 4½ in.).

HEEL SETUP K 12 (14, 15, 16) sts, place the next 24 (26, 30, 34) sts on a separate needle or holder for the instep, place the rem 12 (14, 15, 16) sts with the first for the heel.

HEEL Work a 24 (28, 30, 32)-st Short-Row Heel as instructed on pages 174–175.

FOOT SETUP Sl 1, K11 (13, 14, 15). Begin new rnd at center of heel. Redistribute sts as desired.

FOOT Work even in Stockinette st until foot measures: Child Shoe Sizes 6–8: 3¼ in., Child Shoe Sizes 10–11: 3½ in., Child Shoe Sizes 12–13: 3¾ in., Youth Shoe Sizes 1–2: 4 in., Youth Shoe Sizes 3–4: 4½ in., Women's Shoe Size 5–6: 5 in., Women's Shoe Size 7–8: 6 in., Women's Shoe Size 9–10: 6½ in.

TOE Work a 48 (54, 60, 66)-st Star Toe as instructed on page 177.

FINISHING With yarn threaded in a large-eye needle, fold the hem down and in at the purl ridge, and stitch loosely in place. Weave the loose end in on the inside of the hem. Weave all loose ends in on the inside of the sock. Wash and block the socks.

Dyeing Your Own
SPIRAL
SELF-PATTERNING YARN

You can dye your own self-patterning yarn with colors that spiral down the sock. It's fun and easy, and the results are stunning. Here are a few ideas to get you started, but you can mix and match any dye colors—they're all gorgeous. These instructions use fingering weight yarn, but the process works equally well on sport, DK, and worsted weight yarns.

It's best to use a tube sock, Afterthought Heel, or Short-Row Heel pattern for socks dyed with self-patterning yarn because Flap and Gusset designs, with their changing stitch numbers, disrupt the patterning. Any basic short-row sock pattern (cuff-down or toe-up—see chapter 2 for patterns) will work well with this spiral-dyed yarn. Complicated texture patterns, cables, and lace get lost in this kind of yarn, so plain Stockinette, or a very simple texture, is recommended.

MATERIALS AND TOOLS:
Knit Picks Bare Superwash Merino Wool Sock Yarn, 75% superwash Merino wool/25% nylon, 100 g, 462 yds, #23852 Natural, or any natural or light-colored fingering weight wool or wool-blend yarn, tied in a 44-in. skein (if your yarn comes in a bigger skein, rewind it to 44 in.)

Country Classics Dye—see individual charts for colors
Waste yarn for extra ties
Measuring and mixing spoons
White vinegar
Small bowls—1 for each dye color
Water

1-in.-wide disposable foam brushes—1 for each dye color
Microwave-proof plastic wrap
Microwave-proof gallon resealable bag
Gloves, apron, paper towels
Protected work surface
Microwave

Note: Use dedicated utensils (including the microwave oven) when dyeing yarn. Never use pots or spoons in dyeing that you also use for food preparation. Always wear gloves and an apron, unless multicolored hands and clothes are your current fashion statement. **Do not use any dye utensils, bowls, or pots for food preparation.**

Note: You can apply the dye directly to the dry yarn with a squirt bottle instead of painting it on with a foam brush.

GENERAL SPIRAL SELF-PATTERNING DYE INSTRUCTIONS

1. Cover your work surface with plastic garbage bags or a vinyl tablecloth. Protect the floor around the work area if necessary. Wear old clothing or an apron. Wear gloves.

2. Select your dye colors and mix them, each in a separate bowl: ½ tsp. of dye, 2 tbsp. of white vinegar, and 1 cup of hot water will make a paintable dye.

3. Carefully remove the label from the yarn skein. Reskein the yarn in a 44-in. hank if necessary. Open the yarn skein into a neat oval, making sure that the strands are as even as possible. Using waste yarn, tie the hank in at least four places.

4. Place the open, tied skein on two lengths of microwave-proof plastic wrap that have been laid side-to-side, as shown in the dye charts.

5. Select one color from your chosen chart, and carefully use the foam brush to apply color to the corresponding area on the dry yarn. Note that the color areas are opposite each other on the skein. It isn't necessary to measure the dye area; you can eyeball the sections. Make sure that all the strands of yarn are saturated with dye, but not runny. You can carefully "smoosh" the yarn to distribute the dye through the strands. Use paper towels to soak up excess dye.

6. Select another color from your chart, and paint as above. Note again that the color areas are opposite each other on the skein. Some dye colors should not touch, others should. Refer to individual charts for specific instructions.

7. Repeat with as many dye colors as shown on your chosen chart. There will be some bleeding and mixing of colors at the edges, unless you choose to leave a white area between the colors. See individual charts for instructions.

8. When you are done painting your skein, wrap it with the plastic wrap that is underneath it, bringing the wrap up through the middle of the skein and around the outer edges. Do not allow opposite sides of the wet yarn hank to touch. Use more plastic wrap if necessary to make sure that the entire skein is wrapped in plastic. Place the wrapped skein in a microwave-proof resealable bag. Close the bag, leaving 1–2 in. open for the steam to escape. (**Note:** Bag will explode if closed tightly.)

9. Place the resealable bag in the microwave and heat on high for 1 minute. Allow the bag to rest for 1 minute. Repeat the heat/rest cycle 2 more times.

10. Carefully remove the bag from the microwave (be extremely careful, it will be very hot, and steam may escape from the opening). Allow the skein to cool to room temperature. Rinse the skein in water no cooler than the wet yarn, especially if using feltable yarn. Some dye colors may bleed, so rinse each color section separately until you are sure that there is no dye runoff. Squeeze or spin the moisture from the skein. Allow it to air dry, and wind it into balls.

11. When knit into socks, a spiral of colors will travel down the length of the piece. You may use any fingering weight sock pattern with this yarn, though an Afterthought Heel or a Short-Row Heel will look best because the extra stitches on a heel Flap and Gusset pattern will disrupt the spiral patterning.

PATRIOTIC SPIRAL SOCK YARN

DYE: Country Classics, #41 Cornflower, #33 Ripe Tomato

NOTE: Be sure to leave areas of undyed yarn between each dyed section on the hank.

WATERMELON SPIRAL SOCK YARN

DYE: Country Classics, #31 Very Hot Pink, #34 Strawberry, #51 Desert Rose, #76 Kiwi, #70 Spring Green

NOTE: Be sure to leave an undyed area between the Desert Rose and the Kiwi sections on the hank.

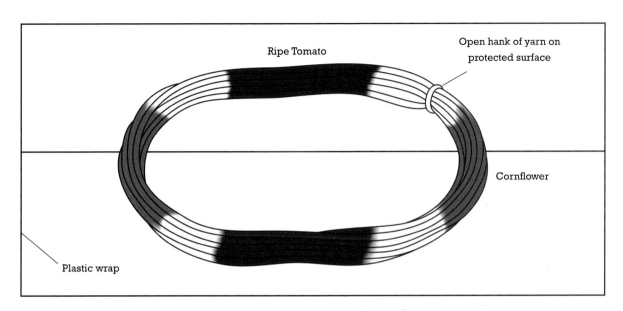

PATRIOTIC

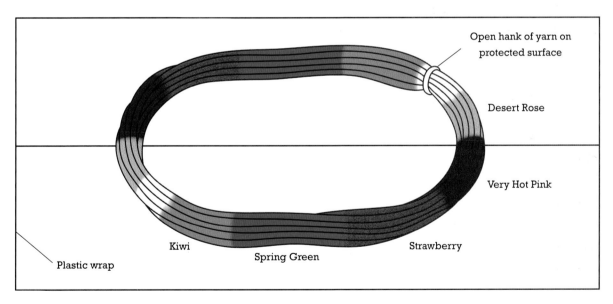

WATERMELON

KNEES *and* TOES

This pattern is head and shoulders above the rest. Keep your tootsies
individually warm and cozy with these knee-length toe socks.

PATTERN DIFFICULTY:
Advanced

YARN: Knit Picks Essential,
75% superwash wool/25% nylon,
50 g, 231 yd., #23698 Burgundy,
2 (2, 3, 3) balls

YARN WEIGHT: Fingering

NEEDLES: Size 2 (U.S.)/
2.75 mm, or size needed to obtain
gauge 1 or 2 circulars or 4 or 5 dpns
as desired

1 size 3 (U.S.)/3.25 mm needle for
casting on

TOOLS: Large-eye blunt needle,
10 safety pins

PATTERN SIZES: Child
(10–11, 12–13), Youth (1–2, 3–4),
Women's Average, Women's Wide
(5–6, 7–8, 9–10)

MEASUREMENTS: Cuff Width
(at widest point): Child: 3¾ in.,
Youth: 4 in., Women's Average·
4¼ in., Women's Wide: 4½ in.;
Cuff Length: Child: 8 in., Youth:
12 in., Women's Average: 14½ in.,
Women's Wide: 15½ in.; Heel-

to-Toe Length (from heel to end
of longest toe): Child Shoe Size
10–11: 5½ in., Child Shoe Size
12–13: 6¼ in., Youth Shoe Size
1–2: 7 in., Youth Shoe Size 3–4:
7½ in., Women's Shoe Size 5–6:
9 in., Women's Shoe Size 7–8:
9½ in., Women's Shoe Size 9–10:
10 in.; Toe Length. Child: 1⅜ in.,
Youth: 1⅝ in., Women's Average/
Wide: 1⅞ in.

HEEL STYLE: Short Row

GAUGE: 9 sts = 1 in., 11 rnds =
1 in. in Stockinette st

Note: It's easier to work the toes with dpns than long
circulars.

Note: Work **Youth** as for **Women's Narrow**; adjust length
according to shoe size.

With a size 3 needle, CO 66 (72, 78, 84) sts. Arrange
on size 2 needles, 1 or 2 circulars or 3 or 4 dpns, as
desired, without twisting the sts, join.

RIBBING: Work 15 (20, 20, 20) rnds in K3, P3 ribbing.

CUFF, CHILD **FIRST RND AFTER RIBBING:** *K9,
K2 tog*, rep around (6 sts dec, 60 sts rem). Work even
in Stockinette st until cuff measures 4 in.

NEXT RND: *K8, K2 tog*, rep around (6 sts dec, 54 sts
rem). Work even until cuff measures 6 in.

NEXT RND: *K7, K2 tog*, rep around (6 sts dec, 48 sts
rem). Work even until cuff measures 8 in.

CUFF, YOUTH Work even in Stockinette st after
ribbing until cuff measures 3 in.

NEXT RND: *K10, K2 tog*, rep around (6 sts dec,
66 sts rem). Work even until cuff measures 6 in.

NEXT RND: *K9, K2 tog*, rep around (6 sts dec, 60 sts

rem). Work even until cuff measures 8 in.

NEXT RND: *K8, K2 tog*, rep around (6 sts dec, 54 sts
rem). Work even until cuff measures 12 in.

CUFF, WOMEN'S AVERAGE Work even in
Stockinette st after ribbing until cuff measures 3½ in.

NEXT RND: *K11, K2 tog*, rep around (6 sts dec,
72 sts rem). Work even until cuff measures 5½ in.

NEXT RND: *K10, K2 tog*, rep around (6 sts dec,
66 sts rem). Work even until cuff measures 7½ in.

NEXT RND: *K9, K2 tog*, rep around (6 sts dec, 60 sts
rem). Work even until cuff measures 14½ in.

CUFF, WOMEN'S WIDE Work even in
Stockinette st after ribbing until cuff measures 4 in.

NEXT RND: *K12, K2 tog*, rep around (6 sts dec,
78 sts rem). Work even until cuff measures 6 in.

NEXT RND: *K11, K2 tog*, rep around (6 sts dec,
72 sts rem). Work even until cuff measures 8 in.

NEXT RND: *K10, K2 tog*, rep around (6 sts dec,
66 sts rem). Work even until cuff measures 15½ in.

HEEL SETUP K 12 (14, 15, 16) heel sts, place the
next 24 (26, 30, 34) sts on a separate needle or holder

for the instep. Place the rem 12 (14, 15, 16) sts with the first for the heel.

HEEL Work a 24 (28, 30, 32)-st Short-Row Heel as instructed on pages 174–175.

FOOT Redistribute sts on needles as desired. Work foot even in Stockinette st until it measures: Child Shoe Size 10–11: 3¼ in., Child Shoe Size 12–13: 3½ in., Youth Shoe Size 1–2: 4 in., Youth Shoe Size 3–4: 4¼ in., Women's Shoe Size 5–6: 4½ in., Women's Shoe Size 7–8: 5½ in., Women's Shoe Size 9–10: 6 in., or until the foot reaches the beginning of the big toe.

TOE SETUP K 12 (13, 15, 17) sts, place next 24, (27, 30, 33) sts on a single needle for the top of the foot, place the rem 12 (14, 15, 16) sts with the first on a single needle for the bottom of the foot. Make absolutely sure that the heel is centered with the bottom needle.

RIGHT FOOT TOES **CHILD:** From the top of the foot, beginning at the right side of the front needle, place 3 sts on a pin for the little toe. Place the next 4 sts on a pin for the next toe. Rep twice more. Place the rem 5 sts on a pin for the big toe. Rep with the bottom needle, placing the same number of sts on each pin as for the corresponding pin for the front of the sock.

YOUTH: From the top of the foot, beginning at the right side of the front needle, place 5 sts on a pin for the little toe. Rep twice more. Place the next 6 sts on a pin. Rep for the big toe. Rep with the bottom needle, placing the same number of sts on each pin as for the corresponding pin for the front of the sock.

WOMEN'S AVERAGE: From the top of the foot, beginning at the right side of the front needle, place 5 sts on a pin for the little toe. Place the next 6 sts on a pin for the next toe. Rep twice more. Place the rem 7 sts on a pin for the big toe. Rep with the bottom needle, placing the same number of sts on each pin as for the corresponding pin for the front of the sock.

WOMEN'S WIDE: From the top of the foot, beginning at the right side of the front needle, place 5 sts on a pin for the little toe. Place the next 7 sts on a pin

for the next toe. Rep three times more. Rep with the bottom needle, placing the same number of sts on each pin as for the corresponding pin for the front of the sock.

1ST TOE (LITTLE TOE) Place 3 (5, 5, 5) sts from the front little toe pin on a single needle. Place the corresponding 3 (5, 5, 5) sts from the bottom little toe pin on a single needle. Beginning at the outside of the toe, K 3 (5, 5, 5) sts, CO 4 sts in the gap, K 3 (5, 5, 5) sts from the bottom needle (10, 14, 14, 14 sts). Distribute sts on needles as desired. Knit the little toe in Stockinette st until it measures ¾ in. (1 in., 1 in., 1 in.).

NEXT RND: *K2 tog*, rep around (5, 7, 7, 7 sts rem). Cut an 8-in. tail. Thread the tail in a large-eye needle, and weave through the rem loops. Tighten and tie off. Weave end in on the inside of the toe.

2ND TOE (NEXT TOE) Place 4 (5, 6, 7) sts from the next front pin on a single needle. Place the corresponding 4 (5, 6, 7) sts from the bottom toe pin on a single needle. K 4 (5, 6, 7) sts from front needle, CO 3 sts in gap, K 4 (5, 6, 7) sts from bottom needle, pick up and K 3 sts along the edge of the little toe gap (14, 16, 18, 20 sts). Distribute sts on needles as desired. Knit this toe in Stockinette st until it measures 1¼ in. (1½ in., 1¾ in., 1¾ in.).

NEXT RND: *K2 tog*, rep around (7, 8, 9, 10) sts rem. Thread the tail in a large-eye needle, and weave through the rem loops. Tighten and tie off. Weave end in on the inside of the toe.

CHILD, WOMEN'S AVERAGE, WOMEN'S WIDE 3RD AND 4TH TOES Rep 2nd Toe.

YOUTH 3RD TOE Rep 2nd Toe.

YOUTH 4TH TOE Place 6 sts from the next front pin on a single needle. Place the corresponding 6 sts from the bottom toe pin on a single needle. K 6 sts from front needle, CO 3 sts in gap, K 6 sts from bottom needle, pick up and K 3 sts along the edge of the little toe gap (18 sts). Distribute sts on needles as desired. Knit this toe in Stockinette st until it measures 1½ in.

NEXT RND: *K2 tog*, rep around 9 sts rem. Thread the tail in a large-eye needle, and weave through the rem loops. Tighten and tie off. Weave end in on the inside of the toe.

BIG TOE Place 5 (6, 7, 7) sts from the last front pin on a single needle. Place the corresponding 5 (6, 7, 7) sts from the bottom toe pin on a single needle.

K 5 (6, 7, 7) sts from the top needle, K 5 (6, 7, 7) from the bottom needle, pick up and K 6 sts in the gap between the big toe and the next toe (16, 18, 20, 20 sts). K in Stockinette st until the big toe measures 1¼ in. (1½ in., 1¾ in., 1¾ in.).

NEXT RND: *K2 tog*, rep around (8, 9, 10, 10) sts rem. Thread the tail in a large-eye needle, and weave

through the rem loops. Tighten and tie off. Weave end in on the inside of the toe.

LEFT FOOT TOES Work as for Right Foot Toes, except divide the sts from the opposite direction, with the big toe sts on the right side of the top and bottom needles.

FINISHING Use the tails from beginning each toe to weave in and tighten any gaps between the toes if necessary. Weave all ends in on the inside of the sock. Wash and block the socks.

AFTERTHOUGHT HEELS

An Afterthought Heel is knitted after the body of the sock has been finished. If you're knitting in the round, you indicate the heel location with a length of waste yarn knit into the sock as you construct it. Remove that waste yarn and pick up the live stitch loops to knit them in the round, the same way you do for a Wedge Toe. Individual instructions for Afterthought Heels are included as necessary in the patterns, though you can also refer to the Wedge Toe section of this chapter for further instructions.

You can also knit Afterthought Heel socks flat, with two needles. Indicate the heel location by binding off the heel stitches on one row, then casting on the same number of stitches on the next row, leaving a precise opening for you to pick up the heel stitches after the rest of the sock is completed.

After binding off a Two-Needle Afterthought Heel, you close the back seam with a Kitchener st, and then sew the remaining sock seam with a Mattress st (see Glossary for instructions for both seam stitches). Individual instructions for Two-Needle Afterthought Heels are included as necessary in the patterns, though you can also refer to the Wedge Toe section of this chapter for instructions.

FLAP & GUSSET HEELS

THE HEEL SETUP The patterns in this book use two methods for getting ready to knit Flap and Gusset Heels. One method selects the heel flap stitches from the first stitches on the needle, which changes the location of the beginning of the round after the heel is completed. The other centers the heel stitches on the back of the cuff. Each pattern specifies which cuff stitches will become the heel stitches. Follow your chosen pattern instructions for the heel setup.

THE HEEL FLAP In general, you work a heel flap over roughly half of the total stitches. For most patterns, you work it back and forth by setting the instep stitches on a separate needle or holder, and working with just the heel stitches. You slip the first stitch

of every row, and purl the rest on the wrong side. You work a combination of *slip one stitch, knit one stitch* (Sl 1, K1) on the right side.

Flap and Gusset Heel Instructions

Though you work this type of heel with short rows, it is different from what is generally termed a *Short-Row Heel*. There are many styles of Flap and Gusset Heels, but this style appears throughout the patterns in this book.

40-Stitch Flap and Gusset Heel

After completing the Heel Flap, and ending with a wrong side (purl) row, turn:

HEEL TURN ROW 1: Sl 1, K24, K2 tog, K1, turn. (Leave rem sts on the needle.)

HEEL TURN ROW 2: Sl 1, P11, P2 tog, P1, turn.

HEEL TURN ROW 3: Sl 1, K12, K2 tog, K1, turn.

HEEL TURN ROW 4: Sl 1, P13, P2 tog, P1, turn.

HEEL TURN ROW 5: Sl 1, K14, K2 tog, K1, turn.

HEEL TURN ROW 6: Sl 1, P15, P2 tog, P1, turn.

HEEL TURN ROW 7: Sl 1, K16, K2 tog, K1, turn.

HEEL TURN ROW 8: Sl 1, P17, P2 tog, P1, turn.

HEEL TURN ROW 9: Sl 1, K18, K2 tog, K1, turn.

HEEL TURN ROW 10: Sl 1, P19, P2 tog, P1, turn.

HEEL TURN ROW 11: Sl 1, K20, K2 tog, K1, turn.

HEEL TURN ROW 12: Sl 1, P21, P2 tog, P1, turn.

HEEL TURN ROW 13: Sl 1, K22, K2 tog, K1, turn.

HEEL TURN ROW 14: Sl 1, P23, P2 tog, P1, turn.

HEEL TURN ROW 15: Sl 1, K23, K2 tog, turn.

HEEL TURN ROW 16: Sl 1, P22, P2 tog, turn. (24 sts rem)

GUSSET SETUP: Sl 1, K11. Begin new rnd at the center of the heel. Change colors if instructed in individual pattern. Redistribute sts on needles as desired.

36-Stitch Flap and Gusset Heel

After completing the Heel Flap, and ending with a wrong side (purl) row, turn:

HEEL TURN ROW 1: Sl 1, K21, K2 tog, K1, turn. (Leave rem sts on the needle.)

HEEL TURN ROW 2: Sl 1, P9, P2 tog, P1, turn.

Work as for 40-Stitch Flap and Gusset Heel until 22 sts rem.

GUSSET SETUP: Sl 1, K10. Begin new rnd at the center of the heel. Change colors if indicated in individual pattern. Redistribute sts on needles as desired.

34-Stitch Flap and Gusset Heel

After completing the Heel Flap, and ending with a wrong side (purl) row, turn:

HEEL TURN ROW 1: Sl 1, K21, K2 tog, K1, turn. (Leave rem sts on the needle.)

HEEL TURN ROW 2: Sl 1, P11, P2 tog, P1, turn.

Work as for 40-Stitch Flap and Gusset Heel until 22 sts rem.

GUSSET SETUP: Sl 1, K10. Begin new rnd at the center of the heel. Change colors if instructed to in individual pattern. Redistribute sts on needles as desired.

32-Stitch Flap and Gusset Heel

After completing the Heel Flap, and ending with a wrong side (purl) row, turn:

HEEL TURN ROW 1: Sl 1, K19, K2 tog, K1, turn. (Leave rem sts on the needle.)

HEEL TURN ROW 2: Sl 1, P9, P2 tog, P1, turn.

Work as for 40-Stitch Flap and Gusset Heel until 20 sts rem.

GUSSET SETUP: Sl 1, K9. Begin new rnd at the center of the heel. Change colors if instructed in individual pattern. Redistribute sts on needles as desired.

30-Stitch Flap and Gusset Heel

After completing the Heel Flap, and ending with a wrong side (purl) row, turn:

HEEL TURN ROW 1: Sl 1, K18, K2 tog, K1, turn. (Leave rem sts on the needle.)

HEEL TURN ROW 2: Sl 1, P9, P2 tog, P1, turn.

Work as for 40-Stitch Flap and Gusset Heel until 18 sts rem.

GUSSET SETUP: Sl 1, K8. Begin new rnd at the center of the heel. Change colors if instructed in individual pattern. Redistribute sts on needles as desired.

28-Stitch Flap and Gusset Heel

After completing the Heel Flap, and ending with a wrong side (purl) row, turn:

HEEL TURN ROW 1: Sl 1, K16, K2 tog, K1, turn. (Leave rem sts on the needle.)

HEEL TURN ROW 2: Sl 1, P7, P2 tog, P1, turn.

Work as for 40-Stitch Flap and Gusset Heel until 16 sts rem.

GUSSET SETUP: Sl 1, K7. Begin the new rnd at the center of the heel. Change colors if indicated in individual pattern. Redistribute sts on needles as desired.

26-Stitch Flap and Gusset Heel

After completing the Heel Flap, and ending with a wrong side (purl) row, turn:

HEEL TURN ROW 1: Sl 1, K14, K2 tog, K1, turn. (Leave rem sts on the needle.)

HEEL TURN ROW 2: Sl 1, P5, P2 tog, P1, turn.

Work as for 40-Stitch Flap and Gusset Heel until 14 sts rem.

GUSSET SETUP: Sl 1, K6. Begin the new rnd at the center of the heel. Change colors if indicated in individual pattern. Redistribute sts on needles as desired.

24-Stitch Flap and Gusset Heel

After completing the Heel Flap, and ending with a wrong side (purl) row, turn:

HEEL TURN ROW 1: Sl 1, K13, K2 tog, K1, turn. (Leave rem sts on the needle.)

HEEL TURN ROW 2: Sl 1, P5, P2 tog, P1, turn.

Work as for 40-Stitch Flap and Gusset Heel until 14 sts rem.

GUSSET SETUP: Sl 1, K6. Begin the new rnd at the center of the heel. Change colors if instructed in individual pattern. Redistribute sts on needles as desired.

22-Stitch Flap and Gusset Heel

After completing the Heel Flap, and ending with a wrong side (purl) row, turn:

HEEL TURN ROW 1: Sl 1, K12, K2 tog, K1, turn. (Leave rem sts on the needle.)

HEEL TURN ROW 2: Sl 1, P5, P2 tog, P1, turn.

Work as for 40-Stitch Flap and Gusset Heel until 12 sts rem. GUSSET SETUP: Sl 1, K5. New rnd begins at center of heel. Change colors if indicated in individual pattern. Redistribute sts on needles as desired.

20-Stitch Flap and Gusset Heel

After completing the Heel Flap, and ending with a wrong side (purl) row, turn:
HEEL TURN ROW 1: Sl 1, K11, K2 tog, K1, turn. (Leave rem sts on the needle.)
HEEL TURN ROW 2: Sl 1, P5, P2 tog, P1, turn.
Work as for 40-Stitch Flap and Gusset Heel until 12 sts rem. GUSSET SETUP: Sl 1, K5. New rnd begins at center of heel. Change colors if instructed in the individual pattern. Redistribute sts on needles as desired.

18-Stitch Flap and Gusset Heel

After completing the Heel Flap, and ending with a wrong side (purl) row, turn:
HEEL TURN ROW 1: Sl 1, K10, K2 tog, K1, turn. (Leave rem sts on the needle.)
HEEL TURN ROW 2: Sl 1, P5, P2 tog, P1, turn.
Work as for 40-Stitch Flap and Gusset Heel until 10 sts rem. GUSSET SETUP: Sl 1, K4. New rnd begins at center of heel. Change colors if instructed in

the individual pattern. Redistribute sts on needles as desired.

16-Stitch Flap and Gusset Heel

After completing the Heel Flap, and ending with a wrong side (purl) row, turn:
HEEL TURN ROW 1: Sl 1, K9, K2 tog, K1, turn. (Leave rem sts on the needle.)
HEEL TURN ROW 2: Sl 1, P5, P2 tog, P1, turn.
Work as for 40-Stitch Flap and Gusset Heel until 10 sts rem. GUSSET SETUP: Sl 1, K4. New rnd begins at center of heel. Change colors if instructed in the individual pattern. Redistribute sts on needles as desired.

SHORT-ROW HEELS

THE HEEL SETUP The patterns in this book use two methods for getting ready to knit Short-Row Heels: after finishing the cuff (for cuff-down socks) or after finishing the foot (for toe-up socks). One method selects the heel stitches from the first stitches on the needle, which will change the location of the beginning of the round after the heel is completed. The other centers the heel stitches on the back of

the cuff (or the sole, for toe-up socks). A few patterns use a different set of stitch parameters for placing the heel within established pattern repeats. Each pattern specifies which cuff (or foot) stitches will become the heel stitches. Follow your chosen pattern instructions for the heel setup.

There is no difference among worsted weight, fingering, or sport weight yarns for Short-Row Heel instructions. You can make any heel narrower (or wider) by working two more (or two less) short rows before turning.

About Short-Row Heels

The style used in this book is a No-Wrap Short-Row Heel, which I find to be very easy to knit and neat when finished, with no holes along the heel shaping.

36-Stitch Short-Row Heel

ROW 1: Turn, Sl 1, P34, turn.
ROW 2: Sl 1, K33, turn.
ROW 3: Sl 1, P32, turn.
ROW 4: Sl 1, K31, turn.
ROW 5: Sl 1, P30, turn.
ROW 6: Sl 1, K29, turn.
ROW 7: Sl 1, P28, turn.
ROW 8: Sl 1, K27, turn.

ROW 9: Sl 1, P26, turn.

ROW 10: Sl 1, K25, turn.

ROW 11: Sl 1, P24, turn.

ROW 12: Sl 1, K23, turn.

ROW 13: Sl 1, P22, turn.

ROW 14: Sl 1, K21, turn.

ROW 15: Sl 1, P20, turn.

ROW 16: Sl 1, K19, turn.

ROW 17: Sl 1, P18, turn.

ROW 18: Sl 1, K17, turn.

ROW 19: Sl 1, P16, turn.

ROW 20: Sl 1, K15, turn.

ROW 21: Sl 1, P14, turn.

ROW 22: Sl 1, K13, turn.

ROW 23: Sl 1, P12, turn.

ROW 24: Sl 1, K11, turn.

HEEL TURN ROW 1: Sl 1, P10, Sl 1, pick up loop in the gap before the next st, P the Sl st and the loop together (HTR 1), turn.

HEEL TURN ROW 2: Sl 1, K10, Sl 1, pick up and K 1 st in the gap before the next st, PSSO (HTR 2), turn.

HEEL TURN ROW 3: Sl 1, P11, work as HTR 1, turn.

HEEL TURN ROW 4: Sl 1, K12, work as HTR 2, turn.

HEEL TURN ROW 5: Sl 1, P13, work as HTR 1, turn.

HEEL TURN ROW 6: Sl 1, K14, work as HTR 2, turn.

HEEL TURN ROW 7: Sl 1, P15, work as HTR 1, turn.

HEEL TURN ROW 8: Sl 1, K16, work as HTR 2, turn.

HEEL TURN ROW 9: Sl 1, P17, work as HTR 1, turn.

HEEL TURN ROW 10: Sl 1, K18, work as HTR 2, turn.

HEEL TURN ROW 11: Sl 1, P19, work as HTR 1, turn.

HEEL TURN ROW 12: Sl 1, K20, work as HTR 2, turn.

HEEL TURN ROW 13: Sl 1, P21, work as HTR 1, turn.

HEEL TURN ROW 14: Sl 1, K22, work as HTR 2, turn.

HEEL TURN ROW 15: Sl 1, P23, work as HTR 1, turn.

HEEL TURN ROW 16: Sl 1, K24, work as HTR 2, turn.

HEEL TURN ROW 17: Sl 1, P25, work as HTR 1, turn.

HEEL TURN ROW 18: Sl 1, K26, work as HTR 2, turn.

HEEL TURN ROW 19: Sl 1, P27, work as HTR 1, turn.

HEEL TURN ROW 20: Sl 1, K28, work as HTR 2, turn.

HEEL TURN ROW 21: Sl 1, P29, work as HTR 1, turn.

HEEL TURN ROW 22: Sl 1, K30, work as HTR 2, turn.

HEEL TURN ROW 23: Sl 1, P31, work as HTR 1, turn.

HEEL TURN ROW 24: Sl 1, K32, work as HTR 2, turn.

HEEL TURN ROW 25: Sl 1, P33, Sl 1, pick up loop in gap between the instep and heel sts, work as HTR 1, turn.

HEEL TURN ROW 26: Sl 1, K17. New rnd begins in center of heel. Change yarn colors if instructed in individual pattern. K17, Sl 1, picking up the loop in the gap between the instep sts and the heel, work HTR 2. Redistribute sts on needles as desired.

32-Stitch Short-Row Heel

ROW 1: Sl 1, P30, turn.

ROW 2: Sl 1, K29, turn.

Work as for 36-St Short-Row Heel until 11 K sts rem after the slipped st.

HEEL TURN ROW 1: Sl 1, P10, Sl 1, pick up loop in the gap before the next st, P the Sl st and the loop together (HTR 1), turn.

HEEL TURN ROW 2: Sl 1, K10, Sl 1, pick up and K 1 st in the gap before the next st, PSSO (HTR 2), turn.

Work as for 36-Stitch Short-Row Heel Turn until 28 K sts rem before HTR 2.

HEEL TURN ROW 21: Sl 1, P29, picking up the loop in gap between the instep and heel sts, work as HTR 1, turn.

HEEL TURN ROW 22: Sl 1, K15, begin new rnd in center of heel unless otherwise noted in individual pattern. Change colors if indicated in pattern. With a new needle, K15, Sl 1, picking up the loop in the gap between the instep and heel sts, work as HTR 2. Redistribute stitches on needles as desired.

30-Stitch Short-Row Heel

ROW 1: Sl 1, P28, turn.

ROW 2: Sl 1, K27, turn.

Work as for 36-Stitch Short-Row Heel until 9 K sts rem after the slipped st.

HEEL TURN ROW 1: Sl 1, P8, Sl 1, pick up loop in the gap before the next st, P the Sl st and the loop together (HTR 1), turn.

HEEL TURN ROW 2: Sl 1, K8,
Sl 1, pick up and K 1 st in the gap
before the next st, PSSO (HTR 2),
turn.

Work as for 36-Stitch Short-Row
Heel Turn until 26 K sts rem
before HTR 2.

HEEL TURN ROW 21: Sl 1, P27,
picking up the loop in gap
between the instep and heel sts,
work as HTR 1, turn.

HEEL TURN ROW 22: Sl 1, K14,
begin new rnd in center of heel
unless otherwise noted in individual pattern. Change colors
if indicated in pattern. K14, Sl 1,
picking up the loop in the gap
between the instep sts and heel
sts, work as HTR 2. Redistribute
sts on needles as desired.

28-Stitch Short-Row Heel

ROW 1: Sl 1, P26, turn.

ROW 2: SL 1, K25, turn.

Work as for 36-Stitch Short-Row
Heel until 9 K sts rem after the
slipped st.

HEEL TURN ROW 1: Sl 1, P8, Sl 1,
pick up loop in the gap before
the next st, P the Sl st and the
loop together (HTR 1), turn.

HEEL TURN ROW 2: Sl 1, K8,
Sl 1, pick up and K 1 st in the gap
before the next st, PSSO
(HTR 2), turn.

Work as for 36-Stitch Short-Row
Heel Turn until 24 K sts rem
before HTR 2.

HEEL TURN ROW 19: Sl 1, P25,
work as HTR 1, picking up the

loop in the gap between the
instep sts and the heel, turn.

HEEL TURN ROW 20: Sl 1, K13.
New rnd begins in center of
heel. Change yarn colors if
instructed in individual pattern.
K13, Sl 1, picking up the loop in
the gap between the instep sts
and the heel sts, work as HTR 2.
Redistribute sts on needles as
desired.

26-Stitch Short-Row Heel

ROW 1: Sl 1, P24, turn.

ROW 2: Sl 1, K23, turn.

Work as for 36-Stitch Short-Row
Heel until 9 K sts rem after the
slipped st.

HEEL TURN ROW 1: Sl 1, P8, Sl 1,
pick up loop in the gap before
the next st, P the Sl st and the
loop together (HTR 1), turn.

HEEL TURN ROW 2: Sl 1, K8,
Sl 1, pick up and K 1 st in the gap
before the next st, PSSO
(HTR 2), turn.

Work as for 26-Stitch Short-Row
Heel Turn until 22 K sts rem
before HTR 2.

HEEL TURN ROW 17: Sl 1, P23,
Sl 1, picking up the loop in the
gap between the instep sts and
the heel sts, work as HTR 1, turn.

HEEL TURN ROW 18: Sl 1, K12.
New rnd begins in center of heel.
Change yarn colors if instructed
in individual pattern. K12, Sl 1,
picking up the loop in the gap
between the instep sts and heel
sts, work as HTR 2. Redistribute
sts on needles as desired.

24-Stitch Short-Row Heel

ROW 1: Sl 1, P22, turn.

ROW 2: Sl 1, K21, turn.

Work as for 26-Stitch Short-Row
Heel until 9 K sts rem after the
slipped st.

HEEL TURN ROW 1: Sl 1, P8,
work as for HTR 1, turn.

HEEL TURN ROW 2: Sl 1, K8,
work as for HTR 2, turn.

Work as for 36-Stitch Short-Row
Heel Turn until 20 K sts rem
before HTR 2.

HEEL TURN ROW 15: Sl 1, P21,
work as HTR 1, picking up the
loop in the gap between the
heel and the instep sts, turn.

HEEL TURN ROW 16: Sl 1, K11.
New rnd begins in center of
heel. Change yarn colors if
instructed in individual pattern.
With new needle, K11, Sl 1,
picking up the loop in the gap
between the instep sts and heel
as, work HTR 2. Redistribute sts
on needles as desired.

20-Stitch Short-Row Heel

ROW 1: Sl 1, P18, turn.

ROW 2: Sl 1, K17, turn.

Work as for 36-Stitch Short-Row
Heel until 9 K sts rem after the
slipped st.

HEEL TURN ROW 1: Sl 1, P8, Sl 1,
pick up loop in the gap before
the next st, P the Sl st and the
loop together (HTR 1), turn.

HEEL TURN ROW 2: Sl 1, K8,
Sl 1, pick up and K 1 st in the
gap before the next st, PSSO
(HTR 2), turn.

Work as for 36-Stitch Short-Row Heel Turn until 16 K sts rem before HTR 2.

HEEL TURN ROW 11: Sl 1, P17, work as HTR 1, picking up the loop in the gap between the instep sts and heel sts, turn.

HEEL ROW 12: Sl 1, K9. New rnd begins in center of heel. Change yarn colors if instructed in individual pattern. Begin with new needle. K9, Sl 1, picking up the loop in the gap between the instep sts and heel sts, work as HTR 2. Redistribute sts on needles as desired.

18-Stitch Short-Row Heel

ROW 1: Sl 1, P16, turn.

ROW 2: Sl 1, K15, turn.

Work as for 36-Stitch Short-Row Heel until 7 K sts rem after the slipped st.

HEEL TURN ROW 1: Sl 1, P6, Sl 1, pick up loop in the gap before the next st, P the Sl st and the loop together (HTR 1), turn.

HEEL TURN ROW 2: Sl 1, K6, Sl 1, pick up and K1 st in the gap before the next st, PSSO (HTR 2), turn.

Work as for 36-Stitch Short-Row Heel Turn until 14 K sts rem before HTR 2.

HEEL TURN ROW 11: Sl 1, P16, work as HTR 1, picking up the loop in the gap between the instep and heel sts, turn.

HEEL TURN ROW 12: Sl 1, K8. New rnd begins in center of heel. Change yarn colors if instructed in individual pattern. Begin with new needle. K8, Sl 1, picking up the loop in the gap between the instep sts and heel sts, work as HTR 2. Redistribute sts on needles as desired.

STAR TOE DECREASES

A Star Toe decreases the foot stitches every other round, at even intervals (usually a multiple of six), generally beginning at the end of the little toe. The decreases form a clearly visible star-shaped design. The final 12 stitches are anchored by sewing yarn through the live loops, tightening and tying off, and weaving the yarn on the inside of the sock.

You work Star Toe toe-up socks in the same manner, by increasing the foot stitches every other round at even intervals, beginning with 12 stitches, and increasing until the proper number has been achieved for your desired sock size. Star Toe Increases also form a clearly visible star-shaped design at the end of the sock. You tighten the 12 cast-on stitches in much the same way that you tighten a Star

Toe Decrease: by sewing through the cast-on loops, tightening, and tying off on the inside of the sock.

You can work nearly any sock with either a Wedge Toe or a Star Toe, as long as you take the difference in foot length into consideration and compensate by knitting ½ in. more (if you're converting from a Star Toe to a Wedge Toe) or ½ in. less (if you're converting from a Wedge Toe to a Star Toe) on the foot before beginning the decreases. You may need to decrease some of the foot stitches before beginning either toe decrease style.

72-Stitch Star Toe Decrease

DECREASE RND 1: *K10, K2 tog*, rep around. (66 sts rem)

Decrease Rnd 2 AND ALL EVEN TOE DECREASE RNDS UNTIL OTHERWISE NOTED: K.

DECREASE RND 3: *K9, K2 tog*, rep around. (60 sts rem)

DECREASE RND 5: *K8, K2 tog*, rep around. (54 sts rem)

DECREASE RND 7: *K7, K2 tog*, rep around. (48 sts rem)

DECREASE RND 9: *K6, K2 tog*, rep around. (42 sts rem)

DECREASE RND 11: *K5, K2 tog*, rep around. (36 sts rem)

DECREASE RND 13: *K4, K2 tog*, rep around. (30 sts rem)

DECREASE RND 15: *K3, K2 tog*, rep around. (24 sts rem)

DECREASE RND 17: *K2, K2 tog*, rep around. (18 sts rem)

DECREASE RND 18: *K1, K2 tog*, rep around. (12 sts rem). Cut a tail 12 in. long. Thread tail in a large-eye needle, and pull the needle through the remaining loops and tighten. Tie off on the inside of the sock.

66-Stitch Star Toe Decrease

Work as for 72-Stitch Star Toe Decrease, beginning at Rnd 3.

60-STITCH STAR TOE DECREASE: Work as for 72-Stitch Star Toe Decrease, beginning at Rnd 5.

54-STITCH STAR TOE DECREASE: Work as for 72-Stitch Star Toe Decrease, beginning at Rnd 7.

48-STITCH STAR TOE DECREASE: Work as for 72-Stitch Star Toe Decrease, beginning at Rnd 9.

42-STITCH STAR TOE DECREASE: Work as for 72-Stitch Star Toe Decrease, beginning at Rnd 11.

36-STITCH STAR TOE DECREASE: Work as for 72-Stitch Star Toe Decrease, beginning at Rnd 13.

30-STITCH STAR TOE DECREASE: Work as for 72-Stitch Star Toe Decrease, beginning at Rnd 15.

24-STITCH STAR TOE DECREASE: Work as for 72-Stitch Star Toe Decrease, beginning at Rnd 17.

WEDGE TOE DECREASES

You work a Wedge Toe by using stitch markers to mark the division between the sole and instep stitches, and then decreasing on either side of each marker. Four stitches are decreased every other round. When the desired number of stitches remains, you divide the stitches on two parallel needles, and close the opening using the Kitchener st (see Glossary for instructions).

You can work nearly any sock pattern with either a Wedge Toe or a Star Toe, as long as you take the difference in foot length into consideration and compensate by knitting ½ in. more (if you're converting from a Star Toe to a Wedge Toe) or ½ in. less (if you're converting from a Wedge Toe to a Star Toe) on the foot, before beginning the decreases.

Wedge Toe final stitch counts will vary depending on the weight of the yarn called for in the pattern and the size sock you are knitting.

Wedge Toe Decrease

On the last row or round before beginning the Wedge Toe Decreases, place the stitch markers as directed in your chosen pattern.

DECREASE RND 1: K to within 2 sts of marker, SSK, move marker, K2 tog, K to within 2 sts of marker, SSK, move marker, K2 tog, K to end. (4 sts dec)

DECREASE RND 2: K.

Rep Wedge Toe Decrease Rnds 1–2 until the proper number of sts rem (refer to individual patterns for the proper number of sts).

Knit to the next marker and arrange the sts, divided evenly on two needles. Use Kitchener st to close the toe opening. Weave all ends in on the inside of the sock.

Appendix

2 Glossary

* : Work the stitch directions within the asterisks (*…*) as many times as the directions instruct.

AFTERTHOUGHT HEEL: A heel worked after the rest of the sock is constructed

BEG: Beginning

BO: Bind off

BO LOOSELY: Bind off the stitches with less tension than used on the rest of the knitted fabric, and usually with a larger-size needle, to form a stretchier bind-off

BOBBLE: A raised stitch, used for visual interest and texture

CABLE: Stitches that you separate and knit separately to form a twist in the pattern. To create the effect, place the directed number of stitches on a cable needle and hold in front of or behind the work as directed, knit the directed number of stitches from the left needle, place the cable needle stitches on the left needle, and work them as directed.

CABLE NEEDLE (CN): A short, straight or curved double-pointed needle used to hold cable stitches

CHART: A diagram grid that provides visual instructions for pattern stitches and/or color patterns. Used in cables, colorwork, beading, and lace knitting.

CIRCULAR NEEDLE: Two knitting needles connected with a flexible cable, which can be used for knitting flat or in the round

CO: Cast on

CO LOOSELY: Cast on the stitches with less tension than used on the rest of the knitted fabric, usually with a larger-size needle, to form a stretchier cast-on

COLORWORK: Stranded, Fair Isle, or intarsia knitting, weaving multiple colors into the knitted pattern

CONT: Continue

CUFF: The top portion of a sock, from the ribbing to the heel

CUFF-DOWN: A method of sock construction in which knitting begins at the upper edge of the cuff, and then down the cuff, the heel, and to the toe

DEC: Decrease, by knitting two (or more) stitches together; slipping one stitch, knitting the next, and passing the slipped stitch over the knit stitch; or SSK, slipping two stitches as if to knit on to the right needle, and then knitting them together

DPN(S): Double-pointed needles

DUPLICATE STITCH: An embroidery method for adding small bits of color to an already completed project by mimicking the actual knitted stitch. You can also use Duplicate stitch to correct small mistakes in stranded knitting. Thread yarn in a large-eye needle and anchor it to the wrong side of the work. Bring the yarn up through the base of the stitch you want to embroider, draw the yarn up and through the base of the stitch above it, and then back down to the base of the original stitch, and tighten. This action covers the original stitch entirely. If the next stitch to be embroidered is adjacent to the one just finished, continue along the row. If the next stitch to be embroidered is farther away, bring the yarn to the wrong side of the work, and either tie off and weave in the end, then move to the next stitch, or strand the yarn loosely to the next stitch to be embroidered. Do not strand over more than five stitches.

EYELET: A deliberate hole made in the fabric by using a yarn over (YO) and then knitting the YO as a regular stitch on the next row or round. A YO is often paired with a decrease, to keep the stitch count the same.

FAIR ISLE: A specific style of stranded colorwork knitting, using two colors per round

FLAP AND GUSSET HEEL: A traditional heel style, where you knit the heel flap flat on approximately half of the sock stitches, turn the heel, and then pick up gusset stitches along the heel flap edge, which you then decrease gradually back to the original stitch number

FLAT: Knitting that you work back and forth, usually on straight needles

FLOAT: The unused strand of yarn in a two-color row of stranded knitting. Carry the float loosely on the inside or back of the work when it's not in use. Do not strand a float more than five or six stitches without anchoring it by twisting it around the active yarn.

FOOT: The area of the sock between the gusset and the toe decreases on a Flap and Gusset Heel sock. The area of the sock between the heel and the toe decreases on a Short-Row Heel sock.

G: Grams

GARTER STITCH: When knitting flat, knit every row. When working in the round, knit 1 round, purl 1 round.

Garter stitch produces a very stretchy fabric.

GUSSET: The area of a Flap and Gusset Heel sock where you pick up stitches along the heel flap edge, and then decrease, usually every other round, until the original number of stitches remains

HEEL: The place in a sock formed, usually by some form of short-row knitting, to accommodate the heel of the foot. It produces a bend in the sock.

HEEL FLAP: A (usually) reinforced flap that you work back and forth before turning the heel on a Flap and Gusset Heel sock

HEEL FLAP EDGE: The edge along which you pick up the gusset stitches

I-CORD: A round knitted cord knitted using two dpns

INC: Increase, usually by picking up a loop from the adjacent stitch on the round below

INTARSIA: A colorwork technique in which you make color changes by tying on new yarn colors and following a chart. Extra colors are not stranded across the back of the work. Usually worked flat.

IN THE ROUND: Knitting on dpns or on a circular needle.

The stitches are joined and the knitting proceeds around the piece, always on the right side.

K: Knit

K2 TOG: Knit two stitches together, by inserting the needle in both at the same time, a method of decreasing the stitch number

K3 TOG: Knit three stitches together, a method of decreasing the stitch number by two

KITCHENER STITCH: A method of weaving stitches together without a visible seam, often used on toes and Afterthought Heels. Divide the stitches on two dpns, with the yarn at the end of one of the needles. Cut about an 18-in. tail, and thread the tail in a large-eye blunt needle. Insert the needle through the first stitch on the front knitting needle as if to purl, pull the yarn through, but leave the stitch on the knitting needle. Insert the needle through the first stitch on the back knitting needle as if to knit, pull the yarn through, but leave the stitch on the knitting needle. Insert the needle in the first stitch on the front knitting needle as if to knit, pull the yarn through, and drop that stitch off the knitting needle. Insert the needle into the next stitch on the front knitting needle as if to purl, pull the yarn through, but leave that stitch on the knitting needle. Insert the needle into the first stitch on the back knitting needle as if to purl, pull the yarn through, and drop that stitch off the knitting needle. Insert the needle into the next stitch on the back knitting needle as if to knit, pull the yarn through, but leave that stitch on the needle. Continue across all of the stitches on the dpns. Weave the end in on the inside of the sock.

LACE: Light fabric with holes made by deliberately increasing and decreasing stitches according to a chart or written directions

LARGE-EYE BLUNT NEEDLE: A tapestry needle with an eye large enough to thread yarn through and a blunt point. Used for sewing seams, performing the Kitchener stitch, doing Duplicate stitch embroidery, tightening and tying off stitches, and weaving ends in.

LT: Left Twist, a cable stitch where the twist travels to the left

M: Meter

MATTRESS STITCH: A method for sewing two pieces of knitted fabric together. With the two edges of the fabric lying flat and lined up, use a large-eye needle threaded with yarn to pick up a bar between the first two stitches on the edge of one piece. Then use the needle to pick up a corresponding bar, and the next bar above it on the edge of the other piece. Continue sewing in that manner, up the seam.

OZ.: Ounce(s)

P: Purl

PATT: Pattern

PICK UP AND KNIT: A method of increasing the number of stitches by picking up a strand from the round below or a loop from an adjacent stitch or by picking up a stitch along a straight edge and knitting it

PICK UP, TWIST, AND KNIT: A method of picking up stitches along a straight edge, often for sock gussets, where the picked-up loop is twisted before knitting to eliminate holes in the fabric

PICOT: A decorative raised stitch, often worked along a folded hem edge

PSSO: Pass the slipped stitch on the right needle back over the stitch knitted right after it, a method of decreasing

REP: Repeat; perform the function the number of times instructed

REPEAT: The portion of a written or charted pattern that is repeated throughout the row as indicated

RIBBING: A stretchy knit fabric consisting of a regular repeat of knit and purl stitches, often found at the very upper edge of the cuff of a sock

RND: Round; a row worked in the round

ROW: A row worked flat

RS: Right side

RT: Right Twist, a cable stitch in which the twist travels to the right

SHORT-ROW HEEL: A heel style worked by knitting back and forth on the same number of stitches, in short rows. There is no gusset with a Short-Row Heel.

SHORT-ROW TOE: A construction style that uses a Short-Row Heel to form a toe, from which you then knit the rest of a toe-up sock

SL: Slip the stitch to the right needle, usually as if to purl. Do not knit the stitch.

ST(S): Stitches

SOLE: The bottom of the foot on a sock. Usually, but not always, worked in Stockinette stitch.

SSK: Slip, slip, knit, a method of decreasing involving slipping two stitches as if to knit onto the right needle, and knitting them together through the back loop (TBL)

STAR TOE: Toe decreases worked at regular intervals, usually every other row or round, that result in a visible star-shaped decrease design

STOCKINETTE STITCH: When knitting in the round, worked by knitting every rnd. When working flat, the right side row is knitted, and the wrong side row is purled.

STRANDED KNITTING: Knitting that uses two or more colors of yarn in a single round, usually worked from a chart indicating which stitches are to be worked

with which color

TAIL: The length of yarn left after tying on or cutting the yarn

TBL: Through the back loop, to knit the stitch from the back of the loop, which twists the stitch

TIGHTEN AND TIE OFF: After pulling the tail through the remaining stitches, pull it tight to close the opening in the stitches. Sew a small knot so that the tail does not loosen.

TOE: The portion of a sock covering the toes, beginning with regular decreases and ending when the stitches are either woven together or tightened and tied off

TOE-UP: A method of sock construction beginning at the toe and knitting up through the foot, heel, and cuff

TOG: Together

TUBE SOCK: A sock without a heel, essentially a tube

TURN: Turn the knitting and work on the other side. Usually at the end of a flat row, but also in the middle of a row for Short-Row Heels.

U.S.: United States knitting needle and shoe sizes

WASTE YARN: Scrap yarn,

Mini Bobble Sock, page 117

usually of the same weight as the yarn being used in the project but of a contrasting color, used to continue the knitting but provide later access to stitches in the middle of the fabric. Waste yarn is not tied in place; you carefully remove it later in order to release the live stitches for picking up.

WEAVE ENDS IN: Thread the tail in a large-eye blunt needle and draw the needle through several loops on the wrong side of the piece. Trim the tail flush with the fabric.

WEAVE THROUGH: Thread the tail in a large-eye blunt needle and draw the needle through the remaining stitches left on the needle(s). Tighten and tie off the yarn, and weave the end in on the wrong side of the piece.

WEDGE HEEL: A style of Afterthought Heel that produces a definite wedge shape in the heel. You usually weave together the remaining stitches using the Kitchener stitch.

WEDGE TOE: A method of decreasing for the toe, which produces a definite wedge shape in the end of the sock. You usually weave together the remaining stitches using the Kitchener stitch.

WS: Wrong side of the work—the back when working flat, or the inside when working in the round

YB: Yarn back; move the yarn to the back of the work.

YD.: Yard(s)

YF: Yarn forward; move the yarn to the front of the work.

YO: Yarn over, a method of increasing the number of stitches or creating deliberate holes in your knitted fabric by wrapping the yarn once counterclockwise around the right needle. On the next round or row, you then knit the YO as for a regular stitch. YOs are often paired with decreases to maintain an even stitch count.

YARNS

ADRIAFIL YARNS

www.adriafil.com/index.html?id_lingua=2

ALPACA WITH A TWIST

www.alpacawithatwist.com

ANGORA VALLEY FIBERS

www.angoravalley.com

BERROCO YARNS

www.berroco.com

BLUE MOON FIBER ARTS

www.bluemoonfiberarts.com

BROWN SHEEP COMPANY

www.brownsheep.com

CASCADE YARNS

www.cascadeyarns.com

CLASSIC ELITE YARNS

www.classiceliteyarns.com

CRYSTAL PALACE YARNS

www.crystalpalaceyarns.com

DECADENT FIBERS

www.decadentfibers.com

DG CONFETTI SUPERWASH

www.dgbcanada.com/index_en.php

FLEECE ARTIST

www.fleeceartist.com

HENRY'S ATTIC

www.henrysattic.com

JÄRBO GARN

www.jarbo.se
www.swedishyarn.com

KNIT PICKS

www.knitpicks.com

LIME & VIOLET

www.limenviolet.com

LION BRAND YARN

www.lionbrand.com

PATONS

www.patonsyarns.com

PHILDAR

www.phildar.com

RIO DE LA PLATA YARNS

www.riodelaplatayarns.com

SHIBUIKNITS

www.shibuiknits.com

SIERRA PACIFIC CRAFTS

www.sierrapacificcrafts.org

YARN TREEHOUSE

www.yarntreehouse.com

NOTIONS

BLUMENTHAL LANSING COMPANY

www.blumenthalstore.com

**CARTWRIGHT'S SEQUINS
& VINTAGE BUTTONS**

www.ccartwright.com

INDEX

Note: **Bold** page numbers indicate a photo, and *italicized* page numbers indicate an illustration. (When there is only one **bold** or *italicized* number of a page range, it indicates at least one photo or illustration.)